Moral Languages from Colonial Punjab

The Singh Sabha, Arya Samaj and Ahmadiyahs

Bob van der Linden

MANOHAR
2008

The Dutch Organization for Scientific Research (NWO)
provided funds towards the production of this book.

First published 2008

© Bob van der Linden, 2008

ISBN 81-7304-759-6

Published by
Ajay Kumar Jain *for*
Manohar Publishers & Distributors
4753/23 Ansari Road, Daryaganj
New Delhi 110 002

Printed at
Lordson Publishers Pvt Ltd
Delhi 110 007

Contents

6 *Contents*

Preface

Upon the whole then, we cannot avoid recognizing in the people of Hindostan, a race of men lamentably degenerate and base; retaining but a feeble sense of moral obligation; yet obstinate in their disregard of what they know to be right, governed by malevolent and licentious passions, strongly exemplifying the effects produced on society by a great and general corruption of manners, and sunk in misery by their vices, in a country peculiarly calculated by its natural advantages, to promote the prosperity of its inhabitants.

CHARLES GRANT in *Observations on the State of Society Among the Asiatic Subjects of Great Britain, Particularly with Respect to Morals and on the Means of Improving it* (1797).[1]

For the majority of Europeans in the early centuries of overseas expansion, the most decisive distinction between them and the people they encountered was not material so much as one of religion. They were Christians, while with very few exceptions the others were heathens. Accordingly, in European accounts much more space was devoted to pointing out differences in beliefs and practices than to explanations or comparisons of scientific and technological prowess (as would happen later in the name of improvement, progress and development, if not evolution). Increasingly Europeans began to identify differing degrees of heathen depravity, though these were 'more difficult to substantiate and compare than the quality of housing, the size of ships and the volume of trade'.[2] Yet idolatry was idolatry. The devil was the same in Africa, Asia and the Americas. Hence, whereas India once often was seen as a land of marvels, by the nineteenth century, most Englishmen (scandalized by such customs as child marriage and widow burning) viewed its people as benighted heathens fit for the civilizing mission and conversion. It was only in early modern times, that the category religion came to be applied universally to all faiths. As a definable entity, religion, described both for its own essence and for the results it produces on society, belongs almost entirely to nineteenth century Western scholarship. Yet a terminology associated with the Western study of religion was imposed on non-Western cultures. Undeniably important to this were processes of modern state formation which officially meant a separation between the religious and the secular (in the Western context, the separation between church and state). But what is religious and what is secular? The use of the category religion to explain human ideas and practices in many places in the world is puzzling. Is it not true that most of what happened under its banner has been very down to earth: economic, political, often totalitarian, xenophobic and generally dependent on charismatic leaders? Whatever the case, the categories religion and secularism, much influenced by the European secular critique of religion since the Enlightenment,[3] have to be handled with care.

In 1962, Wilfred Cantwell Smith in his classic, *The Meaning and End of Religion*, recommended the use of the categories tradition, community and faith instead of religion[4]—being a word he found so muddled in meaning and so modern in coinage as to be useless for any comparative historical study. Twenty years later, however, in *Genealogies of Religion*, Talal Asad argued that in scholarship the use of such terms as those mentioned by Cantwell Smith is not the answer. On the contrary, Asad stressed that these comprehensive concepts always have to be unpacked into their heterogeneous and historically specific elements, reflecting local power relations.[5] All the same, he refers only to the discipline of history and assuming that the study of the latter excludes as W.H. Mcleod put it 'the need for a spiritual interpretation in research',[6] I suggest that in the end there are only the categories of tradition and history. The idea of religion and morality as distinct remains peculiar to the West. South Asian languages, for example, do not have words for religion meaning 'a single uniform and centralized community of believers'.[7] For centuries (and often to the present, if only from the participant's point of view) people in the subcontinent enacted their rituals, pilgrimages and acts of piety without objectifying religion into an exclusive entity. Thus there are words for 'faith, rites, piety, beliefs and gods, but not for an overarching community of believers'.[8] As Harjot Oberoi rightly stressed:

At most, Indian languages yield the word *panth*, a sort of moral collective of believers. But then any tradition could be made up of several conflicting *panths*, and the word does not exactly fit a uniform, centralized, religious community possessing a fixed canon and well-demarcated social and cultural boundaries.[9]

Not particularly surprising in pre-modern South Asia therefore, religion was a 'highly localized affair, often even a matter of individual conduct and individual salvation'.[10] Such labels as Hinduism and Sikhism only emerged during the nineteenth century. Obviously the word 'Hinduism' should be scrupulously avoided because there are only multiple Hindu practices. Even so, because of the Singh Sabha movement there is reason for continuing with 'Sikhism', though the term does not apply to earlier patterns of Sikh belief.

All in all, as far as the idea of religion is concerned, it is time to leave behind the secular–religious binary opposition as mainly a creation of the Enlightenment. In its place one could define religion as traditional morality not on the basis of reason or experience but on some final and transcendental source. In this way, tradition stands in opposition to secularism, which has its ultimate point of moral reference in the world of human knowledge and not beyond but equally has its own orthodoxy and includes the idea of history.[11] Then again, and this is crucial, I take secularization to be a neutral process whereby authority passes from a traditional to a secular source but is not anti-religious in intent. These definitions differ from the idea of secularism put forward by Peter van der Veer, 'as a set of arguments in favour of separation of church and state' with 'a genealogy in the Enlightenment' but working out differently in historical formations worldwide.[12] When trying to understand how traditions changed since the nineteenth century that idea certainly remains bounded by the Euro-centric secular-religious binary opposition. Instead, I see tradition as knowledge handed down from generation to generation, often on the basis of sacred texts that are interpreted by the elites in a certain social hierarchy.

In this view, tradition can be religious as well as secular. The canons of Western literary texts, art and classical music for example are taken as sacred by many and are hierarchically interpreted by scholars. Also it could be argued that, despite all the reasonable thinking involved, such secular notions as democracy, liberalism, progress and nationalism have a transcendent dimension, i.e. one that is not based on reason and experience.[13] Any discussion of tradition in history therefore is sensitive and risky because the propagators of cultural canons generally find it problematic to accept change and those in power never like to give it away. Imperative to this study remains the fact that because of the fast societal changes during the colonial period there emerged a social consciousness among Indian elites that undermined the traditional *status quo*. On the basis of rationally redefined traditions, these elites formed moral identities in order to confront the fast changing world around them. By relying on their own individual reason and invoking the authority of science, Indian elites secularized their traditions.

When we look at social practice, tradition since the nineteenth century appears not very different from other forms of moral knowledge that were authorized by science and spread by modern institutions and practices. Liberalism, for example, cannot be understood unless one recognizes that it began as a moral doctrine of the Protestant dissenter.[14] Also it is worth pointing out that Protestantism perpetuates the category religion because of its 'images of how the world ought to be' and because it heavily influenced traditions worldwide in terms of morality and the rational organization of knowledge and practice. As argued by Ainslee Embree 'much of modern humanistic studies and almost all social science use categories formed in the nineteenth century and imposed upon other societies'.[15] Hence sometimes I have no option but to use terms such as religion and religious nationalism, if not the secular-religious binary opposition, as a whole intellectual heritage cannot be easily discarded. The idea however is to analyse what happened by writing a comparative historical narrative that does not follow the secular-religious binary opposition. Instead the long-term world historical perspective is taken of the period of European expansion in which, a crucial interaction took place between the Christian West and the rest of the world. Since then the West has dominated the world and, as a result, modern non-Western traditions developed along similar universal rational lines.[16] These developments, however, cannot be justified simply by the use of such slogans as secularization or modernization. Undeniably rational forms of knowledge and practice that can be called secular existed in non-Western societies before the coming of the Europeans. Later, non-Western peoples interacted with Western ideas and created their own modern history. In fact, it is probably fair to say that one of the results of the colonial interaction was that non-Western traditional forms of rationality got more space than ever before because this suited the times. Equally, to explain what happened in the non-Western world solely by referring to secularization and modernization does no justice to the different meaning of secularization in the colonial period when local traditions confronted Western science and Christianity.

Because of its preoccupation with secularism, religion, tradition, the colonial state, public sphere, secularization, religious nationalism, etc., this book is largely an exercise in historiography. In the specific context of late nineteenth century Punjab, the logic of these terms often vanishes in the light of the historical sources. How does one construct a narrative without compromising too much with historical detail? How does one use larger labels in a comparative and satisfactory manner? Being a comparative study of three reform movements in the specific context of colonial Punjab, the book's primary aim is to open up a debate about the use of the category religion in relation to modern traditions worldwide. In opposition to Orientalist assumptions about East and West I argue that since the nine 'enth century Indian traditions have been more modern and secular than is generally thought. My introduction of the term moral languages should convey this specifically by making clear the influence of the supposedly objective moral values underwriting modern Western liberal ideas (about the colonial state, the public sphere and the civilizing mission at large), in the definition of non-

Western traditions since the nineteenth century. One of my main arguments will be that in the fast changing colonial culture, Punjabis had to deal with Western science and Christianity but could not just transcend their own modes of thinking. I trust that what follows has not become too antiquarian, written by a grubber for bits of string too short to use but too long to throw away, and instead provides a new perspective on religion in South Asia.[17]

Between 1989 and 1998, I visited the Punjab four times. The first time I stayed only a short while in Amritsar and Lahore en route to China, but long enough to become fascinated both with the British influence as well as the abundance and colour of Punjabi traditions. Subsequently I toured Indian Punjab more extensively during my stay at Jawaharlal Nehru University (Centre for Historical Studies) in 1992-3. There and after I particularly enjoyed the company of Tulsi Bisht, Shruti Kapila, Takashi Oishi and Manoj Tiwary. Special thanks also to Majid Siddiqi. I returned to Indian and Pakistani Punjab for three months in 1996 and once again in 1998. During these visits I mostly was hunting for source materials in a variety of depositories, public and private. The final research was done in the British Library, Oriental and India Office Collections (OIOC), London. For funding, I am thankful to the Amsterdam School for Social Science Research, University of Amsterdam, and the Dutch Organization for Scientific Research (NWO), The Hague.

I am grateful to all who advised and/or assisted me over the years and particularly to Jerry Barrier, Dirk Kolff, Hew McLeod, Dick Plukker and Peter van der Veer for their comments on earlier versions of the book and for providing inspiration at large. At Manohar, I thank Ramesh Jain for publishing my work. Lastly, my gratitude to Damandeep Singh in New Delhi: since 1990, he and his parents, family, friends (in particular Sunny and Meeta, Amit Sengupta and Vidyanidhi Chhabra) and later his wife, Sharmila Purkayastha, welcomed me and the people I brought along. As a result, my stay in India always meant more to me than simply an academic sojourn.

NOTES

1. As cited in Eric Stokes, *The English Utilitarians and India*, 1959; repr. New Delhi: Oxford University Press, 1992, p. 31. Charles Grant was proprietor and Director of the East India Company. He was an evangelist and, on his return to Great Britain, one of the founders of the Clapham sect. This informal group of wealthy, influential families worshipping in Clapham Parish Church, south-west London, successfully lobbied for the opening of India to missionary enterprise (1813) and for the abolition of slavery (1834).
2. Michael Adas, *Machines as the Measure of Men*, New Delhi: Oxford University Press, 1990, p. 64.
3. Roy Porter, *The Enlightenment*, Chapter Four: 'Reforming Religion by Reason', Basingstoke: Macmillan, 1991.
4. A Canadian by origin and an ordained Presbyterian minister, Cantwell Smith lived in Lahore between 1941 and 1949, where he taught at Forman Christian College. At that time he was a scholar of Islam and the author of *Modern Islam in India* (1946), which earlier had been rejected as a Ph.D. dissertation at Cambridge because of its leftist leanings. In a series of books, notably *The Meaning and End of Religion*, he revolutionized the study of religion. Educated at Toronto, Cambridge and Princeton universities, he taught at numerous universities. Until his death in 2000, he remained a doyen among scholars of comparative religion.
5. Talal Asad, *Genealogies of Religion: Discipline and Reasons of Power in Christianity and Islam*, Baltimore: John Hopkins University Press, 1993.
6. W.H. McLeod, 'Crisis of Outrage', *South Asia Research*, 14, 1994, p. 135.
7. Harjot Oberoi, *The Construction of Religious Boundaries: Culture, Identity and Diversity in the Sikh Tradition*, New Delhi: Oxford University Press, 1994, p. 12.
8. Ibid., p. 13.
9. Ibid., p. 14.
10. Ibid.
11. Importantly, since colonial times secularism has a different meaning in India, it is not the absence of religion but a political and social order wherein officially no one religion is preferred to others but all are given equal respect by the state.
12. Peter van der Veer, *Imperial Encounters: Religion and Modernity in India and Britain*, Princeton: Princeton University Press, 2001, pp. 16-18.

13. See on this point in relation to nationalism: Juergensmeyer, *Religious Nationalism Confronts and Secular State*, New Delhi: Oxford University Press, 1994, pp. 15-18.

14. Owen Chadwick, *The Secularization of the European Mind in the Nineteenth Century*, Chapter Two: 'On Liberalism', Cambridge: Cambridge University Press, 1975.

15. Ainslee T. Embree, *Utopia in Conflict: Religion and Nationalism in Modern India*, Berkeley: University of California Press, 1990, p. 117.

16. Cf. Bayly's idea of 'global uniformities' in *The Birth of the Modern World 1780-1914*, London: Blackwell, 2004.

17. See for example: Peter van der Veer, 'Religion in South Asia', *Annual Review of Anthropology*, 31, 2002, pp. 173-87.

Introduction
Tradition, Rationality and Social Consciousness

In 1859, John Beames became District Officer of one of the smallest districts of colonial Punjab, Gujrat.[1] He was also stationed in the districts of Ambala and Ludhiana and remained for two years in the region. In his memoirs he wrote vividly about the times when the colonial administration was still frail:

I looked out and found myself in a tumble-down building of red-brick—not plastered as houses in India mostly are—the British administration in the Punjab was then still so newly established that there had been no time for refinements and luxuries such as plaster. Buildings were hastily run up to serve the emergencies of the moment, and if they tumbled down again as hastily, it did not matter—they were professedly only temporary.[2]

The European part of Gujrat was small, not yet a civil or military lines:

In the European station there were only five houses and a few public buildings. The society was correspondingly small, consisting of Major Adams, the Deputy Commissioner and his wife and child, Major Terence O'Brien, a jolly little fat, round Irishman with a strong Cork brogue (he called his native place 'Cyark') and his wife, a sickly half-caste, and child, and my humble self. There were also two half-caste clerks and their families. For doctor we had a Bengali who spoke English well.[3]

As far as John Lawrence, the famous first Lieutenant-Governor of the Punjab, was concerned, the ideal district officer was

a hard, active man in boots and breeches, who almost lived in the saddle, worked all day and nearly all night, ate and drank when and where he could, had no family ties, no wife or children to hamper him, and whose whole establishment consisted of a camp bed, an odd table and chair or so and a small box of clothes such as could be slung on a camel.[4]

Lawrence was a sort of popular hero but intensely disliked by those who served under him. One of Beames' comrades from the East India Company training college in Haileybury, the then Deputy Commissioner of Ludhiana, G.R. Elsmie, suffered a great deal under John Lawrence's command:

Elsmie imprudently brought a piano to the Punjab with him. Such a refinement was unpardonable, and poor Elsmie was moved five times from one end of the Punjab to the other in the course of two years. 'I'll smash his piano for him', John Lawrence was reported to have said, when he first heard of such a degradation as a Punjab officer having a piano.[5]

The playing of an instrument certainly did not accord with Lawrence's view of an ideal district officer because it was an indication of the lack of grit he expected from his staff. Hence in 1864, when John Lawrence was Viceroy of India, the Lieutenant-Governor of the Punjab, Robert Montgomery, wrote a word of warning, while offering Elsmie a job as judge in Simla:

Simla is full of important people, and there is none so *shrewd* amongst them all as Sir John Lawrence. I do not think he would like you to take part in theatricals. They are hardly fitting the grave sobriety of a Judge, and I shall be glad to hear you eschew them as an actor.[6]

Even so, it should be clear that the staunch Protestant evangelical John Lawrence was influential, but not typical of the British in India. On the contrary, British civilians, 'who had been accustomed to the more civilized conditions of the older and more settled provinces, objected strongly to being turned into homeless, vagrant governing-machines' by this rough and coarse man, who believed that 'personal government was the only form of rule which the rude and simple Punjabis could understand'.[7] After Lawrence's death in 1879, Lieutenant-Governor Charles Aitchison unveiled a massive bronze statue of him on the Mall road in Lahore, holding a sword in one hand, a pen in the other and carrying the inscription: 'Will you be governed by pen or by sword? Choose!'. By then, however, already much had changed. Now the colonial administration was mostly manned by Punjabis and reached deep into rural society. Moreover, Lahore not only had become the headquarters of an important economic and strategic region but, indeed, also the place where since 1884 pianos could be ordered from C. Steiert & Co.

Unquestionably the establishment of the Pax Britannica heavily influenced Punjabi minds. The aim of this study is to learn how traditions changed during the colonial interaction in late nineteenth century Punjab. Though in general the ideas and values assertively propagated by British civil servants and army-men were crucial, I will argue that it was Protestant missionary activity that influenced the making of modern Punjabi identities. Within a few decades of the coming of Christian missionaries, Islamic, Sikh and Hindu traditions were redefined by numerous reform movements through modern institutions and practices. Because the Sikh tradition originated in Punjab and Hindu practices and Islam had specific histories in the region, this gives us an unparalleled opportunity for a comparative historical study about the making of modern South Asian identities. I limit myself, however, to three reform movements, the Singh Sabha (Sikh), the Arya Samaj (Hindu) and the Ahmadiyah (Muslim).[8] Surprisingly, these movements have hitherto not been discussed as similar products of the same regional colonial culture, albeit coming from within three by that time often overlapping Punjabi greater traditions.

From 1873 onwards (the year that the Amritsar Singh Sabha was established), Singh Sabhaites, Arya Samajis and Ahmadiyahs started to define themselves through what I call moral languages. Being minor groups, they created (often with support of the British) bodies of moral knowledge, that was supposed to be eternal. By doing this, they largely rejected the identities existing in Punjabi popular culture at the time. For undeniably the ideas propagated by the Singh Sabhaites, Arya Samajis and Ahmadiyahs did not mesh well with those existing within the larger polytheistic traditions that covered a wide spectrum of beliefs and ritual practices. Instead, the elitist reformers favoured uniformity and homogeneity. To achieve their goal they organized themselves into voluntary movements, opened up educational and other institutions, and appropriated modern modes of communication. What is more, these newly created identities increasingly became crucial in the struggle for authority and status in a fast changing society. Following rivalry between elites for jobs in the administration and urban professions during the 1880s, they provided a useful means of elbowing out adversaries and so became a 'means for individuals and groups to control others or resist such control, for changing society or for blocking change, for affirming or suppressing cultural identities'.[9]

On the whole, I will investigate the dynamics of the Singh Sabha, Arya Samaj and Ahmadiyah moral languages not only 'in a utilitarian way, as the creation of technical terms for precise practical purposes', but especially also 'in a symbolic way, as the expression of a growing group self-consciousness and of a growing sense of distance from the rest of society'.[10] Identities depend on stereotypes of the self and the other, exaggerate whatever makes one community distinct from others, and forge solidarity in the course of conflict with others. The Singh Sabha, Arya Samaj and Ahmadiyah moral languages are no exception. Most reformers saw the world in black and white and hence public meetings often ended up in polemic if not in violence. Most essential to these moral languages remains the dialogue with Western reason which overall led to a stress on rationality in the language used for moral, literary, political or other purposes. Underwriting the moral languages was the fundamental process of strengthening doctrine, conduct and ritual through a dialogic process in which readings of the traditional literature (often as interpreted by European Orientalist scholars) were combined with an understanding that often invoked the authority of science. As a result, there was a growing tendency to treat the Granth Sahib, Vedas and Koran at par with the Bible as scriptures. I examine the Singh Sabha, Arya Samaj and Ahmadiyah self-definitions in the context of a newly emerging liberal public sphere to which the hierarchical system of authority set-up by the Anglo-Indian colonial state provided the backbone. Hence, importantly, I question some assumptions about the colonial state and the public sphere. By using the label Anglo-Indian colonial state, I follow the idea that nineteenth century South Asia found itself in a complicated flux dominated by the interaction between two dynamic civilizations: the regional one and the British imported version of European civilization. On the one hand, the British unleashed different policies following the changes happening in South Asia, Great Britain, and the rest of the world (of Empire), which had effects they could not anticipate. On the other hand, a complex process of responses generated actions of all kinds and in turn influenced the policies of the British (both in Britain and within the Empire). There were closely related worldwide economic, social, political and cultural transformations in which people participated and contributed, not simply as the objects or victims of the successes of others, but by being actively, independently and creatively 'involved in establishing the structures of oppression and exploitation in both India and Great Britain at the same time'.[11] In this way the two civilizations constantly reconstituted each other.

In my view, the creation of an Anglo-Indian colonial state simultaneously was accompanied by the emergence of a public sphere as part of a larger configuration of socio-economic change. As such, I take the formation of both state and public sphere as interrelated and, consequently, query the notion of a neutral, not participating, state in Indian society, as argued for example by Sandria Freitag:

Through the institutions of the state, the British Raj established a structure of rule that interfered, even though it would not participate, in an extraordinary range of activities related to the public arena. Yet where earlier the ruler had fully participated in public arena activity to establish his legitimacy, the imperial state had now withdrawn. In its place it had deputed certain local power-holders to act as its intermediaries.[12]

Or as put more bluntly by Gyan Pandey:

. . . one may note the radically altered nature of the state—and not just of policies, or even politics as a whole—under colonialism. This state is not only far more modern, powerful, centralized and interventionist than any state that had existed before in the subcontinent. It is also far more self-consciously 'neutral' standing above society, and not really part of it than any previous state, a position that no previous state had especially claimed or desired.[13]

Undoubtedly the Anglo-Indian colonial state was something new. Officially ruled from London, as the centerpiece of the British Empire the centralized colonial state claimed absolute authority but even so could not execute its policies without interacting with (i.e. being part of) South Asian society. Like European states, the colonial state functioned through intermediaries, was more bureaucratic and therefore perhaps could be called more impersonal than any of the earlier states, but that does not mean it was neutral and standing above it all. On the contrary, state institutions and actions were at the heart of what happened in modern South Asia. Yet to come back to my use of the term Anglo-Indian colonial state, while one should certainly not suppress the political and military domination of both the colonial and post-colonial states in South Asia,[14] I stress that power is very rarely a one-way process and that consent is needed as power does not descend from above. It rises from below, from within society.[15] Also the position of a neutral colonial state taken by Freitag, Pandey and others remains much similar to the official rhetoric of British colonial policy as put forward in Queen Victoria's 1858 Proclamation (see Chapter Two). It is likewise comparable to the idea of secularism as propagated since 1947 by the independent Indian state. Also the idea of a neutral Anglo-Indian colonial state fits in with a long existing mode of thinking that views states in terms of their sovereignty instead of their military, legal, educational and bureaucratic institutions and practices acted out in the public sphere.[16] The Anglo-Indian colonial state functioned on the basis of human agency, often with pre-planned results but, importantly, many times also with unintended consequences. The latter in particular should always be kept in mind when aiming to write history without drawing too easy conclusions in hindsight. This book follows the idea that the processes of state formation took place simultaneously with the emergence of a liberal public sphere, all together with fast changes in socioeconomic circumstances. This option at the same time questions the idea of the public sphere as a corollary to the state, as put forward by Sandria Freitag.[17] In the newly emerging liberal public sphere, dominant state institutions and practices continually interacted, competed and often overlapped with voluntary ones.

In concert, they constituted a modern hierarchical colonial culture. Through law, education, military service and other forms of state involvement the British propagated their civilizing mission whose liberal terms were to dominate South Asian society ever since.

Even so, to what extent can one use the term liberal public sphere to make clear the workings of a more or less modern universal process in nineteenth century South Asia? To what degree is it of value for the comparison with developments in the West? Decisive to any answer to these questions remains the growing dominance of scientific knowledge as spread through modern institutions and practices by the colonial state and/or voluntary associations. Closely related, 'liberal' is used to stress the importance of the dissenter in modern South Asia. Liberalism remains an extremely difficult concept to define but central to it for instance remain fundamental assumptions in favour of improvement, education, law and individual rational beings leading a self-conscious life.[18] Most important, however, remains the fact that liberalism opposes tradition and privilege because at its core there is the belief that the tests of reason and usefulness should be applied to all institutions and that nothing can be justified solely on the grounds of convention. Having said this, it should be emphasized that I do not use the term liberal public sphere to imply any making of a Habermasian debating public sphere, open to all arguments. That idea solely concerns an ideal type incompatible with modern (racist) politics of difference and power relationships worldwide: interesting for the debate but far off from daily practice. Every modern society creates its own specific public sphere as embodied in state and voluntary institutions and practices.[19] As such, because colonial rule was based on the racist politics of difference, in particular after the 1857 Revolt, liberalism in British India was conservative: authoritarian, evangelical and motivated by race and class. British rule supposedly stood for innovative reform, while India represented sheer inertia. Yet, ironically, the roles were reversed. British officials were preoccupied with law and order, which in practice meant keeping traditions as they were, while their Indian counterparts increasingly appealed to the dynamic aspects of Western liberalism. In the long-term, therefore, the most important feature of the liberal public sphere in South Asia remains the passionate moral commitment to community and tradition in the context of a powerful centralized representative governmental state. Be that as it may, alertness is needed. My use of the adjective liberal above all should be understood from a comparative rather than idealistic perspective. While Indian electoral politics had an unusually long gestation period, Indian society largely remained illiterate and dominated by caste. Admittedly, from the 1860s until 1937, Indian political power was limited to a narrow franchise, while the British retained effective control. In comparison with other former colonized societies however, the public sphere in South Asia (India in particular) certainly proved to have some liberal and democratic features.

The British civilizing mission was to introduce The Law as Rudyard Kipling put it.[20] This was a hard and thankless task he argued, a burden shouldered by a small and dedicated band of British civil servants who 'devoted themselves completely to their tasks in almost unbearable conditions, hoping for no reward beyond their pay, and no recognition for endless patience and un-wearying self-sacrifice'.[21] Kipling admired the men who did the real work and whose laureate he became. Their justification was their work, to be performed in obedience to a government of order and control, not of whim or personal preference. Civilization and 'the Law', then, were virtually synonymous. Civilization was possible only if one played the game according to the rules laid down by time, history, precedent, all of which amounted to 'the Law'. For the British, civilization was a question of objective morality, of external form, of behaviour rather than sentiment, of duty rather than whim. The British civilizing mission was principally one of extending the sense of civic virtue simultaneously in metropolis and colony. As John Stuart Mill put it in his essay *Civilization* (1836):

Consider the savage: he has bodily strength, he has courage, enterprise, and is often not without intelligence; what makes all savage communities poor and feeble? The same cause which prevented the lions and tigers from long ago extirpating the race of men—incapacity of co-operation. It is only civilized beings who can combine. All combination is compromise: it is the sacrifice of some portion of individual will for a common purpose. The savage cannot bear to sacrifice, for any purpose, the satisfaction of his individual will. . . . It is not difficult to see why this incapacity of organized combination characterizes savages, and disappears with the growth of civilization. Co-operation, like other difficult things, can be learnt only by practice: and to be capable of it in great things, a people must be gradually trained to it in small.[22]

Since the beginning of the nineteenth century the British were dedicated to the elevation of mankind. Raised to the summit of the world by their own improvement, they believed in progress and thought they held its keys. The idea of duty was paramount to the muscular Protestant morality propagated by those trained in the public schools and the universities of Oxford and Cambridge. Undoubtedly, the British desire to reform and elevate was a true energy but at the same time it was the duty of masters belonging overwhelmingly to the Churches of England, Scotland, and Ireland ruling an Empire of multifarious beliefs. Protestants regarded all ignorance as evil, if only on the grounds that it prevented men and women from understanding the word of God. Sometimes, especially in the middle of the nineteenth century, their duty was powerfully Old Testament in style: soldiers stormed with Bibles in their hands, administrators sat like bearded prophets at their desks. By the 1890s they were more subdued, but still devoted to the principle that the British were some sort of chosen people, touched on the shoulder by the Great Being and commissioned to do His will in accordance with a worldview wherein decency, fortitude, grit, civilization, Christianity and commerce all blended into one.

Most significant to this study is the fact that indigenous voluntary movements tended to incorporate parts of the British civilizing mission in their moral languages.[23] The words spoken by Bhartendu Harishchandra (1850-85) during his celebrated 1884 Ballia speech, 'Bharatvars ki Unnati Kaise ho Sakti Hai?' (How can India Progress?), are a pointer in this direction. Unequivocally advocating social reform as a prerequisite of progress (*unnati*), the following excerpt definitely sums up what happened in the South Asian mind during the nineteenth century, especially when keeping in mind that Harishchandra not only was crucial to the development of modern Hindi, but also a tireless critic of British rule:

Take your chance during these times of British rule and great progress to reform yourselves, otherwise stay as you are. And that reform should also be such that there will be progress in all cases. In religion, in the household, in work outside the home, in one's daily work, in courtesy, in conduct, in physical power, in intellect, in society, in the child, in youths, in the old, among women and men, among rich and poor, throughout Indian society, within every caste and in all regions, let there be progress. Get rid of all practices that hinder you on this path, even if people call you worthless or shameless, a Christian or corrupt. Only look at the suffering conditions of your country and do not listen to their words.[24]

During the colonial interaction, elitist Indian reformers thus more or less became conscious of some kind of past, effectual in the present and determined for the future.[25] The point, however, is that, as Sudhir Chandra put it, 'the West became a persistent factor for the colonized within their attempt to recover their tradition and selfhood'.[26] The earlier autonomy of Indian thought was no longer possible, as individuals now were either resigned or enthusiast *vis-à-vis* the British civilizing mission. In modern India, the final framework of validation came from the West: 'Faith in colonialism despite an understanding of its exploitativeness—this was the paradox of educated consciousness in colonial India.'[27] Moreover, the 'oppressive present' of the colonial interaction initiated a momentous epistemological change by creating the idea of a traditional India in South Asian minds:

At the plane of collective cultural life, time was fractured into past, present and future; and tradition, plucked out of this continuum, was created selectively out of different points in time past. Alienation from tradition—from one's own culture—lay in a consciousness of the need to belong to this newly constructed tradition.[28]

Importantly, in perceiving the reality of British rule, elitist Indians adopted an idealized view of the Anglo-Indian colonial state, without making any difference between an alien and a native government. Many accepted and even welcomed British rule as a divine dispensation. This way of thinking did not arise solely out of profits from 'collaboration' but generally out of a belief in the instrumentality of British rule in bringing improvement.[29] In addition to Western science and technology, elitist Indians particularly were attracted to the supposed superiority of Western liberalism. After some time, however, a different perception of the nature of British rule developed. Beginning as a vague sense of patriotism and as an abstract discussion on the disadvantages of colonial rule, it culminated in the first decades of the twentieth century in a definite version of a future free from British domination (*swaraj*). Ashis Nandy, Partha Chatterjee and Gyan Prakash argued that in the crystallization of this dominant social consciousness, elitist Indians heavily drew from Western reason.[30] What needs to be emphasized, however, is that the moral rearmament of Indian self and community also was influenced by Christian morality. As C.A. Bayly put it:

The debate between Partha Chatterjee, who insists that Gandhi was part of the post-Enlightenment rational episteme and Ashis Nandy, who sees him as an essential Indian figure, surely misses the point. It was Christian moralizing which informed Gandhi's encounter with the West, not the West's rational episteme. In fact, that secular post-Enlightenment rationality has been greatly exaggerated in recent writings on the British Empire.[31]

Conversions to Christianity were few, yet the impact of missionary criticism of Indian society, the dominance by Christian missionaries of print culture, schools, hospitals and orphanages were profoundly unsettling for the established South Asian order. Furthermore, the civilizing mission, to which elitist Indians often were attracted at large, was saturated with the Christian morality of nineteenth century liberal Europe.

Nandy, Chatterjee and Prakash seem too preoccupied with a negative understanding of Enlightenment. The basic message of Enlightenment thinkers was to use one's own critical reason and think individually against traditional authorities. Yet, it should be stressed that simultaneously they acknowledged that there was more than reason alone. At best, Enlightenment thinkers argued that 'experience and experiment, not a priori reason, were the keys to true knowledge' and also believed that 'divorced from experience and sensitivity, reason equally led to error and absurdity'.[32] All simple-minded extremes were criticized. Opposed to what is commonly thought, therefore, the Enlightenment never was a perfect project for human progress. Dogmatic ideas in this direction, leading towards twentieth century totalitarian regimes, solely developed afterwards. In fact, Ashis Nandy even argued that because of the European racist and one-sided construction of non-Western peoples, 'the idea of a brave new world was first tried out in the colonies'.[33] In contrast, in this book I understand the Enlightenment as a liberal, pro-science, rational, non-dogmatic and open philosophical approach to life that wrestles with perennial questions rather than bringing solutions, in order to gain a reasonable understanding of the functioning of man and the world. No doubt Enlightenment thinkers were worldly moral beings who wanted to use their critical reason to create a better world. They saw modern state formation embedded in representative community groups and institutions as the most effective and socially responsible medium for the improvement of human life. Even so, I suggest, their view on reason, morality and transcendence was different from the dogmatic reasoned moralities propagated by the British civilizing mission and Indian moral languages.

Though I clearly take the confrontation between indigenous traditions and Western science and Christianity as most crucial to modern South Asian history, following the historian's vocation, I also see much continuity within the disruptive historical flux. Of course, there were great social and intellectual changes through which Indian localities became incorporated into the wider world (of Empire), yet these often happened on South Asian terms, not just because the British Raj really was a limited one but also because Indians increasingly became familiar with the fast changing circumstances. Hence particularly significant to this study remains the continuity in language drawn from the Indian past in communicating contemporary understandings. For it should be clear that, although I will use the word language and terms like polemic, rhetoric, symbol and meaning extensively,

Indians (like the British) never were free to concoct words and symbols out of the blue. On the contrary, for they were obviously bound (if not prisoners) by their own values and those they came to know after interacting with the British. By focusing on the Singh Sabha, Arya Samaj and Ahmadiyah moral languages, I aim to make clear how these reform movements made certain rational forms of tradition available through modern disciplinary institutions and practices for the communication of modern identity politics.[34] To reach this goal, I concentrate on the period of social reform when the customs and institutions of a traditional society were secularized, the political spirit was still very much that of loyalty to the British and the route taken not necessarily leading to religious nationalism[35] (a term indeed that solely reinserts the dichotomy between modernity and tradition in a different manner, as if religion made the difference[36]). Specifically in relation to the process of redefinition of tradition, the period of social reform remains the most crucial one in modern South Asian history. It was then, during high colonialism when world events became increasingly interconnected and interdependent, that East and West encountered each other most directly and set the pace and pattern for the secularization of the subcontinent. Ever since, forms of human action undoubtedly adjusted to and came to resemble each other across the world. Hence, while assuming that the history of South Asia is part of world history (as it should nowadays when it is so easy to have a wider look at the globe), I situate the Singh Sabha, Arya Samaj and Ahmadiyah movements squarely within the complex world of opportunities, constraints and motivations they shared in different degrees with those others within non-Western secularizing traditions.

Fundamental to this study and the nature of intellectual history in general remains the relationship between social and intellectual change. Was the creation of the Singh Sabha, Arya Samaj and Ahmadiyah moral languages the result of new forms of rational knowledge or of fast changing social circumstances? What were the social changes that lay beneath the willingness of Punjabis to abandon notions that previously were conceived as necessary to their very existence or, more specifically, moral authority?

Although the study is divided into two parts, the Social Process and the Intellectual Texture, the two are part of one complicated configuration of change. In the end, however, I assume that in the dialectic between ideas and society 'there are times when ideas are not just legitimizers of action taken for other reasons but also a prime force in directing the deeds of men'.[37] For that reason, it is not my idea to take the daily struggles for authority and status (read: power) literally as the most significant engines of change in late nineteenth century Punjab. On the contrary, by treating British and Punjabi reformers as expressions of a dominant social consciousness, I stick to an alternative approach, albeit with sweeping metaphysical implications. For as Clive Dewey put it in his masterly *Anglo-Indian Attitudes: The Mind of the Indian Civil Service* (1993), such an approach

> implies that vested ideas, rather than vested interests, are the great determinants of human behaviour; it denies that men can see complex things—societies, economies, polities—'as they really are', without invoking elaborate theories to explain their chaotic impressions; and it dismisses 'common-sense', the last refuge of the pragmatist, as low-grade ideology: a rag bag of rules of thumb, culled from forgotten thinkers.[38]

Accordingly, I hope the narrative proposes rather than imposes and, since I too remain one of its readers, reads as a collection of arguments organized musically around a continuous line of thought, with themes recurring in different keys that eventually orchestrate a particular point of view.

The study is divided into two parts. Part I describes the social process of the making of a liberal public sphere in late nineteenth century Punjab under the Pax Britannica. The importance of the context of the British Empire is particularly stressed. First, I discuss the incorporation of the Punjab, a strategic and agri-culturally fertile imperial region. Second, I describe how the Anglo-Indian colonial state reached the root of Punjabi rural society for the collection of its land revenue. Both processes created profound change in the structure of Punjabi society and in the minds of its inhabitants. Furthermore, Christian missionary activities set example and pace in terms of modern institutions and practices in general, and in the propagation of the values of nineteenth century European liberalism in particular. Both state and missionary activities made elitist Punjabis sensitive to the civilizing mission and, first in the cities, induced them to focus on programmes of reform and revitalization. Anglo-vernacular education and print culture created a subculture of public men that became central to the creation of a Punjabi public sphere.

In Part II, the focus shifts to the redefinition of Punjabi traditions through the examples of the Singh Sabha, Arya Samaj and Ahmadiyah moral languages. Reformers criticized existing traditions and rationally defined themselves through moral languages that invoked the authority of Western science and increasingly stirred the public mind. Politically, it aims to make clear how the reformers' choice of a particular vernacular to spread their message and definition of their moral languages in history, strengthened the identities of communities in which women had a subordinate position. Their emergent social consciousness was much self-centered. It wrestled with Western science and Christian morality and as a result led to comparative polemics with missionaries and importantly, other communities. Although this resulted in Punjabi politics transcending former regional ones and becoming part of the larger world, simul-taneously it lead other Punjabis to attain their political goals and thus make use of traditional authoritative sacred symbols. Even so, in the context of the relationship between social and intellectual change I will show how the identities created by both colonizer and colonized belonged to the one and the same colonial culture. In other words, certain dominant values that simultaneously were vital to the making of a liberal public sphere were more or less shared by the British and Indians alike and, despite all continuity of indigenous traditions, the moral lan-guages to a great extent shared the terminology of the civilizing mission. Finally, I will attempt to make clear how, despite the massive changes in the material world, the structure of social consciousness since the nineteenth century 'has not undergone anything like the same rapid transformation' and 'shown an amazing persistence'.[39]

NOTES

1. Some may know John Beames as the officer who intensely despised Richard Temple, insulting him by imitating him at a dinner party (when the latter visited Cuttack in 1874 as the new Lieutenant-Governor) and which Beames himself always believed to be the cause of his ill success during the later part of his career. Yet he is probably best remembered as one of those influential nineteenth century comparative linguists of the new Indo-Aryan languages (i.e. author of *A Comparative Grammar of the Modern Aryan Languages of India*), whose dated works today are more frequently cited in South Asia than in the West.

2. John Beames, *Memoirs of a Bengal Civilian*, 1896; London: Eland, 1961, p. 96.

3. Ibid., p. 100.

4. Ibid., p. 102.

5. Ibid., p. 103. Following John Beames, Elsmie's name generally is misspelled as 'Elmslie' and I have corrected it here.

6. G.R. Elsmie, *Thirty-Five Years in the Punjab, 1858-1893*, Edinburgh: David Douglas, 1908, p. 105. Later, in 1871, Elsmie wrote: 'Our life is exceedingly monotonous, and though not unpleasant it does not afford much material for talking or writing. Conversational powers get very rusty in India. There are no subjects for light conversation out here. No music, no pictures, no popular preachers, nothing going on of any sort. I miss music very much' (ibid., p. 160).

7. Beames, *Memoirs*, p. 103.

8. It is important to mention the heterodox character of the Ahmadiyahs. From the beginning this movement was rejected by orthodox Islam, which could not accept the claim of its founder Mirza Ghulam Ahmad (1839-1908) to be a prophet following Muhammad. In fact, in 1975 in Mecca, Ahmadiyahs were declared to be non-Islamic.

9. Peter Burke, *The Art of Conversation*, New York: Cornell University Press, 1993, p. 26.

10. Ibid., p. 25.

11. David Washbrook, 'South Asia, the World System, and World Capitalism', *Journal of Asian Studies*, 49, 1990, p. 489. Cf. Bernard S. Cohn, *Colonialism and its Forms of Knowledge: The British in India*, New Delhi: Oxford University Press, 1996, p. 4 and Peter van der Veer, *Imperial Encounters: Religion and Modernity in India and Britain*, Princeton: Princeton University Press, 2001, p. 8.

12. Sandria B. Freitag, *Collective Action and Community: Public Arenas and the Emergence of Communalism in North India*, New Delhi: Oxford University Press, 1990, p. 53. Cf. David Gilmartin who followed Freitag's thesis directly in relation to the Punjab: 'Seeing

itself as a mediator standing outside the structure of society, the British government withdrew in the nineteenth century from any direct role in the operation of local public arenas' in 'Partition, Pakistan, and South Asian History: In Search of a Narrative', *Comparative Studies in Society and History*, 40, 1998, p. 1075.

13. Gyanendra Pandey, *The Construction of Communalism in Colonial North India*, New Delhi: Oxford University Press, 1992, p. 16. Earlier Ranajit Guha spoke of the 'absolute externality of the state in colonial India' in 'Dominance Without Hegemony and its Historiography', *Subaltern Studies*, VI, New Delhi: Oxford University Press, 1989, p. 274.

14. Among the post-colonial states, the political and military hegemony of the state is particularly clear in Pakistan, where rather than the constitution or political parties (like in India), the bureaucracy and the army became the central institutions in the building of an independent state and public sphere. Moreover, the fact that Pakistan inherited from the colonial past an army dominated by Punjabis reinforced regional differences and increased estrangement from the centre.

15. Lloyd I. Rudolph and Suzanne Hoeber Rudolph, 'The Coffee House and the Ashram', in *Civil Society and Democracy*, ed. Carolyn M. Elliot, New Delhi: Oxford University Press, 2003, p. 379.

16. Hence I disagree with the idea that 'history is the grand narrative of the modern nation-state' as put forward by Peter van der Veer in 'Writing Violence', in *Contesting the Nation: Religion, Community and the Politics of Democracy in India*, ed. David Ludden, Philadelphia: University of Pennsylvania Press, 1996, p. 250 (and afterwards repeated by David Gilmartin in 'Partition, Pakistan, and South Asian History: In Search of a Narrative', *Journal of Asian Studies*, 57, 1998, p. 1070). For it is exactly this teleological view of history that keeps us from learning what really happened in South Asia, ruling out, for example, all social forms that the West did not view as belonging to the realm of the state. Cf. Ranajit Guha, *History at the Limit of World History*, New York: Columbia University Press, 2002, especially Chapter Three and D.H.A. Kolff, *Indië en de Wereldgeschiedenis*, Leiden: Universiteit Leiden, 2003, p. 6.

17. Freitag, *Public Arenas*, p. 177. Following Michel Foucault and in many ways similar to Freitag, Peter van der Veer takes the state as 'totalizing and individualizing at the same time' and 'to be analysed as a structural effect'. 'The boundaries of the state are notoriously difficult to define. The state appears to be a sovereign authority above and outside society, but Foucault has pointed out that the modern state works internally through disciplinary power not by constraining individuals and their actions but by producing them. The individual,

civil political subject is produced in churches, schools, and factories'. (*Imperial Encounters*, pp. 32-3).

18. Thomas R. Metcalf, *Ideologies of the Raj*, Cambridge: Cambridge University Press, 1995, Chapter Two: 'Liberalism and Empire' and C.A. Bayly, *The Birth of the Modern World 1780–1914*, London: Blackwell, 2004, Chapter Eight: 'The Theory and Practice of Liberalism, Rationalism, Socialism, and Science'.

19. See for example Rudolph and Rudolph, 'The Coffee House', on Gandhi's unique talents to give newer shape to institutional forms and means associated with liberal and democratic spheres, p. 381.

20. Bonamy Dobrée, *Rudyard Kipling: Realist and Fabulist*, London: Oxford University Press, 1967, pp. 65-70.

21. Ibid., p. 72.

22. John Stuart Mill, 'Civilization', in *The Collected Works of John Stuart Mill*, ed. J.M. Robson, vol. 18, Toronto: University of Toronto Press, pp. 122-3. According to authoritarian liberals like James Fitzjames Stephen, who wrote *Liberty, Equality and Fraternity* (1872) in reply to Mill, the latter had too naïve a faith in civilization. For Stephen society not only rested upon a consensus of shared opinions but also upon authority, a large measure of mere acceptance by a crowd incapable of conscious decision, of what a trustworthy and responsible 'gifted few' said. Mill's theory, on the contrary, destroyed all faith in authority. See further: Owen Chadwick, *The Secularization of the European Mind in the Nineteenth Century*, Cambridge: Cambridge University Press, 1975, Chapter Two: 'On Liberalism'.

23. In *Rhetoric and Ritual in Colonial India: The Shaping of the Public Sphere in Surat City, 1852-1928*, New Delhi: Oxford University Press, 1992, Douglas Haynes stresses the pervasive liberalism (read: propagation of improvement) of Indian nationalism. Something which to a lesser degree I like to extend to modern traditions in the subcontinent. Cf. Guha, 'Dominance without Hegemony'.

24. Bhartendu Harishchandra, 'Bharatvars ki Unnati Kaise ho Sakti Hai?', in *Bhartendu Samagra,* ed. Hemant Sharma, Varanasi: Pracharak Granthavali Pariyojan, 1987, p. 1011.

25. Instead of such modern categories as public intellectual, cultural entrepreneur or identity politician, I decided to stick to reformer to stress the moral content of the colonial interaction in terms of the civilizing mission and moral languages. Particularly critical in this context is the fact that elitist Indians generally accepted a respondent role while dealing with Western forms of thought and being loyal to their own newly defined traditions at the same time.

26. Sudhir Chandra, *The Oppressive Present: Literature and Social Consciousness in Colonial India*, New Delhi: Oxford University Press, 1992, p. 71.

27. Ibid., p. 46.

28. Ibid., p. 5.

29. K.N. Panikkar, *Culture, Ideology, Hegemony: Intellectuals and Social Consciousness in Colonial India*, London: Anthem Press, 1995, p. 72.

30. One paragraph by Ashis Nandy on what he labelled the 'second colonization' remains crucial here: 'Modern colonialism won its great victories not so much through its military and technological prowess as through its ability to create *secular hierarchies* incompatible with the traditional order. These hierarchies opened up new vistas for many, particularly for those exploited or cornered within the traditional order. To them the new order looked like—and here lay its psychological pull—the first step towards a more just and equal world. That was why some of the finest critical minds in Europe—and in the East—were to feel that colonialism, by introducing modern structures into the Barbaric world, would open up the non-West to the modern critical-analytic spirit. Like the 'hideous heathen god who refused to drink nectar except from the skulls of murdered men', Karl Marx felt, history would produce out of oppression, violence and cultural dislocation not merely new technological and social forces but also *a new social consciousness* in Asia and Africa. It would be critical in the sense in which the Western tradition of social criticism—from Vico to Marx—had been critical and it would be rational in the sense in which post-Cartesian Europe had been rational. It is thus that the a-historical primitives would one day, the expectation went, learn to see themselves as masters of nature and, hence, as masters of their own fate'. *The Intimate Enemy: Loss and Recovery of Self under Colonialism*, New Delhi: Oxford University Press, 1983, p. ix (emphasis mine). Cf. Partha Chatterjee, *Nationalist Thought and the Colonial World: A Derivative Discourse?*, London: Zed Press, 1986 and *The Nation and its Fragments: Colonial and Post-Colonial Histories*, New Delhi: Oxford University Press, 1993; and Gyan Prakash, *Another Reason: Science and the Imagination of Modern India*, Princeton: Princeton University Press, 1999.

31. C.A. Bayly, *Origins of Nationality in South Asia: Patriotism and Ethical Government in the Making of Modern India*, New Delhi: Oxford University Press, 1998, p. 285. Bayly refers to Nandy, *The Intimate Enemy* and Chatterjee, *The Nation and its Fragments*.

32. Roy Porter, *The Enlightenment*, Basingstoke: Macmillan, 1991, p. 3.

33. Nandy, *The Intimate Enemy*, p. x. Cf. D.H.A. Kolff, 'A British Indian Circumambulation', *Itinerario*, 16, 2, pp. 92-3.

34. Instead of nationalism, the term identity politics is used to avoid the implication of nationalism that an individual's loyalty to one or more political group(s) leads to the formation of an independent state. As Malcolm Yapp put it: 'Political identities may be realized in this way

but they may be and are accommodated in many other fashions' in 'Language, Religion and Political Identity: A General Framework', in *Political Identity in South Asia*, ed. David Taylor and Malcom Yapp, London: Curzon Press, 1979, p. 1.

35. Mark Juergensmeyer, *Religious Nationalism Confronts the Secular State*, New Delhi: Oxford University Press, 1994 and Peter van der Veer, *Religious Nationalism: Hindus and Muslims in India*, Berkeley: University of California Press, 1994.

36. In 1914 Protestant missionary J.N. Farquhar included a Chapter on religious nationalism in *Modern Religious Reform Movements in India*, a classic study that undoubtedly influenced the subsequent study of religion and society in South Asia, if only because it served as starting-point for Kenneth W. Jones, *Socio-Religious Reform Movements in British India*, Cambridge: Cambridge University Press, 1989.

37. Robinson, 'Islam and Muslim Separatism', in *Political Identity in South Asia*, ed. David Taylor and Malcom Yapp, London: Curzon Press, 1979, p. 81.

38. Clive Dewey, *Anglo-Indian Attitudes: The Mind of the Indian Civil Service*, London: Hambledon Press, 1993, p. vii.

39. Chandra, *The Oppressive Present*, p. 15.

PART I

THE SOCIAL PROCESS

*(The Creation of a Liberal Public Sphere
Under the Pax Britannica)*

CHAPTER ONE

Authority, State and the Civilizing Mission

A FERTILE REGION AT THE AFGHAN BORDER

The Punjab is perhaps the best regional example of how the colonial interaction shaped and transformed virtually every aspect of life in South Asia, including the indigenous inhabitants' intellectual horizons (only the cities of Calcutta and Bombay are comparable examples).[1] The region changed so much during a relatively short period that in order to see what happened during high colonialism, it is particularly useful to choose the Punjab as an area of research. Its proximity to Afghanistan, where the British and the Russians played their Great Game, and its fertile heartland influenced its development.[2] The former was the main factor in the British Indian army's decision taken after the 1857 Revolt (when the Punjab remained loyal to the British) to concentrate its recruitment in the province. As a result, although the Punjab comprised only around a tenth of British India and its population, its significance as a strategic and wealthy border province was disproportionate. Situated in the north-west corner of the subcontinent, the Punjab was geographically clearly defined, with the Himalaya in the north, the Thar Desert in the south, the Jamuna in the east and the Indus in the west. The literal meaning of the Persian term *Panj ab* or five rivers was meant to signify the land through which the Jhelum, Chenab, Ravi, Beas and Sutlej rivers flowed. In fact, Punjab was a land of six rivers but by name the Indus was not included. It was Mughal Emperor Akbar who named the tracts of land between these rivers, respectively, from east to west, the Bist-Jullunder, Bari, Rechna, Jech and Sindh-Sagar *doabs*. The alluvial soil of these tracts, additionally irrigated by wells and canals, formed the productive heartland of the region. Capricious weather none-theless regularly led to a shortage of rainfall in the growing season, resulting in lower crop yields, crop failures and sometimes famine. Partly because of the latter problem, the British decided that the Punjab was an ideal area for the construction of a system of irrigation canals. After annexation, work first began on restoring and extending the Punjab's canal system as developed under Mughal and Sikh rule (the Bari *doab* canal, for example, was extended for some 400 km). By the 1880s, canal construction had reached a high point, as several canals, including the western Jamuna, the lower Chenab, and many smaller ones, were built, modified or extended. Most areas adjacent to the canals were neatly laid out in plots of land with market places, towns and villages spaced at regular intervals along the roads and railways that developed rapidly during the same period. These canal colonies indeed represented a new environment and way of living, as Prakash Tandon put it in his most readable autobiography, comparing his birthplace Gujrat with a newly created colony town that during the first decades of this century would develop into one of the largest wheat markets in the world:

Sarghoda was a much cleaner and healthier city than Gujrat. It was planned, well laid out and had plenty of light and air. Its streets and lanes were wide and straight. Somehow the clean, hygienic, impersonal layout seemed to mould the population into the pattern that the settlement officer of the late Victorian period must have had in mind. There was more social and political awakening in Sarghoda; its municipal affairs were better run; its communities had started new schools. The singing and dancing girls were moved out of the city, first near the canal bank, and then still further away. It was typical of the new spirit of Sarghoda that its biradaris (brotherhoods) tried to stop wasteful expenditure at weddings by banning fireworks, and had they got away with this they would probably have stopped music and entertainment as well. But with all this Sarghoda was drab and had none of the colour of Gujrat, neither the city not its people.[3]

Meanwhile, a million Punjabis from the central districts around Amritsar and Lahore (two cities that expanded remarkably during colonial rule) migrated to the canal colonies. These emigrants regularly sent money home and, alternatively, agri-cultural products of the home regions found a ready market in the canal colonies, where farmers specialized in cultivating a small variety of cash crops such as tobacco, sugarcane, cotton and wheat (which became the region's main export commodity).[4] While the extension of the total cultivated area of the province outstripped the rate of population growth, many (although indeed far from all) Punjabis in the old as well as the new regions experienced an unprecedented rise in their standard of living.

Closely interlinked with the construction of the canals and colonies, was the impact of army recruitment on the Punjab's economic, social and political life.[5] Soon the region replaced the older military recruitment areas in north India and by 1914 three-fifths of the troops came from the Punjab. This process occurred not only because the region's loyalty during the 1857 Revolt but generally because it was believed there existed a martial tradition in the area, as generations had been forced to fight in order to survive at the one and only existing overland gateway to India. Even so, of greater importance seems to have been the fact that the region was situated next to British India's main theatre of war at the time: Afghanistan. On the way from Lahore to Kabul, Rawalpindi was the centre of military activity with the biggest cantonment in South Asia (in fact, it still is the headquarters of the Pakistani army). Because of the comparable terrain and climate, recruits especially from west Punjab not only were more suitable but, in particular, also cheaper, as soldiers serving on the frontier from other parts of the subcontinent had to be paid extra foreign-service allowances.[6] The increased prosperity that irrigation had brought to the Punjab also meant that far fewer volunteers for army service were turned away on medical grounds. At the same time, the vast increase in land available for agriculture enabled the British to set large areas apart solely for the purpose of breeding horses and cattle for the army. Importantly, though army recruitment in the Punjab was mostly based on pragmatic policies, it also became enshrined in the mythology of India's martial races. In reality, according to Lieutenant-Governor James Douie, recruitments in the case of Sikhs belonging to the Jat caste had more to do with an abundance of energy than what G.F. MacMunn saw as inbred martial skill:

The Jat is a typical son of the soil, strong and sturdy, hardworking and brave, a fine soldier and an excellent farmer, but slow-witted and grasping. The Sikh Jat finds an honourable outlet for his overflowing energy in the army and in the service of the Crown beyond the bounds of India. When he misses that he sometimes takes to dacoity. Unfortunately he is often given to strong drink, and, when his passions or his greed are aroused, can be exceedingly brutal.[7]

More noteworthy than such stereotypes however is the close relationship between the British Indian army and the Punjab which increased the rural population's prosperity as soldiers sent money home to their villages. Besides, servicemen and their retired comrades invested their savings or received pensions, land or government office as a reward for their loyalty. They gained powerful political influence within the restricted electorate, particularly through the cross communal Punjab Unionist Party which would dominate Punjabi politics during the decades preceding Partition.[8]

Although road and railway construction primarily served British strategic needs, linking military outposts, cantonments and major cities (the last part of the Grand Trunk Road from Lahore to Peshawar at the Khyber Pass was completed in 1863-4), Punjabis obviously benefited from the improved communications.[9] On the whole, the Punjab became part of British India's internal and external trade system. Faster circulation of agricultural products at a cheaper rate, and a greater equalization of prices and market integration followed, while the total cultivated area expanded. Throughout the province the trend was to substitute inferior crops by more commercial ones, especially wheat, cotton, and sugarcane. The control of credit, carts, storage facilities and agricultural capital brought opportunities to rural entrepreneurs. Again mostly as a benefit of the military presence, the British took the initiative in the development of the region's natural resources (to be found mostly in the Himalayan foothills). Large borax deposits along with iron ore and coal were discovered and exploited, while in 1903-4 British investors set-up 35 refineries to process saltpetre (used in explosives and in leather tanning).[10] Now divided between India and Pakistan, the Punjab is still the most prosperous region of each country. Though the British were largely responsible for many of the changes in its economic structure, it has to be stressed that many Indian entrepreneurs (contractors mainly) were involved in seeking higher profits. For example, during extreme famine conditions in the second half of the nineteenth century, Indian entrepreneurs continued to export grain (from the Punjab granary in particular) to the much more profitable European market, not only diminishing the availability of grain in the subcontinent, but driving prices even higher. All in all, more important than these general socio-economic changes following canal irrigation and army recruitment was the British hierarchical system of authority which brought its inhabitants into close contact with their rulers.

AUTHORITY REACHING THE ROOTS OF RURAL SOCIETY

In 1803, when the Mughal Emperor accepted British protection and the Marathas remained the only obstacle to British supremacy, the East India Company had become the strongest force in South Asia. During the following fifty years it emerged as the paramount power and with the conquest of the Sikh kingdom of the Punjab, British territorial expansion became coterminous with the subcontinent's natural frontiers in the north-west. After the 1857 Revolt, the Company was dissolved and India was placed under the Crown. Never before had such a vast part of South Asia been officially ruled by one central government, holding the monopoly on international relations, which is a fundamental characteristic of any colonial state. Undoubtedly, the Anglo-Indian colonial state was more powerful, centralized and interventionist than any other former Indian state. Yet what made it most peculiar in comparison to other colonial states, was the fact that it focused mostly on the management of the internal markets and, continuously, on inland government.[11] British India was an atypical colony, as until the twentieth century, foreign trade never was more than a low percentage of the gross national product. Unlike in the Netherlands East Indies, therefore, the fiscal basis of the Anglo-Indian colonial state could not be based on a taxation of commodities meant for the world market nor on the imposition of duties in harbours.[12] Instead, in British India only the land revenue could finance the maintenance of the colonial state. As Baden-Powell argued at the time, it was 'certainly *not* easy to find other sources of revenue': income-tax or a tax on traders and professions, were the main alternatives but these presented 'great difficulties'.[13] Thus as in the Mughal Empire, throughout the later nineteenth and into the twentieth centuries also land revenue was the financial basis of the state, producing over 40 per cent of its revenue.[14] Importantly, unlike the Mughals, the British constructed an administrative hierarchy reaching the root of Indian agrarian society for its collection.[15]

Indispensable to this process of 'going native' (and again, though in different degrees, characteristic to the whole colonial world) was the creation of a body of scientific knowledge of South Asian society.[16] A vast amount of empirical knowledge of what the British thought to be the structure and functioning of Indian society was collected, mostly for the cadastral record. Investigations into the nature of land tenure were made: who did or who should own the land? What did the land produce? How much revenue could one collect? What were the past procedures? With whom should the collection be arranged? These and other questions were crucial to the Anglo-Indian colonial state, whose income largely depended on the land revenue, and to which colonial knowledge had to provide the answers. Thus the British spent much time on the determination of existing rights to the land rather than the creation of new ones, though, as James Douie made clear, nowhere in the Punjab did individual pro-prietary rights amount to full ownership 'except where the land-revenue has been redeemed'.[17] The major innovation of the British administration therefore was the legal recognition of an individual's property rights.

The British quest for revenues deeply influenced the lives of ordinary people, making them more conscious of the presence and character of colonial rule and generating great discontent. Trigonometrical and topographic surveys were held, maps were drawn and pre-existing records (containing social and economic information, appraisals of population and area, agricultural and craft production, and discussions of history and government) were summarized. All this knowledge was formalized in series of district gazetteers, and, since 1871, in the decennial census, on which the gazetteers in later years depended for most of their statistical data. Used by the independent Indian and Pakistani governments, the formal categories produced by this process of inclusion-by-definition decisively influenced the course of later history. Not only was the knowledge of Indian intermediaries (scholars, teachers, priests, lawyers, merchants and bankers), who had worked together with the British since the late eighteenth century, incorporated in this body of colonial knowledge. They themselves also became part of the colonial system: the daily running of the district was in the hands of Indian officials (who according to John Strachey had improved their standard of morality because they were relatively well-paid) and there is no doubt that it was they who often exercised the real power.[18] Also the colonial state began to patronize the holders of what they found to be the Indian tradition, those related to indigenous religious, educational, legal or other institutions. In this way, a political and cultural framework was created that embodied the Anglo-Indian colonial state's imperative to control the lives of Indians without necessarily sharing their values.

In fact, most probably more than elsewhere in South Asia, principles of authority also were articulated in the Punjab:

> Every section of society, from the handful of great landlords to the mass of peasant proprietors, co-operated with the district officers; and their collaboration enormously enhanced the power of the state for every public purpose.[19]

After annexation and in the spirit of the 'patronage bureaucracy' of Robert M. Bird and James Thomason,[20] the imperatives of a stable rural base through nurture of indigenous village communities and their customs lay at the heart of the Punjab tradition of administration.[21] Though much has been written about the founding members of the Punjab administration (John and Henry Lawrence, Robert Montgomery, Richard Temple and Donald McLeod to name a few), it should be stressed that in the long term it were not so much the intellectual capacities of these military doers but of their successors that proved important to the establishment of colonial authority in the region. Nonetheless, what remains significant is that from now on the colonial state came into close contact with village life, often to the great surprise of Punjabi villagers themselves. As one contemporary put it:

The villagers were, to begin with, frightened of the new conquerors. Women would hide their children. But fear soon gave way to curiosity and then to controversy. What were these Angrez log (Englishmen) up to? Their ideas were quite unlike those of rulers in the past. They began by doing the oddest things, like consulting each peasant about the land he possessed and giving him a permanent title to it, with a fixed revenue which was remitted in years when crops were bad. The officers moved about freely unguarded and without pomp and show. The visiting officials pitched their tents outside the villages, and held their office under a tree where anyone could approach them. Accompanied by just one or two persons they would ride on horseback for hours, inspecting and talking to the people. Most of them had learned Punjabi well, and some quite fluently.[22]

Subsequently, during the 1860s and 1870s, the British defined a specific tribal system on the basis of which, they said, the Punjabi village communities were organized. By linking up with native institutions like these, they believed, 'they could not only present themselves as legitimate indigenous rulers, presiding over an unaltered "traditional" society, but they could also harness the Punjab's distinctive social forms, above all in the settlement of canal-colonies, to the creation of a prosperous land'.[23] At the same time, a system of customary law was developed.[24] The idea behind the 1872 Punjab Laws Act was to use custom as the foundation for a system of personal law to be incorporated into the overall system of law enforced by the colonial state. Anglo-Indian law thus rested on two contradictory principles of social involvement. On the one hand, the colonial state was the agent of an expanding commercial society which brought India into the world market. On the other, the state depended for purposes of control on the maintenance of a traditional base.[25] In this way, British policy overall had the effect of drying up the pragmatism and natural flexibility of South Asian traditions, creating much more rigid and bureaucratic versions of them in the process.

On the basis of these colonial constructs, village community, tribal system and customary law, the British built a hierarchic system of administration. The five Punjab divisions were divided into districts and these again into *tahsils* of around 150 villages each, under the control of *tahsildars*, who held revenue and judicial powers. At the lower end of the administrative hierarchy, there were the *zails*, consisting of between ten to thirty village communities and forming the key units of the system. Control rested with the *zaildar*, who supervised the village headmen and also acted as head of police. These *zaildars* generally were the leaders of the local dominant tribes and often also landowners. Subsequently, some *zaildars* produced families of local influence, who used their position to claim leadership. The administrative influence of the *zaildars* guaranteed that the positions, though initially not hereditary, passed from father to son. Thus by and large, at the turn of the century, British policy had produced a class of rural leaders, tied closely to the administration and exercising their authority in a tribal idiom. The further framework for this structuring of rural Punjabi politics took place with the creation of the category of agricultural tribes in the 1901 Alienation of Land Act. Already for some time, the British worried (and not only in the Punjab) about the large-scale sale of land for debts owed to moneylenders as result of the fact that the British wanted their revenue in cash and introduced the usual assessment based on long-term averages rather than sharing the risk of each harvest with the peasantry. They saw that these moneylenders were intruders in the Punjabi village communities and therefore banned the sale of land to anyone other than a member of a registered agricultural tribe. In reality, agricultural enterprise was largely financed by rurally based investors, who secured their capital from those who had profited from the expansion of cash crop farming. As a result, a large section of the middle peasantry consolidated itself, overall leading to an egalitarian pattern of landownership right up to the end of British rule. Afterwards, the protection of agricultural tribes through the 1901 Act made it even easier for this class (as well as the region's landowners) to dominate the supply of credit and the power that accompanied it. Even so, according to S.S. Thorburn, the British mission was unsuccessful for the poverty-stricken Punjabis of the lower strata.

In spite of our science, our unique experience in governing Asiatics, and the unselfish devotion to duty of our Anglo-Indian officials, we have failed to fulfil our primary obligation as rulers, the doing of the greatest good to the greatest numbers.[26]

The Revolt of 1857 led to a conservative drift in British policy, which led to the cultivation of alliances with the so-called natural leaders of Indian society. Accordingly, the Punjab's influential top ranking individuals and groups were incorporated into the bureaucracy. The Punjab's leaders (and the Sikhs in particular) proved to be loyal and were rewarded: princes, chiefs, landowners, and families of note were made *zaildar*, honorary magistrate, member of one of the *darbars* held in the province or tied to the British system of rule in other ways (for example through Punjabization of the British Indian army from the 1880s and the education of the Punjab's young elites at Aitchison Chiefs' College in Lahore).[27] In the countryside most of these leaders were tribal chiefs or landowners or both, while in the towns and cities they usually owned considerable residential property, commanded credit or controlled broad urban factions. Only after they had been properly ranked and labelled, and frozen into place, so the British believed, would these leaders, exercise their traditional authority. The colonial state also patronized Punjabi religious and educational institutions. Ian Kerr, for instance, has described the close relationship between the state and the most holy Sikh shrine, the Golden Temple, in Amritsar.[28] Similarly, David Gilmartin has discussed how the British, after linking their rule to ideas about local tribal authority, came to participate in the functioning of many rural shrines of Sufi *pirs* by establishing close connections with those in authority at the shrine, usually the lineal descendants of a particular saint.[29]

Still, the functioning of this system of patronage was increasingly undermined. This was partly because the British preoccupation with what they believed to be traditional India encouraged them to ignore, or wish away, or disregard, the alternative India that was coming into being: urban, educated, modernizing, radical, middle-class and nationalist (the Bengali variety in particular).[30] Subjects to be discussed later such as evangelicalism, Anglo-vernacular education, new modes of communication (railways, post offices, telegraph, print culture), urbanization and, moreover, the way the British assessed what were legitimate interests meriting political representation, proved to be crucial to Punjabi responses to the newly created order.

Increasingly they would see in the categories used by the British, something they could use profitably. Broader identities emerged, which transformed the character of regional politics, as Punjabi elites responded to Western science and Christianity and their local ties increasingly gave way to more universal commitments. Importantly, they did not formulate their programmes independently but competitively amongst each other and in confrontation with the British. If they wanted to lead Punjabis, however, they often had to connect to local languages and sacred symbols to communicate their message and ultimately it were these identity politics also that triumphed with the Partition of India. I will return to all this in the subsequent chapters, but for now wish to give a general description of the traditional world of the Punjab.

THREE GREATER TRADITIONS AND PUNJABI POPULAR CULTURE

Punjab offered an unparalleled case for a comparative historical study: only here can one compare the three greater traditions of Islam, Hinduism and Sikhism, each with a long specific history in the region.[31] This in the first place because Punjab was the homeland of the Sikhs. Moreover, what is often forgotten is that Islam and Hinduism in the region showed characteristics that differed remarkably from other parts in South Asia. From the Indus civilization onwards, the Punjab underwent five millennia of human history. Many invaders followed the Aryans on their way to the fertile *doab* of the Yamuna and Ganga rivers. Since the twelfth century the Punjab also has been a region of Indo-Islamic interaction. It formed a frontier province of respectively, the Ghaznavid Empire, the Delhi Sultanate and the Mughal Empire after the battle of Panipat in 1526. Lahore experienced its high noon thereafter, when Mughal Emperors held their courts there. While there is no general explanation for the collapse of Mughal power, within the Punjab the Sikhs at least profited from it; alternatively, their emergence as a powerful community was crucial to its further decline. Except for the so called *nirguna sants*, Guru Nanak (1469-1539) did not find anything commendable in the major forms of contemporary belief and practice, whether Hindu or Muslim. Something new was needed and, following his moral fervour, Nanak created an ideology and started a movement, which under his nine successors evolved into the Sikh Panth. In 1603-4 the fifth Guru, Arjan, compiled the Granth Sahib and in 1699 the tenth Guru, Gobind Singh, established the institution of the Khalsa of initiated Sikhs. Thus came about the concept of the saint-soldier[32] (which simultaneously meant that women 'were inadvertently depreciated as full-fledged followers of the Sikh tradition'[33]). Under the leadership of Maharaja Ranjit Singh (1781-1839), a Sikh Empire was established in 1799 that, subsequently, with the help of a body of European and American professional instructors (many of whom veterans of Napoleon's army), ruled Punjab and Kashmir until the British annexation of 1849. Although central Punjab, which contained the most prosperous tracts of the region, was the stronghold of the Sikhs,[34] Muslims outnumbered both Hindus and Sikhs together in that same area. During the decade after annexation, around a quarter of the population was Sikh in the Amritsar, Ludhiana and Ferozepore districts. Loss of political power initially had led to large scale re-conversion to Hinduism but gradually the Sikhs got back their strength and self-confidence. In fact, by the beginning of the twentieth century, they had gained a political influence disproportionate to their numbers, mostly because of their eminent roles in agriculture and the British Indian army.

The emergence of the Sikh faith alongside Islam and Hinduism and the constant invasions however did not lead to a weakening of the caste system in the Punjab.[35] Undoubtedly, Brahmans did not dominate the Hindu social hierarchy and indeed their status was so depressed in the eastern part of the province that some even took to the plough. On the whole, this low position (except in the Himalayan foothills) resulted not only from the fact that they had to compete with Muslim and Sikh leaders but also because they lacked the economic power which temples in Hindu-dominated areas elsewhere provided. Much more powerful within the Hindu community were the commercial castes: the

Khatris in particular, followed by Aroras (western Punjab) and
• Banias (eastern Punjab), who according to S.S. Thorburn, un-
deservingly profited most from the hard labour of the Punjabi
peasant.[36] Under colonial rule, however, their position was increasingly challenged by Rajputs and Jats, who had become rich
peasants or found jobs in the British Indian army. The majority
of the Punjab's population, nonetheless, was Muslim (and, as
opposed to what is generally thought, the Punjab army consisted
of Muslim recruits from west Punjab instead of Sikhs). They
were organized, the British observed, on a tribal basis of which
the largest were again the Jats and Rajputs (being those Hindus
who had embraced Islam mostly between the fourteenth and
sixteenth centuries). Other important tribes (besides the traditional Sayyid and Sheikh elites) were the Pathans, Awans,
Baluchis and Gujars. These tribes mostly were to be found in
the western Punjab where there also were large Muslim landowners. At the same time, it has to be stressed that particularly
in rural Punjab, religious boundaries were extremely fluid. People
did not see themselves simply as Muslims, Hindus or Sikhs. On
the contrary, these categories often overlapped (as noted also by
the leading ethnographer and administrator of the Punjab, Denzil
Ibbetson, when recording religious statistics for the 1881 Punjab
census).[37] The widespread influence of Sufism remains a most
interesting aspect of Islam in the Punjab. Especially in the countryside, all communities without distinction regarded Sufi *pirs*
as sacred. Almost every village in central Punjab contained a
shrine dedicated to Pir Sakhi Sarvar (who was believed to be a
patron of young children). In the same way, Punjabi (generally
written in the Persian-Arabic Nastaliq script), in which such
Sufi poets like Bullhe Shah, Sultan Bahu and Shah Husain
composed, was both a literary and a spoken language transcending religious boundaries. Members of all communities
shared in many of each others' celebrations, coming together,
for example, at the festivals honouring Sufi saints as Baba Farid
of Pakpattan and Hazrat Datta Ganj Bakhsh, whose recently
renovated *dargah* remains the largest and most popular Sufi
shrine in Lahore up to today. In addition, songs, proverbs and
folk tales provide further evidence of this shared popular culture.

At the end of the nineteenth century, Richard Temple collected many of these among illiterate Punjabis, hearing numerous versions of the same stories in different villages.[38] A more famous genre than these folk tales were the *qissas* or tragic love tales of Hir and Ranjha, Sassi and Punnu, and Sohni and Mahival. All in all, rural Punjab and in particular the central areas shared an overall popular culture. Standards of behaviour, categories of thought, conceptions of time, notions of purity and impurity and of the sacred and the profane were not marked by great differences. Besides honouring Sufi *pirs* and taking part in each others' celebrations, many Punjabis followed common beliefs bordering on animism and fetishism concerning different spirits, witchcraft, divine intercession, the need to pay attention to omens and the merit to be gained through pilgrimage. These beliefs had been there for many centuries and were older than all formal theologies.[39]

Obviously much of this shared popular culture remained in the new cultural configuration. Social reform was controversial: it often was subversively resisted and laughed at.[40] According to John Strachey, Indians largely kept to their own traditional way because they detested progress at large:

I never heard of a great measure of improvement that was popular in India, even among the classes that have received the largest share of education. No one who has lived, as I have done for the better part of my life, among the people can have towards them feelings other than those of sympathy and affection and respect. They have qualities which deserve all admiration, but they are intensely conservative and intensely ignorant, wedded, to an extent difficult for Europeans to understand, to every ancient custom, and between their customs and religion no line of distinction can be drawn. We often deceive ourselves in regard to the changes that are taking place. We believe that our western knowledge, our railways, and our telegraphs must be breaking up the whole fabric of Hinduism, but these things, as I have said before, have touched only the merest fringe of the ideas and beliefs of the population of India. The vast masses of the people remain in a different world from ours. They dislike everything new, they dislike almost everything that we look upon as progress, and they live, for the most part, in blind ignorance of the aims and ideas of their rulers.[41]

Despite all continuity, the three greater Punjabi traditions and the shared popular culture increasingly were under attack by the reformist politics of the colonial state and, more important to this study, by indigenous voluntary movements in the emergent public sphere.[42] Among the latter movements, the Arya Samaj remains the best known within the Hindu community and beyond, but will be extensively dealt with later. Most influential among Muslims was the Anjuman-i-Islamia. It was founded in 1866 in Lahore by followers of the famous reformer, Sayyid Ahmad Khan (1817-98), who had established the Aligarh movement and in 1884 visited the Punjab to collect funds for this project and to deliver speeches. It opened schools with an Anglo-vernacular curriculum (of which Islamia College in Lahore remains the best known), emphasized female education, loyalty to the British and subsequently opposed the Indian National Congress. Another two important modern Muslim reform movements active in the Punjab were the Deobandi and Ahl-i-Hadith. The former followed the ideas of the reformist ulema associated with a Theological Academy founded in the town of Deoband in 1867. Its offshoot, the Tablighi Jama'at (preaching society) is probably the most widely followed Muslim movement today.[43] The Ahl-i-Hadith or people of the tradition, who declared their preference for authentic prophetic traditions over the four law schools, descended from the Wahhabis of Sayyid Ahmad Shahid and had fought against the Sikhs during the 1820s. They were strict Muslims and opposed anyone (but particularly Ahmadiyahs) indulging in *taqlid* or accepting authority from sources not found in the Koran and the *hadith*. Indeed, compared to Muslim groups like these, Ahmadiyah membership was small. Yet, the movement is worthy of study because of its very active propaganda in both the spoken and the written word and, closely related, particularly also its importance as an Islamic missionary movement.

Undeniably, the Singh Sabhas were the most important reform movement within Sikh history. Yet, already there had been some reformist ferment among the Sikhs after annexation with the Nirankari and Namdhari movements, both established some influence in the countryside.[44] Minor movements, they still exist and therefore have to be mentioned, especially also because they got their inspiration towards purification and the past from ascetics who were raised to the position of Gurus by their followers. Accordingly, both movements produced distinct successions of Gurus afterwards and thus clearly opposed the subsequent Singh Sabha emphasis upon the ten Gurus (as stressed in the 1925 Gurdwara Act: see Chapter Three). Otherwise interesting remains the fact that Baba Dayal Das, founder of the Nirankaris, like the Singh Sabhaites later, believed that the Granth Sahib should be the only visible focus for the Sikhs. He rejected the militant Khalsa ideal as conflicting with the spiritual teachings of Guru Nanak and so threatened the Sikh tradition as propagated by Maharaja Ranjit Singh. The millenarian Namdharis were similar to the Nirankaris but unlike the latter often used physical force, and so the colonial government closely watched them. Their leader, Baba Ram Singh, opposed the British at least for their killing of cows for beef and, subsequently, when in 1872 some Namdharis attacked Muslim slaughterhouses and butchers' shops, more than fifty protestors were blown from the gun. Though Baba Ram Singh himself was not involved, he was exiled to Rangoon afterwards.[45]

The history of socio-religious reform in the Punjab obviously started before the Singh Sabha, Arya Samaj and Ahmadiyah movements. Yet, what makes the latter movements interesting for a comparative historical study is that from within three different greater traditions they closely interacted with each other, with Christian missionaries and with the colonial state in fast-changing social and intellectual circumstances. It was because of the latter that their actions transcended earlier regional forms of politics and increasingly adapted to the intellectual ideas introduced by the British. Punjabis could not get away from the results of modern science and technology which were to be seen all over the region. Their intellectual response to the dominant colonial culture certainly defined the direction of Punjabi politics. Chapter Two will describe some of the most vital underlying processes (Christian missionary activities, Anglo-vernacular education, print culture and the emergence of Punjabi voluntary associations), while Part II will focus upon how the Singh Sabhas, Arya Samaj and Ahmadiyahs stirred up Punjabi minds. Previous to that, however, I wish to discuss the wider context: the creation of a liberal public sphere in the Punjab under the Pax Britannica. In particular, how the British perception of the material superiority of their own culture, as manifested in scientific thought and technological innovation, had decisive consequences for the way they viewed and tried to shape nature and communities in the Punjab.

SHAPING NATURE AND COMMUNITIES

Because of scientific discoveries and technological advance since the Renaissance, Europeans increasingly adhered to a world-view that elevated man above nature, 'a conception long prominent in some strains of the Judeo-Christian philosophical tradition'.[46] Otherwise, as part of a long term attempt to Christianize the masses, during the complex sixteenth century process of the Reformation, the church tried to undermine and control popular belief in the enchanted natural world.[47] Afterwards, during the Enlightenment, early modern scientists began to proclaim that it was the destiny of man (who after all was not an animal) to dominate nature. After all, the divinely created natural world was knowable through the senses. Relying on observation and experiment, scientists believed it was possible to reveal the laws of nature that governed the world and all that was in it. From here it was indeed a small step to the idea that nature was nothing more than a quantitative and mechanistic mass; a resource to be exploited and its utility to be maximized through science and productive labour. Soon Westerners began to define the status of societies worldwide on the basis of the level of control over nature through scientific investigation, the level of efficiency in the use of natural resources and the application of machine power.

In the colonial context all this meant that most British began to look at their own 'vastly superior understanding of the workings of nature' as the crucial justification for their 'monopolization of leadership and managerial roles in colonized societies'.[48] Hence when in 1878 the Empress-bridge across the Sutlej was opened, the Bishop of Lahore hailed it as 'a temple of science', a monument to the Christian virtues of faith, patience and hard work. Those who had undertaken much of the labour, between five and six thousand Indian labourers, were treated to a feast of sweetmeats. The bridge was described in the *Pioneer* as 'exactly the kind of work that makes the natives look up to and feel the superiority of the English, who are able to control and bridge the wildest rivers'.[49] The British were underscoring not only their power over nature but, simultaneously, over traditional Punjabi communities. Like the region's rivers, these communities had to be 'controlled and guided, led and regulated' by scientific administration, 'rather than as allies of government in a common project of rational environmental domination'.[50] So while the Anglo-Indian colonial state was backed by modern forces (the army and the police), both the recognition and the protection of a society composed of numerous traditional communities was crucial to control. This played a fundamental role in the shaping of liberal institutions in the late nineteenth and early twentieth centuries. For, whatever may have been the starting principle and however narrow its distribution, the introduction of electoral representation surely represented one means by which traditional communities were lured into the public sphere and the bureaucracy. Penetrating deep into South Asian society to collect the land revenue, the Raj introduced local and provincial elections to legitimize its position and maintain support among local elites. This was partly a response to pressure from educated Indians, but the central concern of the British was the maintenance of the underlying structure of the Anglo-Indian colonial state.

As in Europe, the public sphere in South Asia overall became dedicated to the promotion of the material and moral progress to which the British, consciously or not, were committed. From the beginning of the nineteenth century, the British (the utilitarians in particular) assumed rule by law as pivotal to any lasting change for the better. In fact, by 1882, India's commercial, criminal, and procedural laws were completely codified, whereas England still awaited a criminal code, and the vast majority of English law remained non-codified, in the form of statute or common law. Indeed, the British often were able to do in South Asia what they were unable to do at home. The Benthamite and

Utilitarian desire for unity, precision and simplicity in law reached great heights in the subcontinent, making Anglo-Indian law far superior in order, clarity and system to its English counterpart. But what did this mean for Indian society? As said earlier, the Anglo-Indian colonial state primarily focused on inland government rule and, hence, the lasting influence of Utilitarianism in South Asia is to be found in the colonial state's hierarchic system of authority, of which the size and activities in the 1870s proved to be the nearest realization in English experience of Bentham's vision of the state of law and order.[51] Not that all this meant a complete transplantation of Western ideas on Indian ground. On the contrary, the British undoubtedly were influenced by South Asian circumstances. As argued earlier in this chapter, while Utilitarian theory touched Indian ground because of the collection of the land revenue, the British defined tradition through Anglo-Indian law. So they sought to preserve a conception of South Asian society as they first saw it, enforcing values as seen rooted in tradition from antiquity that placed the family and community above the individual. In this way, Anglo-Indian law accommodated both the assimilative ideals of liberalism (with its optimistic assumption that South Asia could be transformed on the basis of a European model) and the excluding insistence upon Indian difference in a personal law.[52] Yet, while according to utilitarians human nature was the same throughout the world, subsequently evolutionary theorists like Henry Summer Maine 'repudiated the utilitarian vision of an infinitely manageable human nature' and argued instead that societies were different though comparable, and had followed distinct historical paths progressively 'from status to contract'.[53] This is relevant as over time these comparative and historicist social theories of Maine and his contemporaries were converted into moral and political ones. The fact that Mahatma Gandhi (1869-1948) and other nationalists afterwards propagated the idea of the village community (to give but one example) shows the influence of these social theories in the South Asian public sphere.

Like that of law reform, the creation of a public education system was surrounded by many of the same difficulties and contradictions. Obviously the colonial government could not introduce the teaching of Christianity directly into the schools it sponsored, and instead therefore introduced English literature as the central element of the school curriculum to boost the moral tone. A remarkable situation indeed, as early Victorian human-istic study in English schools centred on (Greek and Latin literatures) instead of English. As a result, as Gauri Viswanathan argued, cultural value was handed over in the emerging South Asian public sphere, 'from belief and dogma to language, experience and history'.[54] Though the public education system only concerned a small part of the population, I nonetheless want to stress that many of the moral ideas introduced through this system ultimately reached a much wider circle. This hap-pened, through the educational activities (in both English and the vernaculars) of indigenous voluntary movements, which not only became increasingly active in the urban public sphere but later also started to penetrate the countryside. These movements were part of a process in which the establishment of the Pax Britannica in the Punjab stood for the growth of a more stable, settled and hierarchical society at the expense of the unsettled, the popular and the fluid situation of old.

The Punjab had been part of the larger Central Asian world of trade and nomadism for centuries but, partly to counter the advent of the Russians in the region, the British attempted to encourage and control this network.[55] Passes were opened, trading posts established, banditry was controlled and the frontier tribes were pacified. Though nomadism continued, in western Punjab particularly many tribal traditions were uprooted. In the same way, British policies changed the lives of the people living in the northern Himalayan parts of the province. By the 1880s, the shepherds and cowherds of Chamba and Kangra found that forests and wastes had become state property. From now on, their rights were defined, the rhythms of their movements controlled, and their spatial mobility restricted. Throughout the province, animals were enumerated, registered, and branded, and in 1903 the Punjab Military Transport Act was passed, legalizing government rights over all transport animals. In the end, few Punjabis continued their earlier herding activities and most turned to more settled modes of life. Some nomads took to wage labour (earning small sums by digging canals or building roads); some became part time peasants or expanded their cultivation to supplement a declining income, while others concentrated on trade. As was to be expected, particularly the construction of a system of canal irrigation and colonies in central and south-west Punjab changed much of the existing pastoral economy. Here pastoralists were expelled on a grand scale and for a prolonged period these uncouth folk carried on a battle with the early peasant migrants. Yet they also would live in a Punjabi village community afterwards. The days when no one thought of wearing anything but a *lungi* (i.e. a rectangular cloth worn wrapped round the waist up to the ankles) by men and turbans were gone and from now onwards one would dress in a more civilized manner. Similarly, thatched huts which could be left behind, or moved, with every change of encampment were replaced by clean mud plastered houses, while the village head-man often would have a verandah supported on masonry pillars to make clear his newly acquired position in society.[56]

Though pastoral life often was romantically immortalized in Punjabi *qissas*, in many colonial writings pastoralists were objects of contempt: lazy, improvident and wretched as cultivators, lawless, wild, and generally cowards. The lazy pastoralist was defined in opposition to the sturdy and industrious Sikh peasant, cultivating his field with care and yielding revenue to the state. Indeed, it is here again that European ideas about man and nature come to the front: notions about work and leisure, good and evil, order and beauty. Undoubtedly, earlier mentioned late nineteenth century evolutionist ideas had strengthened this association between the pastoral nomad and the primitive. The evolutionist scheme saw the movement from savagery to civilization as an evolution from tribe to state, where family, property and territory were established at different stages of this linear movement. Throughout the Punjab, the Anglo-Indian colonial state opposed nomads, pedlars and herdsmen and attempted to discipline and settle them. Watched, hounded, harassed and frequently prosecuted by the police, nomads lived a life of endless persecution, particularly after the Criminal Tribes

Acts of 1871 and 1911 gave legal sanction to official action against wanderers. Again seen as a group phenomenon, tribes stigmatized as habitual wanderers were expected to stay confined in their village communities. Licences of leave were to be issued, but only to those who pursued an 'honest' livelihood. By 1881, the census counted 16,039 individuals, belonging to seven criminal tribes (when India gained independence it inherited, as a legacy of the colonial period, 3.5 million individuals belonging to 128 'criminal tribes'). Interestingly, the 1871 Act included eunuchs as well. According to James Fitzjames Stephen (who as Law Member drafted the Act), there existed an 'organized system of sodomitical prostitution, of which these wretches are the managers', and that no measure to force them to adopt 'honest pursuits' would be too severe. During the discussions preceding the Act, many resented the eunuchs' alleged kidnapping and castration of children, yet what disturbed the participants as much as criminal behaviour (and what the Act hence forbade), was the practice of eunuchs appearing in public dressed in female clothes. For once and for all, one should not only live long and happily in some village but at the same time stick to one's sexual nature as well, because for most Victorians (and increasingly elitist Indians) sexual ambiguity and a life of 'wandering without leave' were disgusting and intolerable.[57] Despite the efforts to discipline and settle criminal tribes, however, during the beginning of the twentieth century Punjab officials noted little progress:

The crime committed by wandering tribes continues to increase; no real surveillance can be maintained over these groups, and the law as it stands is a direct encouragement to them to continue wandering, as so long as they have no fixed place of residence they cannot, however criminal, be registered under the Criminal Tribes Act.[58]

During the establishment of the Pax Britannica, the civilizing mission reached a climax with the emergence of reformatory settlements in the Punjab, where people would be taught the virtues of discipline, hard work, and cleanliness. The most incorrigible characters were placed in a central prison-like re-formatory, the reasonably well-behaved in industrial settlements, and the best in new agricultural settlements in the canal colonies.

Significantly, besides the Salvation Army, indigenous voluntary movements like the Arya Samaj, the Singh Sabhas and the Anjuman-i-Islamia responded positively to the government's invitation to become involved in these reformatory settlements to produce moral peasants. By the end of 1919, more than half of the agricultural and industrial settlements were more or less administered by indigenous associations with government assistance. These however did not spend anything more than the amount of the government grant. Primarily they were concerned with making converts and therefore particularly focused on the appointment of teachers and the establishment of mosques, gurdwaras and temples.[59] Alternatively, the softer side of the civilizing mission was to be found in museums and exhibitions. In museums Indians were confronted with the scientific order of things as perceived by Europeans (who after all knew more about South Asia) and saw themselves represented as tribes and castes living close to the soil and following archaic and chaotic forms of knowledge. When in the London India Office in 1869 and shown the photographs in *The People of India*, Sayyid Ahmad Khan, for instance, was horrified to see his countrymen portrayed as the 'equals of animals'.[60] For Punjabi common folk, the Lahore Museum was the 'wonder house' and, indeed, increasingly a popular spot to wander around. By 1905 the museum had 300,000 visitors a year and these were not only men for for since 1901 every first Monday of the month was reserved for women (in 1905-6 almost 4,000 women visited the museum on these Mondays).[61] Alternately, those who had followed Anglo-vernacular education undoubtedly were heavily influenced by the museum's orderly world and indeed often rejected the notion of their country as an ethnographic museum. The Lahore Museum took its educational function very seriously: apart from housing the Science Institute and allowing the Society for Promoting Scientific Knowledge to use its lecture hall, it instituted a series of magic lantern lectures.[62] The most visited and historically more interesting lectures, however, took place during the 1910-20s. Reserved for women in purdah, these not only concerned science but travel and, indeed, the education of women too. Much in the same way, exhibitions instructed

Punjabis how to improve agricultural production. At these exhibitions, indigenous products and knowledge were scientifically classified and organized in order to make clear their utilitarian value, while in turn the latest gadgets from the West were displayed so that Punjabis would know where they would be going if they did their best. In fact, the Lahore Museum originally was hastily constructed for the Punjab exhibition of 1864-5.[63]

CONCLUSION

Because the Punjab became a crucial strategic and fertile agricultural region soon after its annexation, its inhabitants became familiar with Western ideas and practices, science and technology. Even if they could not understand its results, they certainly were impressed with the roads, railways, bridges, irrigation canals and telegraph. Otherwise, Punjabis were confronted with the world of science because of the ever-growing body of colonial knowledge about their society that accompanied processes of Anglo-Indian colonial state formation. The latter was particularly important because the legitimacy of the British depended on the preservation and at times creation of local elites and indigenous rituals and symbols of authority. The establishment of the Pax Britannica certainly was a multifaceted process, riven with contradictions. The limited Raj often was forced to compromise as it worked in the context of Punjabi social classes and conditions. It was closely related to struggles inside society for status, privilege, and power. Competing forces were not established solely by the British and hence to be put under the label of divide and rule, nor were they controlled by them. On the contrary, the British increasingly became busy trying to contain Punjabi forces and in the twentieth century became more reactionaries than initiators, when the niches within the public sphere inhabited by certain groups and interests cutting into and contradicting the policies of the colonial state had become too large. Importantly, many aspects of pre-nineteenth century Punjabi culture continued to exist. Through simultaneous processes of acceptance, accommodation, adaptation and rejection, Punjabis rationally redefined their traditions, while incorporating

European thought at the same time.[64] Within this new cultural configuration, then, there were three dominant interrelated continuities. First, the formation of the Anglo-Indian colonial state that provided the spine to the emerging liberal public sphere. Second, the fact that through modern institutions and practices, a rational mode of knowledge authorized by Western science came to dictate Punjabi society. And third, the tendency among leading Punjabis to organize themselves into new self-identifying voluntary groups. Indeed, perhaps the fast changes in society made Punjabis anxious for the re-imposition of some moral order. This at least would partly explain both the popularity of indigenous voluntary reform movements and the British Indian army as the 'only kinds of order with which the villagers were familiar, above the level of the family; and the only kinds of order which were compatible with the patriarchal authority pervading the average villager's day-to-day life'.[65] In order to understand the ideas and activities explored by the Singh Sabhas, Arya Samaj and Ahmadiyahs, however, further investigation into the creation of a Punjabi public sphere remains crucial.

NOTES

1. Colonial Punjab was divided into five divisions (Lahore, Jullunder, Rawalpindi, Delhi and Multan), each subordinate to a commissioner. These were further grouped in twenty-nine districts with a deputy commissioner in charge. The five frontier districts were separated in 1901 to form the North West Frontier Province and Delhi district a decade later, when the government of British India shifted, with great pomp, its capital from Calcutta to New Delhi. In the Punjab were also forty-three native states, where British law was not applied and overall the colonial interaction was of a different kind.

2. Rudyard Kipling has described the exciting atmosphere of the Great Game beautifully in *Kim*, 1901; repr. Harmondsworth: Penguin, 1987. Kipling worked as a journalist in the Punjab for the *Civil and Military Gazette*, a sister newspaper of the larger and very profitable *Pioneer* at Allahabad. His first stories came out of that experience and were published locally.

3. Prakash Tandon, *Punjabi Century*, London: Chatto & Windus, 1961, p. 161 (translation mine).

4. Soon after annexation considerable quantities of potatoes were produced in the tracts around Lahore and adjustment to the Western presence therefore also meant the incorporation of the potato into the Punjabi diet. Ian Kerr, 'Urbanization and Colonial Rule in 19th-Century India: Lahore and Amritsar, 1849-1881', *Punjab Past and Present*, 14, 1980, 223. Cf. Bayly's idea of 'global uniformities' in relation to food in *The Birth of the Modern World 1780–1914*, London: Blackwell, 2004, pp. 18-19.

5. In 'Some Consequences of Military Expenditure in British India: The Case of the Upper Sind Sagar Doab, 1849-1947' in *Arrested Development in India: The Historical Dimension*, ed. Clive Dewey, New Delhi: Manohar, 1988, Clive Dewey shows in detail how defence spending in the Punjab galvanized the economies and flattened the societies of the areas in which it was concentrated.

6. Ian Talbot, *Punjab and the Raj, 1849–1947*, New Delhi: Manohar, 1988, Chapter Two.

7. G.F. MacMunn, *The Armies of India*, 1911; repr. New Delhi: Heritage, 1991, p. 129; James M. Douie, *The Panjab, North-West Frontier Province and Kashmir*, 1916; repr., New Delhi: Seema, 1974, p. 104.

8. On the Punjab Unionist Party: Talbot, *Punjab and the Raj*.

9. Generally railway tracks demarcated British civil and military lines from the Indian old city areas in major cities. In Lahore, in fact, the station itself was designed as a fort in which the British could take refuge in case of a revolt.

10. *Imperial Gazetteer of India*, Provincial Series: Punjab, vol. 1, 1908; repr. New Delhi: Atlantic, 1991, p. 76.

11. D.H.A. Kolff, 'Zuid-Azië na 1945', in *De Wereld na 1945*; ed. D.F.J. Bosscher, H. Renner, R.B. Soetendorp and R. Wagenaar, revd. edn., Utrecht: Spectrum, 1992, pp. 478-9.

12. The Dutch state could deal with its financial problems at least for a hundred years after the introduction of the Cultivation System in 1830, i.e. the production of valuable cash crops on lands previously used for subsistence rice cultivation, to be sold on the international market through government monopolies.

13. B.H. Baden-Powell, *The Land Systems of British India*, vol. I., Oxford: Clarendon Press, 1892, p. 344.

14. Judith M. Brown, *Modern India: Origins of an Asian Democracy*, New Delhi: Oxford University Press, 1894, p. 124.

15. Most Empire builders probably thought that India was worth governing well, and this atypical colony increasingly became the jewel in the crown. Nearly half of all Indian government revenues were spent on the maintenance of the British Indian army. At no cost to the British tax payer, these 'English barracks in the Oriental seas' could be widely launched—from Abyssinia to Hong Kong—to protect

imperial trade and communications between Europe and Australasia. In fact, during the Second World War two and a half million Indians (the largest unrewarded volunteer force that ever existed) fought to defend the interests of the British Empire. Moreover, almost as important as the British Indian army for the functioning of the Empire were the crucial movements during high colonialism of Indians with administrative skills and expertise (they ran subordinate state bureaucracies and professions in the colonial territories from Malaysia to the Persian Gulf and East Africa), India also controlled the capital and indentured labour system.

16. Seminal here have been the essays by Bernard S. Cohn also collected in *An Anthropologist Among the Historians and Other Essays*, New Delhi: Oxford University Press, 1987; and *Colonialism and its Forms of Knowledge: The British in India*, New Delhi: Oxford University Press, 1996.

17. James M. Douie, *Panjab Settlement Manual*, Lahore: Civil and Military Gazette Press, 1899, p. 58.

18. John Strachey, *India: Its Administration & Progress*, London: Macmillan, 1911, pp. 91-3.

19. Clive Dewey, *Anglo-Indian Attitudes: The Mind of the Indian Civil Service*, London: Hambledon Press, 1993, p. 202.

20. Peter Penner, *The Patronage Bureaucracy in North India: The Robert M. Bird and James Thomason School, 1820-1870*, New Delhi: Chanakya, 1986.

21. Among the 'mythological' works about the Punjab tradition, P.H.M. van den Dungen's *The Punjab Tradition: Influence and Authority in Nineteenth Century India*, London: George Allen & Unwin Ltd., 1972, probably remains the most reasonable. The latest is Harold Lee, *Brothers in the Raj: The Lives of John and Henry Lawrence*, Karachi: Oxford University Press, 2004.

22. Tandon, *Punjabi Century*, p. 12 (translation mine).

23. Thomas R. Metcalf, *Ideologies of the Raj*, Cambridge: Cambridge University Press, 1995, p. 129.

24. The first official and most famous compendium of customary law was published in 1881: C.L. Tupper, *Punjab Customary Law*, 3 vols., Calcutta: Government Printing, 1881.

25. David Gilmartin, *Empire and Islam: Punjab and the Making of Pakistan*, New Delhi: Oxford University Press, 1988, pp. 13-14.

26. S.S. Thorburn, *The Punjab in Peace and War*, 1883; repr. Patiala: Punjab Languages Department, 1970, pp. 261-2.

27. Lieutenant-Governor Robert Montgomery commissioned Lepel Griffin to record the lineages of these Punjabi 'natural leaders'. *The Punjab Chiefs*, 2 vols., Lahore: Civil and Military Gazette Press, 1865, was the result.

28. Ian Kerr, 'British Relationships with the Golden Temple, 1849-1890', *Indian Economic and Social History Review*, 21, 1984, pp. 320-42.

29. Gilmartin, *Empire and Islam*, Chapter Two.

30. Generally Bengalis were ridiculed by their fellow countrymen for aping the British. Yet they were the first to question the legitimacy of colonial power and therefore were not liked by the British. Consequently, the latter contrasted the Bengalis with such Indian martial races as the Sikhs with whom they supposedly had much affinity. In the words of John Strachey: 'it has often been said, and it is probably true, that Bengal is the only country in the world where you can find a population among whom personal cowardice is looked upon as in no way disgraceful', in *India*, p. 151.

31. Once again, Islam is a tradition, Sikhism was moulded into one; but because of the multiplicity of Hindu practices Hinduism remains a non-definable term in the Indian context.

32. The word Sikh comes from the Punjabi verb *sikh*, to learn. Basically therefore a Sikh is one who learns and follows the path of liberation taught by Guru Nanak and his nine successors. In 1699, the tenth Guru, Gobind Singh, formed the *Khalsa* at Anandpur. Thereafter all who had undergone the initiation ceremony retained their hair uncut and carried weapons were *Khalsa* Sikhs and called themselves Singh (lion). Ever since, Sikhs of the *Khalsa* are distinct from Sikhs who are unitiated but do not cut their hair (and often wear a turban) as well as those Sikhs keep who even less to outward Sikh forms and codes of belief and discipline (*Rahit*). See W.H. McLeod, *Who is a Sikh?: The Problem of Sikh Identity*, New Delhi: Oxford University Press, 1989, Chapter Seven.

33. Doris R. Jakobsh, *Relocating Gender in Sikh History: Transformation, Meaning and Identity*, New Delhi: Oxford University Press, 2003, p. 42.

34. According to B.H. Baden-Powell, Sikh rule had flattened central Punjabi society and rendered the former tribal system irrelevant. See *The Land-Systems of British India*, vol. II, p. 617.

35. For the background of the Punjabi castes mentioned in this study. See H.A. Rose, *A Glossary of the Tribes and Castes of the Punjab and North-West Frontier Province*, 3 vols., 1919; repr., Patiala: Punjab Languages Department, 1990. This work is based on the census reports written by Denzil Ibbetson (1883) and E.D. MacLagan (1892) and because of its detailed anthropological descriptions, during the past decades became an important primary source for the investigation of contemporary Punjabi popular culture (see particularly Harjot Oberoi, *The Construction of Religious Boundaries: Culture, Identity and Diversity in the Sikh Tradition*, New Delhi: Oxford University Press, 1994).

36. S.S. Thorburn, *Musalmans and Moneylenders in the Punjab*, 1886; repr. Lahore: Book Traders, n.d., p. 35.
37. *Census of India*, Punjab, 1881, p. 101.
38. The original writings of the scribes employed by Temple to write down *The Legends of the Punjab* (1886; repr., Patiala: Punjab Languages Department, 1988) now are part of the British Library, Oriental and India Office Collections, London: Private Papers, MSS Eur. F 98/4, Richard Temple.
39. Oberoi, *The Construction*, Chapter Three.
40. See further on how this happened specifically among Punjabi women: Doris R. Jakobsh, *Relocating Gender in Sikh History* and Anshu Malhotra, *Gender, Caste, and Religious Identities: Restructuring Class in Colonial Punjab*, New Delhi: Oxford University Press, 2002.
41. Strachey, *India*, p. 555.
42. When Arya Samajis and Singh Sabhaites over time increasingly turned towards the Punjabi countryside to propagate their reforms, they often didactically used the traditional literary *qissa* form mentioned above. Malhotra, *Gender, Caste, and Religious Identities*, pp. 71-81.
43. Barbara D. Metcalf, *Islamic Revival in India: Deoband, 1860-1900*, Princeton: Princeton University Press, 1982.
44. The 1891 Punjab census counted 10,500 Namdharis, who are also known as Kukas (shouters) because their acts of worship often resulted in states of ecstasy in which they would dance and cry out.
45. The foundation and development of both the Nirankaris and Namdharis was significantly affected by caste. The Nirankaris comprised mainly Khatris and Aroras. The Namdharis were either Ramgarhias or poor Jats. Today they are almost all Ramgarhias.
46. Michael Adas, *Machines as the Measure of Men: Science Technology and Ideologies of Western Dominance*, New Delhi: Oxford University Press, 1990, p. 210.
47. R.W. Scribner, *The German Reformation*, Basingstoke: Macmillan, 1992, pp. 8-10.
48. Adas, *Machines as the Measure of Men*, p. 205.
49. *Indus Valley State Railway: Administration Report*, Roorkee, 1879, Appendix I.
50. David Gilmartin, 'Models of the Hydraulic Environment: Colonial Irrigation, State Power and Community in the Indus Basin', in *Nature, Culture and Imperialism: Essays on the Environmental History of South Asia*, ed. David Arnold and Ramachandra Guha, New Delhi: Oxford University Press, 1996, pp. 226-7.
51. David Skuy, 'Macaulay and the Indian Penal Code of 1862: The Myth of the Inherent Superiority and Modernity of the English Legal System Compared to India's Legal System in the Nineteenth Century', *Modern Asian Studies*, 32, 1998, pp. 513-57 and Eric Stokes, *The English*

Utilitarians and India, 1959; repr., New Delhi: Oxford University Press, 1992, Chapter Four.

52. Metcalf, *Ideologies*, pp. 35-8.
53. Ibid., p. 68.
54. Gauri Viswanathan, *Masks of Conquest: Literary Study and British Rule in India*, New York: Columbia University Press, 1989, p. 117.
55. Neeladri Bhattacharya, 'Pastoralists in a Colonial World', in *Nature, Culture and Imperialism: Essays on the Environmental History of South Asia*, ed. David Arnold and Ramachandra Guha, New Delhi: Oxford University Press, 1996, pp. 49-85.
56. Malcolm Darling, *The Punjab Peasant in Prosperity and Debt*, 1925; repr. Bombay: Oxford University Press, 1947, pp. 123-4. In his Introduction to the 1978 reprint, Clive Dewey called this work 'simply the best book on peasant indebtedness ever written'.
57. As cited in Metcalf, *Ideologies*, p. 125.
58. *Report on the Administration of the Punjab and its Dependencies, 1898-1906*, Lahore, Punjab Government Press, 1905-6, p. 18.
59. Andrew J. Major, 'State and Criminal Tribes in Colonial Punjab: Surveillance, Control and Reclamation of the "Dangerous Classes"', *Modern Asian Studies*, 33, 1999, pp. 657-88.
60. G.F.I. Graham, *The Life and Work of Syed Ahmad Khan*, 1885; repr., Karachi: Oxford University Press, 1974, p. 129. In 1868 the Government of India published *The People of India*, an eight-volume work of 468 photographs, each of which was accompanied by a brief account of what was supposed to be that group's essential character.
61. Percy Brown, *Lahore Museum Punjab: A Descriptive Guide to the Department of Archaeology & Antiquities*, Lahore: Civil and Military Gazette Press, 1908, p. 2.
62. These lectures were important meeting grounds for Protestant evangelicals, who built up libraries of slides and lent them out (with suitable scripts) to anyone willing to make use of them.
63. Prakash, *Another Reason*, Princeton: Princeton University Press, 1999.
64. Brown, *Modern India* and C.A. Bayly, *Rulers, Townsmen and Bazaars: North Indian Society During the Age of British Expansion, 1770-1870*, New Delhi: Oxford University Press, 1992, pp. 498-9 (Epilogue to the 1992 Indian Edition).
65. Dewey, 'Some Consequences of Military Expenditure in British India' in *Arrested Development in India: The Historical Dimension*, ed. Clive Dewey, New Delhi: Manohar, 1988, p. 154.

CHAPTER TWO

A Subculture of Punjabi Public Men

PROTESTANT EVANGELICALISM AND PUNJABI VOLUNTARY MOVEMENTS

Would like to know what you are actually doing so as to give a more Christian stamp to your government, and leaven your people with Christianity. People in this country are watching your proceedings attentively, looking upon you as a worthy successor of John Lawrence, and in earnest in doing all you can to make known that only name whereby men can be saved. Whilst you have so much power, do, my dear friend, exert it to the utmost for good.

> MR. TUCKER of the London Church Missionary Society
> in a letter to Robert Montgomery, dated 22 July 1861.[1]

During 1859-65, Robert Montgomery was Lieutenant-Governor of the Punjab and ever since, a large district and its capital town are named Montgomery in his memory. He had spent more than seven years as collector in Azamgarh (near Benares) under the direct authority of his brother-in-law, James Thomason. Between 1843 and 1853, the latter was Lieutenant-Governor of the North-Western Provinces and became known as the co-founder of the patronage bureaucracy in northern India. After the annexation of the Punjab in 1849, Thomason released twenty-eight officers to assist in the settlement of that region. More than half came from either Ulster or from Scotland and, like Thomason, all were Protestant evangelicals.[2] Surprisingly, Montgomery was appointed personally by Governor-General Dalhousie himself. Thomason received the following letter signed by Henry Elliot, secretary to Dalhousie:

Governor-General's Camp
Allahabad
12th March 1848

My dear Thomason,

Will you order up Montgomery from Cawnpore immediately? He will
be a Commissioner of some sort, probably of the Lahore Division, on
Rupees 2,400 a month—the Board of Administration will consist of
the two Lawrences and Mansel.

Yrs. sincerely,
H.W. Elliot.

P.S. The G.G. will not declare his policy yet but within a fortnight I
fancy you will receive a public letter calling for the selected Civilians.
He will not take Temple.[3]

One might expect that to be appointed by the Governor-General
in this way meant that Montgomery (like his colleagues) was a
senior official but, on the contrary, his name was unknown
outside the East India House in London. Hence Elliot's postscript
remains interesting as Dalhousie definitely made clear he did
not want such a senior official as Richard Temple. Montgomery
succeeded John Lawrence as Lieutenant-Governor but, according
to John Beames, he was 'a much milder, more refined and civilized
man' who gradually mitigated the extreme rigour of Lawrence's
system.[4] Even so, Montgomery also was a man of his times and
hence could not help the fact that throughout the second half of
the nineteenth century a quasi-official Protestant Christian evangelical administration ruled the Punjab.

   True, the British argued that the power and authority of the
government should never be used to promote missionary goals.
A distinction was made between the public and private personalities of officials, restricting the public personality to the
observance of neutrality, while allowing the private personality
the right to follow the promptings of personal conscience. Yet,
as stated earlier, much can be argued against this proclaimed
neutrality of the state in South Asia. Queen Victoria's proclamation of 1858 to the princes, chiefs, and people of India,
for example, shows how Janus-faced the colonial policy towards
Indian traditions was:

Firmly relying ourselves on the truth of Christianity, and acknowledging with gratitude the solace of religion, we disclaim alike the right and the desire to impose our convictions on any of our subjects. We declare it to be our royal will and pleasure that none be in anywise favoured, none molested or disquieted, by reason of their religious faith or observances, but that all shall alike enjoy the equal and impartial protection of the law. . . . And it is our further will that, so far as may be, our subjects, of whatever race or creed, be freely and impartially admitted to offices in our service, the duties of which they may be qualified, by their education, ability, and integrity, duly to discharge.[5]

Here was the principle of religious neutrality and equality of all traditions, and also a public pronouncement that Christianity formed the foundation for British government in South Asia.[6] But could it have been otherwise? Culturally, the British in India (including the so-called secular ones) were Christians, as most Indians perceived them anyway, whatever the official statement. Though they might not be actively devout themselves, they nonetheless had been brought up in a society that firmly believed the Christian way to be the only truth. Therefore, the complicating fact for late nineteenth century Europe was the claim that 'you could have a morality without Christianity' (and be an atheist), while 'the morality which you must have was Christian morality'.[7] The point is that, at one time or the other, the policy of religious neutrality towards Indian traditions had to come in conflict with the programme for promoting the material and moral progress of the subcontinent and, hence, with the Christian faith which they believed to be the foundation for such progress. To be neutral demands sympathy and no doubt this was difficult for a ruler convinced of his own righteousness and ability and on the whole morally outraged by the practices tolerated by Indian traditions. The policy of religious neutrality particularly was violated during the process of state formation in the second half of the nineteenth century. By then, not only had the British intensified their relationships with indigenous institutions and individuals, but Indians themselves were increasingly seeking contact with the state for financial support and legitimacy.

In line with the evangelical revivalist movement that sought to advance a notion of muscular Christianity, the British reached the Punjab as conquerors and rulers not as traders. They were cocksure, knew what they came for, and were determined to do their duty and bring civilization to this corner of the Empire. As for the missionaries, they believed that 'British rule in India was an act of divine providence for the benefit of the Indian people'.[8] Accordingly, they made use of the contacts they had with government officials (British missionaries obviously had closer links with them than their American counterparts). In terms of the civilizing mission, the colonial government and the missionaries certainly had similar goals. This had much to do with the fact that Protestant evangelicalism had experienced a crucial shift in its social theology during the nineteenth century. Instead of stressing Biblical doctrines of inherent personal sinfulness, guilt and divine punishment, evangelicals generally gave more importance to practical service to others through the duty of hard work and self-denial. This translated into a muscular Christianity that showed military overtones in such hymns as 'Onward Christian Soldier' and in the idea of the Salvation Army with its uniforms, titles and military ranks. Often in contemporary Indian writings, the hard work and character of the British and Europeans in general is praised.[9] To what extent therefore did the British and the missionaries in particular by doing their duty give the moral example of how one should behave as a modern public citizen? How successful were they in spreading the idea that 'one should not be content with one's welfare alone, but should look for one's welfare in the welfare of all'? These questions certainly remain imperative to emerging social consciousness in South Asia because, as I will discuss in subsequent chapters, the latter led to the creation of moral languages which often overlapped with the British civilizing mission and hence proved fundamental to the making of a liberal public sphere devoted to the idea of improvement. Christian missionaries also underscored 'secular philosophies of equality' with their 'insistence on men's quality before God, both in the matter of sin and in freely bestowed rather than earned salvation'.[10] This is important to mention as it would inspire Indian elites to protest against the racial exclusiveness claimed by the British.

Evangelism started in the Punjab when in 1834 American Presbyterians set-up the first major mission beyond Delhi in

Ludhiana. It became the headquarters for later expansion into the Punjab and a centre for education, publishing and proselytism. Naturally there were almost no Christians in the Punjab at the time, but this would soon change.[11] To aid missionary efforts, British officials in 1852 helped with the foundation of a Church Missionary Association in Lahore under the leadership of Henry Lawrence.[12] The major missionary societies in the region were well established Protestant evangelical ones: the Church Missionary Society of England, Anglicans from the Church of England, Presbyterians from the Church of Scotland and two north American Presbyterian denominations. With amazing speed they published tracts, pamphlets and books in Punjabi, Hindi, Urdu, Persian and Kashmiri. Next to grammars, dictionaries and translations of the scriptures, they published tracts in which they attacked indigenous beliefs and practices. An extensive network of mission schools was established, recognized and supported by the government and fundamental to the spread of Western education and Christian ideas, if not a channel for catechizing. Overall, missionaries stressed the importance of learning to read as a process though which Punjabis could be improved: getting 'younger tender minds' to read parables containing 'simple, moral truths' of Christian belief was considered the most suitable method of instruction, far more effective than direct preaching. In addition, missionaries opened up hospitals and orphanages, and regularly preached at the market and village fair, where they were seen as a public spectacle, 'involving as they did camels, tents, magic lanterns, and in some instances women preaching in public to women'.[13] Perhaps the best illustration of the direct link between government and mission in terms of the civilizing mission, however, were the Christian model colonies with modern farming facilities. All in all, in the Punjab church and state together probably violated the traditional world more than elsewhere in the subcontinent. Though, in terms of causality, the activities of the evangelists cannot be taken as the final determining agency, they surely worked as a catalyst in the emerging militancy of Punjabi traditions during the last quarter of the nineteenth century.

The Church Missionary Society (CMS) was the largest Christian association in the Punjab and remains most important for this study because it was very active in and around Amritsar and Lahore. In Robert Clark, it had a leader who staunchly conformed to Protestant evangelicalism and its 'formidable, but intellectually narrow, millenarian, exclusive theology'.[14] In 1852, he arrived in Amritsar, which at that time was the largest city in the region and chosen as mission headquarters. One reason behind this choice was the dominant presence of Sikhs. Many British officials and missionaries erroneously saw Sikhism as 'a waning religion, that will soon belong to history' and hence as a community ripe for conversion.[15] As one British contemporary wrote:

The Sikh faith and ecclesiastical polity are surely following the way of the Sikh political ascendancy. There were two elements in the old *Khalsa*, made up as it was of the followers of Nanuk, the first Sikh prophet, and of those who held to Gooroo Govind, the second great religious leader. The first were inferior in number but zealous in faith; the last were of later and less profound convictions. These were the 'Singhs' or Lions, who embraced the Grunth because the sword lay within its leaves, and became converts to a religion which had war for its profession and plunder for its promises. With the disappearance of the *Khalsa* prestige, these votaries have fallen off; they joined in hundreds, and have deserted in thousands. The ranks of the Hindooism receive them again, and their children will never drink the *pahul* (*Khalsa* initiation rite) at Umritsar. Only the disciples of Nanuk still perpetuate in the Five Rivers the memory of a faith which was the Islam of Hindooism.[16]

The fact that during the early decades after annexation there were comparatively many Sikh converts, however, was more because of their numerical dominance in Amritsar and its surroundings. For as described by G.R. Elsmie, Punjabis generally remained untouched by Christian preaching: 'the people come to see the sight, remain perfectly quiet, get up and go away, but have no more intention of turning Christian than flying over the moon'.[17] In thirty years, the CMS created a chain of mission stations, similar to military outposts across the North-West Frontier. As Robert Clark put it,

Our frontier line of Missions is like one of the great Punjab canals, which is made to irrigate and fertilize the waste and barren lands which lie *on both sides* of its course, and we remember that, with very few exceptions, there are absolutely no Christian Missions beyond us.[18]

Because of the location of their missions in these dominantly Muslim areas, CMS missionaries especially focused on Islam which according to Clark was 'but a heresy of Christianity' and to be conquered by the word of God 'preached in the power of the Holy Ghost with simplicity and fidelity'.[19] On the whole, evangelicals denounced anything that stood in the way of the propagation of the Gospel as sin, and generally followed a negative policy of reform: 'an opposition to slavery and paganism as much as to sexual wrongdoing and drunkenness'.[20] Their stern morality was immutable, sacrosanct and certainly closed to compromise, especially when over time it was 'infused by secular Victorian values, the very uncertainties of which added an even more compulsive element to the quest for a more ordered, spiritualized society'.[21]

It did not take long before Punjabis reacted negatively to Christian conversions. When during the 1880s thousands of Punjabi men (and some women) began to demand baptism from missionaries (especially in the central districts), this alarmed indigenous leaders and led to anti-missionary feelings. Of more importance than these increasing emotional tensions, however, was the fact that the Christian missionaries introduced new forms of organization and action to the region. Voluntary associations of course were not new to South Asia. For many centuries, indigenous movements had 'drawn individuals to them on the basis of belief rather than birth'.[22] What made a fundamental difference was that Christians 'carried with them the concepts and forms of weekly congregational meetings held by structured societies with formal membership and sets of written rules'.[23] Indeed, 'it was the presence of mission institutions that set-off the most profound Indian reaction to the mission presence'.[24] In fact, in 1877 the Punjab was the first province to have a Native Church Council.[25] It was established by the CMS, which delegated to it some responsibilities for appointing, transferring and fixing the salaries of Indian clergy. It became a forum for urging that Indian ordinands should be granted equal status with Western missionaries, but it would take some more decades before the time was ripe for an indigenization of Christianity in the region. Importantly, all this happened in the context of a politico-legal frame within which the new organizational forms could originate and sustain themselves. Associations registered with the government had the legal right to own property and conduct business. A complex network of English-oriented law came into being, which gave legitimacy and permanence to an unfamiliar form of social organization based on voluntary membership and individually assumed contractual obligations. Fundamental to the whole process was the Registration of Societies Act of 1860: conservative within the Western tradition, this law was revolutionary in the South Asian context. Modern Indian voluntary associations, *sabha, anjuman, samaj,* were established throughout the subcontinent, with officers, constitutions, bye-laws and annual reports. In the Punjab, this generally happened first in Lahore and Amritsar, from where the different movements then spread their message to the rest of the province.

While the Christian voluntary association provided Indian society with the example of a new form of organization with a legalistic character, missionaries presented new forms of action as well. Apart from educational and social work, they particularly were in search of converts and of local leaders against whom they could prove their one and only truth through polemical debates. As Sayyid Ahmad Khan put it in his well known Urdu treatise on the causes of the 1857 Revolt, *Asbab-e-Baghavat-e-Hind* (1859):

The missionaries took on new forms of preaching. They printed and circulated controversial religious books, in the shape of questions and answers. Holy men of other faiths were spoken of in these books in a most offensive manner. In Hindustan it was the custom that everyone preached and explained his views in his own religious place or house and if anyone wished he could go there to listen. But the method of the missionaries was exactly the opposite. They used to go to public meeting grounds, places of pilgrimage and fairs, to preach, while no one hindered them solely out of fear of the authorities. In fact, in some districts it became the custom to escort the missionaries with a *chaprasi* (peon) from the local police station. Besides, the missionaries were not satisfied to talk only about their New Testament, on the contrary, in violent and abusive language they began to attack the holy men and places of other creeds, insulting the feelings of those who listened to them and so sowing the seeds of unrest in the hearts of the people.[26]

Indigenous movements nonetheless became used to these practices and copied them, and thus seriously compromised with their opponents. This permitted, importantly, the growth of diverse, specialized and autonomous associate groups, wherein action came to be based on pragmatic wisdom and techniques typical of successful entrepreneurship. Undoubtedly, the example given by the Christian missionaries of the functioning (and success) of being organized into a voluntary association was decisive. When subsequent voluntary movements increasingly confronted each other, Christian missionaries and the state, they surely created a disturbing legacy for Punjabi society.

More difficult to answer but central to this study remains the question to what extent Christian morality influenced the moral languages propagated by these movements. What can be said with certainty is that 'the overwhelming majority of missionaries were not wandering preachers in search of converts but institution-builders presiding over churches, schools, and hospitals'.[27] It was not in the open air but, as today, in an institutional setting that Punjabis met Christian missionaries. Particularly teachers and medical personnel were responsible for the broader Christian moral influence in Punjabi society. The fact that, over time, the majority of them were Indian (running colleges such as Delhi's St. Stephen's College and Lahore's Forman College up this day) only makes clear the long term effect. Yet in the opinion of Christian missionaries, Indians on the whole failed to come up to the standard of Western liberalism and science that Christianity had absorbed. Accordingly, they viewed mission stations as centres for the diffusion of technical skills and, if the natives were thought to be clever enough, scientific knowledge. In so far as the missions were successful, their attraction lay in this moral superiority that was based on financial resources and scientific superiority: theology won few converts. The Christian polemic therefore should be seen as a highly concentrated and specific moral form of general infiltration of the subordinated society that was decidedly influential among Indian elites. Progressively the latter took a rational stand towards the British (missionaries) and other Punjabi communities. Hence, they incorporated new methodologies into their moral languages whereby, importantly, the grounds for their debates simultaneously became more and more individualistic. As a result, traditional loyalties were often strengthened because the relationships between Christian missionaries and mutually exclusive Punjabi groups became growingly antagonistic. All this induced anxiety and produced change in Punjabi society. That this was much the result of the spread of Anglo-vernacular education and print culture is argued below.

ANGLO-VERNACULAR EDUCATION
AND PRINT CULTURE

. . . we may trust that the English or Western education will not impair the originality of the educated, nor lessen the chance of their self-development. It would be sad if these men were confined to springs of thought belonging not to themselves but to their masters: in that case their mental growth would be sickly and stunted. We can never desire that they should be intellectually prostrate before us in servile imitation. But there is no probability of this happening; on the contrary, while abandoning some of their own, and adopting others from us, they are likely to cherish the essence of nearly all that is indigenous. Already this development of theirs is moving in what must be called Asiatic lines—as the lines are not exactly European—and will probably diverge still more in an Oriental direction.

RICHARD TEMPLE in *Men and Events of
My Time in India* (1882).[28]

The role of English language education has unquestionably been fundamental to the making of modern South Asia. Everyone knows the importance of English as a link language in contemporary India and Pakistan, despite the roles of Hindi and Urdu. As far as early British policy is concerned, the debate between Orientalists (who wanted to continue instruction through the traditional classical languages, Arabic, Persian and Sanskrit) and Anglicists (who wished to use English) was crucial. More important, however, was the acceptance of Macaulay's Minute on Education of 1835, which recommended the spread of Western learning through English, and of Charles Wood's Education Dispatch of 1854, which banned Bibles from the schools and decreed that government education should be exclusively secular.[29] Eventually the Orientalists lost to the Anglicists at the level of higher instruction, while at the levels of primary and secondary education, they lost to regional vernaculars, which anyway remained inferior in status to Anglo-vernacular education.[30] In reality, however, the role of the colonial government was limited. Attempts to organize a modern system of education were principally (and this remains crucial) the result of private initiative. The government confined its role to that of assisting private (mostly missionary) enterprise, hoping that through the education of the indigenous elite modern knowledge would filter down to the masses. In pre-colonial days, Muslim mosques, Hindu temples and Sikh gurdwaras often had their own schools.[31] In the colonial period the British patronized many of these institutions. One of the proposals of Charles Wood's Dispatch was to give grants-in-aid to schools carried on by voluntary effort, provided that they accepted government inspection and guidance for the secular part of their work. What the British found lacking in Indian systems of education was moral instruction. Hence their policies favoured the patronage of what was deemed to be secular learning even in institutions they defined as religious, though they allowed the management of the latter to give such religious instruction to their pupils as they thought appropriate. In the end, nonetheless, it were Christian missionaries who took the greatest advantage of government aid, especially in the Punjab where in 1883, three decades after Wood's Dispatch, thirty of the thirty one aided Anglo-vernacular secondary schools (including all of the government aided high schools) were Christian missionary institutions.[32]

Besides the dominance of mission schools, the introduction of Christian morality was strengthened by the British adherence to Anglo-vernacular education. Wherever the public education system was offered (in mission, state or indigenous schools), in most places it meant a combination of the knowledge of vernacular languages with that of English language and culture. As a result, a tiny but influential bilingual (if not polyglot) privileged elite was educated for whom language skills were a form of capital. This remains crucial because it offered the new patron of learning (the so-called neutral colonial state) the possibility to invent, as Gauri Viswanathan has argued, an entire academic discipline for the teaching of English literature as the formative moral influence on the colonized elite,[33] which would have far-reaching consequences for the emergence of new indigenous literary forms and moral languages. On the whole, a single vision inspired public education in India from its beginning and would continue to do so, as we all know, up to today. At the heart of it was a belief in the unquestioned superiority of Western civilization, science in particular. For Indian students, 'salvation lay only in the abandonment of their decadent traditions and acceptance of the values of the West'.[34] The textbooks invited students to identify themselves 'not with the backwardness of the Indian past but with the enlightenment of the British present'.[35] Because the British had brought peace and justice to the subcontinent, it was argued, 'they were worthy of imitation, being, with few exceptions, a noble, brave, and self-sacrificing people'.[36] Over time, many Indian students accepted the invitation, if only because a working knowledge of English meant more salary. Well known in this context are the Indian social reformers, who since the beginning of the nineteenth century glorified Western civilization in comparison to their own. In *Musafiran-e-Landan* (1869), for example, Sayyid Ahmad Khan, not only praised the workings of British society, but compared it with everything to be found in South Asia: the difference being, for him, like that between a talented and beautiful boy and a wild and dirty animal in rags.[37] However, as the educated gained experience with the realities of British rule (especially the racial inequality within the Raj), gratitude often changed to bitter disappointment.

Anglo-vernacular education at the same time brought a growing dependence on the printed word. The printing press came to the subcontinent as part of a full blown technology and therefore did not take centuries to develop as it did in Europe. Obviously it led to a standardization of languages as typography arrested linguistic drift. Crucial to this process was the publication of grammars, dictionaries, etymologies and other reference works often by Christian missionaries.[38] Otherwise, the way it happened through local linguistic knowledge and scripts certainly remains an interesting subject for further study. At the end of the eighteenth century, the first dictionaries and grammars not only standardized Indian languages but also made it possible to set them in type. The casting of type fonts was completed soon afterwards and quickened the production of inexpensive printed texts. Translations of scriptures and commentaries into the vernacular languages now became available to a wider, though still limited, literate audience than could read Sanskrit, Arabic or Persian. For a growing number of Punjabis the printed word replaced the oral, person to person and often ritual modes of transmission of knowledge. People once prohibited by birth from education (like women) now had access to knowledge formerly only studied by a small elite.[39] By and large, there emerged a concern for the rational understanding of a text as opposed to rote learning or, to put it differently, for the meaning instead of the sound of a word. The well-known reformer and literary figure of the Urdu language, Muhammad Husain Azad (1830-1910), for example, was fed up with the extensive use of hyperbole made for effect and not intended to be taken literally. Azad worked for the Punjab Education Department where he produced school books in Urdu. Over time he was exposed to Victorian ideas of what poetry should be, which decisively influenced his criticism of Urdu poetry. Properly in the Aligarh tradition, he propagated in *Ab-e Hayat* or Water of Life (1880) a preference for natural (*necharal*) writings embodying an aesthetic of realism, whether in its depiction of history or the external world.[40] Otherwise, Azad certainly experienced the societal changes around him as an 'oppressive present':

There are many thoughts and themes in English that our language cannot express. That is, the enjoyment they produce in the English language can't be fully conveyed in Urdu. Which in reality is a result of the weakness of the language, and this is a cause of the greatest shame for its native speakers.[41]

On the whole, it was under the influence of English modes of writing that new genres like biographies, novels and poems emerged, and the literati became aware of the rationality of the language used (both in writing and speech).

In 1911, nearly 600 books were published in Urdu, over 450 in Punjabi and about 80 both in English and Hindi. These included not only traditional forms of prose and poetry but also new literary genres like the novel. The political and socio-cultural concerns of Punjabis, however, came to be reflected most in journalism. A total of 209 newspapers (though few were of real importance and many little more than advertising sheets) owned by Punjabis were published in 1903: 31 in English, 1 in English and Urdu, 164 in Urdu, 6 in Hindi and 7 in Punjabi. The leading papers were more or less mouthpieces of various groups criticizing each other and the colonial government in their editorial columns. The *Tribune* and the *Observer* (both published in English from Lahore) respectively were the leading Hindu and Muslim papers. On the whole, more than half of printed publications were published in Lahore (with Amritsar following after a wide margin).[42] Newspapers framed opinion, impassioned it. The weight of the press was not argument but assertion; not the making of opinion but its strengthening. It was through the press that Punjabi elites first confronted questions about the identity, size and location of their audience and their relation to a potentially infinite, literate community. Over time, successful newspapers led to a group of relatively independent social commentators (on a quasi regular contractual basis) that certainly was most critical to the emergence of a public sphere. Indeed, importantly, a waspish native press made it less and less easy for the Raj to implement policies which impinged on Indian sensibilities.

Undeniably the new modes of communication influenced the issues and strategies of those involved in South Asian traditions. Indian elites increasingly became involved with both Anglo-vernacular education and print culture. As during the European Reformation, modern printing techniques led to the creation of scriptures. Complex sets of teachings were summarized and put into print, furnishing a basic statement of belief for a particular community. Furthermore, as print shaped the popular dissemination of religious teachings and an entire style of religious education, it also fostered sectarianism. Printed works made room for internal debate, whipped up differences and generally advanced the extent to which tradition became part of public debates. The importance of an oral debate was often found less in the event itself than in the formulaic presentation of the event in publications. Otherwise, 'printed texts made possible ever more detailed standards for correct knowledge and behaviour: the medium permitted the message'.[43] As in sixteenth century Europe, print culture disseminated elite norms through a widespread circulation of what might be called high cultural texts and textual norms, particularly through the aspirations of upwardly mobile groups as part of the processes later described as Sanskritization and Ashrafization, among Hindus and Muslims respectively.[44] All the same, it should be stressed that print culture did not influence Indian traditions so much as it did Western Christianity since the Reformation. Hence, a word of warning about the uniformity and authority of the printed word in the dissemination of well defined bodies of moral doctrines. For indeed up to today Indian traditions to a great extent continued to be transmitted orally and hence the way new ideas were spread was far less defined or coherent. Personal discussion of ideas enabled Indians to make their own choices of the ideas they heard, to impose their own understanding on them, rendering the content of the message more diffuse and complex. Partly, of course, this could be compensated for by the speaking skills of a reformer in the use of rhetorical devices of repetition and recapitulation, and in seeking to attract his audience to return for further speech, in which poorly understood points might be clarified or reinforced. If this was sufficient to create any uniformity in faith remains unsure. What is certain is that it created fervour and impatience for change. Otherwise, by the 1880s, there were only around 55,000 Indians (on a total population of 195 million) who wrote and spoke English with relative skill and had at least a passing familiarity with the cultural assumptions and values of the West.[45] In relation to this, two contemporary Indian authors not only described how knowledge of English became a status marker but, more interestingly, also how in reality few Indians had a genuine proficiency in the English language, despite their own confidence in it. In 'Dilli Darbar Darpan' (1877), Bhartendu Harishchandra comically describes what he saw at the Delhi *darbar* (where Queen Victoria was declared Empress of India, *Kaisar-i-Hind*) the Prince of Luharu unhesitatingly rattling away in English doing a lot of damage to grammar and idiom.[46] Similarly, Nazir Ahmad (1836-1912) voiced his criticism of Sayyid Ahmad Khan's Westernized way of life and belief in natural philosophy in a satirical novel called *Ibn-ul-Vaqt* or The Time Server (1889). In it, for example, he describes how his main character, who thinks he has become quite an Englishman already, understands English in a most peculiar way and, after desperate efforts to learn it, cannot converse in it without difficulty even at the end of his life.[47] Further, because of the linguistic knowledge of a small but influential group of Indians, not only the English language but also, and more significantly, the South Asian languages changed linguistically in crucial ways (see Chapter Four).

The English spoken in South Asia obviously has travelled its own idiosyncratic journey since the guardians of its purity left. Anyone who has been there must have picked up some peculiar colloquial examples. Interestingly, as the British up to just fifty years ago had their Anglo-Indian language, of which *Hobson-Jobson* (1886) remains the legendary memorial,[48] many English words, in turn, have taken on new Hinglish meanings. Indian English indeed went through a similar development as American English, creating its own grammatical rules, syntax, vocabulary and, moreover, a fascinating body of literature. My point is that one should imagine how difficult it was during the early colonial period to come to terms with a language created in a distant world. Driven by curiosity about and the need to understand Western civilization and science, for example, Arya Samajis Pandit Guru Datta Vidyarthi and Lala Ruchi Ram Sahni (both became Assistant Professors of Science at Lahore's Government College) while students in Lahore, wrestled with the foreign concepts in John Stuart Mill's *Utilitarianism* (1861):

We read and re-read Mill's small book line by line, or paragraph by paragraph, discussing, arguing, differing or agreeing in the end, as we went along. Now and again, we could not 'do' more than a sentence or two in the course of one hour, for either we could not agree as to what the author's real meaning was or, for some other reason, the whole time was taken up with the discussion about all the implications of the passage or how far we could ourselves accept his lead.[49]

Learning a new language means learning to analyse one's experience of reality in a completely different manner. Moreover, learning to read is different from learning by reading. While English became increasingly important in South Asia, it has to be stressed that there were many different (often imaginative) and conflicting readings of English texts. In the next chapters, when discussing the Singh Sabha, Arya Samaj and Ahmadiyah moral languages, I will give some examples of how each interpretation of English works was dependent on who was reading them, in what state, with what knowledge and with what purpose. But for now I turn to the cultural and administrative centre of the region, the city of Lahore, where there emerged a subculture of elitist Punjabi public men.

THE BRAHMO SAMAJ AND
ANJUMAN-I-PUNJAB IN LAHORE

Colonial rule encouraged urbanization in the Punjab, especially in those places that became British administrative centres. Much of it came in the new parts of the towns and cities, the civil and military lines outside of the old mostly Mughal city walls. Actually, the region counted only three cities, which controlled most of the long distance trade and some manufacturing: Lahore, Amritsar and Delhi. Smaller towns like Rawalpindi, Multan, Ambala, Jullunder, Patiala and Sialkot served as centres of specialized manufacturing. Lahore was the centre for various engineering, educational, police and railroad administrative units, an Episcopal See of the Church of England and the headquarters of an army division. Accordingly, the city attracted a constant stream of visitors from other parts of India and Europe, many of whom spent their time there lecturing and debating cultural, economic and political themes. After his visit to Lahore in 1867, twenty-three year old Charles Dilke, whose political career ended prematurely because of a typical Victorian adultery scandal, wrote the following interesting statement in his immensely popular *Greater Britain* (1868): 'Lahore has been a British city for nineteen years. Bombay for two centuries and more; yet Lahore is far more English than Bombay.'[50] Though this might seem a strange thought at first, Lahore was a city with large civil and military lines where one clearly could see 'the complexities, the internal stratification and the attitudinal differences that characterized British society at home'.[51] True, the city was much smaller than Calcutta or Bombay, but its population had grown, after annexation, by 60 per cent (Amritsar's only 25 per cent) between 1855 and 1881 to 149,369 and subsequently reached 474,181 in 1901.[52] Yet, because of its time of annexation, Lahore was an imperial provincial capital, architecturally displaying the pomp and splendour of the Raj (as is still visible) and the centre of cultural and intellectual life in north-west India. In this urban setting, a vital interaction took place between Englishmen from different social and professional backgrounds and an equally various indigenous elite. A sub-culture came into existence dominated by a new Lahori elite who had followed Anglo-vernacular education, immersed themselves in print culture and, generally, found employment in one or the other government institution. As Prakash Tandon put it:

Lahore was the first town to start schools and Colleges, and although educational facilities spread all over the Punjab, higher education in arts, science, medicine, law, engineering, teaching and veterinary science was concentrated in Lahore. Each generation, my grand-uncle, father, uncle and we ourselves, studied at Lahore. When you settled in a profession or service, most of your colleagues were old friends from Lahore; you married into some family whose sons and daughters had been to Lahore. Gradually people also began to retire to Lahore. Thus Lahore came to acquire a very special position in our society. There was an overall class of Punjabi professionals who had been educated in Lahore, and this was not a caste of birth and inheritance, for in many Colleges, especially those started by charitable trusts, there was a large number of students from humble homes in towns and villages.[53]

Members of this Lahore elite belonged to the upcoming class of Indian public men, who together formed a power bloc the like of which had never existed in pre-colonial society.

While the Anglo-Indian colonial state penetrated deeply into Punjabi society and its officials defined a large body of knowledge of the region and its inhabitants, its workings obviously also became more bureaucratic, more reliant on the archive. The creation and maintenance of the archive gradually was aided by private indigenous initiatives along government lines. On the whole, the archival depth of Lahori society (and thus of the Punjab at large) was reinforced with the building of public and private libraries, as well as all sorts of (mostly government) institutions housing an ever-increasing amount of documents and statistics.[54] An impetus to the creation of this collective memory unmistakably was the remarkable growth of the legal profession. Following colonial numbers and terminology, around the turn of century, the Punjab was 'the most litigious province' of British India, relatively to the population: 'in 1901 the number of suits instituted was 11.4 per 1,000 of the population, the next highest figure being 9.6 in Bombay'.[55] Though what happened in courts no doubt remained mysterious and, above all, costly for most Punjabis,[56] the point is that legal cases led to a more widespread desire for written standard and validated documentation. Similarly, in this Lahori version of the emerging world of Indian public men, scientific knowledge and standard time (as celebrated by the clock tower in cities and towns throughout the subcontinent) were internalized in ways that were qualitatively new. While, generally, the different modes of knowledge and of spreading information speeded up the awareness of time, some among the Punjabi public figures began to keep personal diaries. Later these notes would develop into autobiographies, introducing a new literary genre. In an interesting study, Judith Walsh studied over a hundred of these autobiographies written in English, groping for 'the psychological consequences of growing up in British India for those who had to combine the heritage of their traditional world with the pressing realities of foreign power and Western education'.[57] While documents and statistics can give us facts of change, these autobiographies (despite their obvious limitations) tell us much about what it all meant for those involved. In the reconstructed sphere of self-identity, Macaulay was beginning to win the day.

Still, more intriguing in relation to the Singh Sabha, Arya Samaj and Ahmadiyah movements, remain the activities of those public men who were specifically religiously involved. There emerged so-called lay leaders within the different traditions, who often had urban professions in the field of law, journalism or teachings, while the more successful among them were able to support themselves by their managing, writing or preaching activities. They came to be seen as experts, even though they did not receive traditional teaching or initiation like the heirs of the traditional (mainly orally transmitted) modes of learning. These lay leaders were crucial, as they were not just engaged in aping the West but also in exploring and constructing avenues to come to terms with the altered historical situation. Though they would replace traditional leadership, characteristically, they identified with communities rather than with the Western educated class as a whole. Obviously these patterns of participation more or less reflected existing identities but membership of one of the newly emerged voluntary associations strengthened that identification. Even so, during the 1860s and 1870s, some of the associations established in the Punjab were joint societies (between Hindus, Muslims and Sikhs), while on the whole Muslims (unlike in Calcutta, Bombay and Madras, the majority in the region) were more involved than Hindus and Sikhs in associations during this period.[58] Rapid social change, however, meant that all this would soon belong to the past, as Sikhs and Hindus became more and more active in public life and the perceptions of the different communities of themselves and one another shifted.

The Brahmo Samaj (dominated by Bengalis) and the Anjuman-i-Punjab (being a mutual effort of Punjabi elites and the British) were the two most important movements during those early decades of colonial rule. They were at the heart of the process of coming to terms with the changing cultural environment and provided platforms where influential Punjabis could hone their skills at oratory, public campaigns, lobbying with the government and so on. Bengalis followed in the footsteps of the British into the Punjab. Most of them settled in the towns, where they, as Brahmo Samajis, came to dominate the social and intellectual world. The Brahmo Samaj or Society for the Transcendent Deity was established in Calcutta by Rammohun Roy (1772-1833). He clearly was a precocious young man, for already at a young age he wrote a Persian tract which criticized idolatry and polytheism and echoed the rational deistic thought imbibed during his earlier Islamic study in Patna. Afterwards, importantly, Roy became acquainted with the Serampore missionaries. He learned English, helped them with the translation of the New Testament in Bengali and set himself to study Christianity (especially its Unitarian variety).[59] In *The Precepts of Jesus: A Guide to Peace and Happiness* (1820), he accepted the morality preached by Christ but rejected his deity and miracles. In 1821, in fact, he started a mission for the propagation and defence of Hindu Unitarianism, which nonetheless had little success and soon was dissolved. Though influenced by Christian Unitarianism, at the same time he felt that the sacred Hindu works contained fundamental truths. What remains crucial, however, is that on the basis of his own individual rational judgement, Roy chose to substitute some of these works (relying heavily on the Vedas and the Upanishads) for priests as the sources of proper knowledge. Translations of them in printed vernaculars as well as English circulated widely in Bengal and eventually beyond. Rammohun Roy established the Brahmo Samaj in 1828 but soon after that left for England, where he died five years later. The movement remains one of the first signs that Indians (in this case Hindus) were now reassessing their heritage. Its members were theists and opposed idol-worship, emphasizing spiritual devotion to God rather than elaborate external ritual. At the same time they appreciated Western science and especially Christianity. Subsequently, however, the Brahmos separated from the mainstream of Hindu society and practice, developing into a distinct community of faith governed by its own marriage laws and famous for its activities in the field of social reform.

The Lahore Brahmo Samaj was founded in 1863. Besides the missionaries and the government, they were the first to own a printing press for the propagation of their ideas. Despite being

Bengali speakers, Brahmo Samajis were willing to make use of Urdu and Punjabi but increasingly advocated Hindi in the Devanagari script. Nonetheless, while being outsiders and mostly in government service, Brahmos faced the same problems as had the missionaries in attracting Punjabis. Though Bengalis provided a lifestyle and Brahmos the specific institutions for adaptation, Bengalis remained aloof from Punjabis and the Brahmo Samaj especially generated much criticism from local Hindus. Most Punjabis rejected the latter because of its tolerance towards other faiths and particularly its use of Christian moral overtones. Such a mix gave little comfort to Hindus surrounded by proselytizing traditions and fearful of Christian conversion. Instead, Punjabi Hindus as well as Sikhs were much more attracted to the Arya Samaj, a movement that definitely was much influenced by the Brahmo Samaj, particularly in its quest for both female education and the propagation of Hindi.

Quite different from the Brahmo Samaj was the Anjuman-i-Punjab. It existed principally in Lahore between 1865 and 1888 as an important voluntary association of both Europeans and indigenous elites. Lieutenant-Governor Donald McLeod made the original call for membership but Dr. Gottlieb Wilhelm Leitner undoubtedly was the pivotal character behind the movement.[60] Leitner was a Hungarian who had lived in Turkey, received a Ph.D. from the University of Freiburg in Germany, and lectured in Arabic, Turkish and modern Greek at King's College, London.[61] In 1864 he came to Lahore and became principal of the Government College. With McLeod's backing, the association soon consisted of over three hundred members, mostly drawn from the Punjab's major towns and cities. A parliamentary report on the Punjab University movement states that the Anjuman was officially founded for the 'diffusion of useful knowledge, the discussion of subjects possessing literary and scientific interest and for the free expression of native opinion on questions of social and political reform'.[62] Accordingly, one of its first important projects was the establishment of a free public library at a time when printed books were still scarce. From 1865 to 1882, nonetheless, the central issue of the Anjuman remained one of higher education: the so-called Oriental movement for the creation of an Oriental University in Lahore (the Prince of Wales, who then was the President of the London Sanskrit Text Society, became the patron of the association). Overall the movement wanted to reinvigorate indigenous learning and spread Western knowledge through the vernaculars instead of English. Yet, such people as the famous Lahori Sikh aristocrat, millionaire and philanthropist, Dyal Singh Majithia (1849-98) strongly opposed Leitner's plans, especially through his *Tribune* newspaper.[63] Instead, they fought for the establishment of an English-language university comparable to those of Calcutta and Bombay. Partly because of this opposition the government decided not to establish an Oriental university in Lahore but Panjab University in 1882 and with Dr. Leitner as its registrar. The University was recognized by Calcutta University as an English-language institution offering Asian language degrees as well. In fact, being the fourth university in South Asia (after Bombay, Calcutta and Madras Universities, all three founded in 1857), Panjab University was somewhat ahead of its time. Until 1904, the former three universities solely examined aspiring degree candidates. They offered no courses and, instead, let students fulfil the required classes at any number of affiliated colleges, before presenting themselves for examinations. Panjab University, on the contrary, was a teaching university, though other things remained the same: Europeans obviously ruled it at the top, while according to Bhagat Lakshman Singh (1863-1944), Indians working below them were only *jo hukm huzurs* (those who did whatever the Europeans wanted).[64]

All in all, the establishment of an Oriental University in Lahore was too exotic for a government committed to the spread of useful learning through education in India. A policy that certainly was detested by Leitner as he made clear in his evidence before the Punjab Education Commission of 1884 in relation to education in government schools:

After leaving the middle school, a boy . . . knows arithmetic, Urdu and Persian, if not a little English, all of which may be said to be 'useful' to him, whilst he has acquired some information regarding history, geography, and elementary science, which, also, cannot be affirmed to be 'useless'. He has also learned the elements of mensuration, which is a 'practical' acquirement for him, especially if he wishes to become a sub-overseer, overseer or engineer. He has also, if he has studied English, read Cunningham's Sanitary Primer, and if he has practiced the lessons contained in it, that knowledge too is 'practical'.[65]

By the times a student is finished with high school, Leitner continues, he has acquired more information but otherwise has become:

less suited for a 'useful' and 'practical' career, than when he passed the middle school. His distaste to all physical exertion, except to that of the pen, has grown, and he is more unwilling than before to return to his father's shop.[66]

Even so, despite Leitner's mockery and the refusal to establish an Oriental university, the Punjab government came to appreciate the Anjuman-i-Punjab as a dependable loyal representative of public opinion and a deposit of 'native knowledge'. While to some extent the movement was a reaction against the loathing of everything coming from the East as put into words by Macaulay, the Anjuman clearly suited the British quest for knowledge of India. Most issues brought before the Anjuman by the government reflected some current need for confirming the native viewpoint on cases such as the prevention of female infanticide; an inquiry from the Punjab census office how best to determine the age of Hindu and Muslim youths; the availability of Persian literary works for government publication; the marriage of minor girls or widow remarriage.[67] Muhammad Husain Azad played a crucial role during these discussions. The Urdu teacher of Leitner, the Anjuman-i-Punjab made his career. In 1869 Leitner appointed him Assistant Professor of Arabic at the Government College. He presented twenty-two papers at Anjuman meetings discussing a great variety of subjects (the Anjuman published a total of 142 papers). One of his lectures turned out to be the most memorable and controversial meeting in the Anjuman's history. On 9 May 1874, Azad straightforwardly called for the reform of Urdu poetry based on English models, aiming at moral instruction and presenting a natural picture of feelings and thoughts (*necharal poitri*). Supported by the Director of Public Instruction, Colonel W.R.M. Holroyd, he proposed to start Victorian style gatherings for poets: a new *mushairah* series. While at the traditional *mushairah* poets read their verses by pre-arrangement in identical forms before an audience of connoisseurs and patrons, the Anjuman invited poets to compose on such themes as hope, patriotism, justice and indeed civilization. Undoubtedly, these meetings symbolize Lahore's uniqueness in terms of the colonial interaction and a significant hub for the development of modern Urdu.[68]

The Brahmo Samaj and the Anjuman-i-Punjab were experimental voluntary movements organized mostly by Lahori public men. The Brahmo Samaj was dominated by Bengalis and the Anjuman-i-Punjab by Punjabis working together with British officials (though over time some Anjuman members, especially through Dr. Leitner's newspaper, the *Indian Public Opinion*, became somewhat critical of the government and began voicing their own felt needs). A more straightforward political movement at this time was the Lahore Indian Association, which had moved to the Punjab from Bengal in 1877 and was dominated by Hindus and Brahmo Samajis in particular. It criticized the British in the *Tribune* but initially did not find much response among educated Punjabis. However, when in 1883 the government tried to authorize the Ilbert Bill, many Punjabis assembled to support the Indian Association. The Bill that would permit Indian magistrates jurisdiction over Europeans met much opposition from Europeans, who demonstrated and formed defence associations. In turn, the Indian Association accused the Europeans of intolerance. In the light of a study about the period of social reform, however, the Brahmo Samaj and Anjuman-i-Punjab definitely remain more important organizations for us. Babu Navincandra Rai (1838-90) played a central role in both of them and undoubtedly stands among the most influential figures in the intellectual history of nineteenth-century Punjab. He was one of the founders and President of the Lahore Brahmo Samaj and according to Bhagat Lakshman Singh

an intellectual man of a unique personality. By his learning and scholarship and by his wide and liberal sympathies, he had made the Samaj a centre of attraction for all the youngmen who were for harmony and accord and who had no faith in the efficacy of the attempts for the regeneration of India by the building of a national creed on the debris of the dead and decadent ancient beliefs, mostly based on superstition and idolatrous rituals. The Brahmo Samaj stood for this liberalism. Hence to belong to the Brahmo Samaj or to rank amongst its sympathizers was to belong to the intellectual aristocracy of Lahore. The Brahmo Samaj Mandir (temple) was, thus, the only place where one could hope to meet Indians of advanced views on religion and social reform.[69]

Navincandra Rai worked for the British government and was a prolific writer of Hindi school books. As Assistant Registrar of the Punjab University College and superintendent of the Lahore Oriental College, he became closely involved in the activities of the Anjuman-i-Punjab. As Ulrike Stark rightfully stresses, however, Navincandra Rai especially was important as a pioneer of female education and promoter of Hindi.[70] Particularly important in this context remains his *Laksmi-Sarasvati Samvad* (1869), a textbook for girls that included a combination of moral instruction and scientific knowledge, mainly geography. Through his social reformist activities, Navincandra Rai proved an inspiring predecessor for later Punjabi reformers in the field of education, female uplift and, in the case of Arya Samajis such as Lala Lajpat Rai,[71] the propagation of Hindi.

CONCLUSION

I have described some of the most vital features of the emerging liberal public sphere in the Punjab under the Pax Britannica. Critical remains the idea of modern disciplinary institutions and practices spreading the word of the civilizing mission to the bottom of rural Punjabi society. This happened not only through government initiative but also of Christian missionaries and local voluntary organizations. Because the goals of the different agencies often opposed each other, the formation of state and public sphere was an extremely complicated process. This in turn was because the great socio-economic changes related to army recruitment and commercialization of agriculture in particular incorporated the Punjab into the wider world of the British Empire. Specifically within the region, however, the colonial state's hierarchical system of authority proved decisive in terms of the rule of law and order. With the fast emergence of schools, printing presses, orphanages and hospitals, the civilizing mission reached deep into society. Urbanization also was crucial in relation to the making of Punjabi moral languages. Particularly in Lahore, Amritsar and Delhi, the Punjabi elites were confronted with Western institutions and practices, with science and technology. Given modern education, as far as possible in the various (mission-) schools, an intensive interaction of ideas took place between Punjabis and the British. Traditions were rationally questioned and a subculture of Punjabi public men increasingly began to make clear what mattered for the future and what did not. Moreover, in the case of lay leaders, the question was how one should behave oneself during these fast changing times. Numerous voluntary associations emerged and, at the early stage, the Brahmo Samaj and Anjuman-i-Punjab undoubtedly set an example in showing Punjabis new forms of organization and debate. Soon, however, they were replaced by such movements as the Singh Sabhas, the Arya Samaj and the Ahmadiyahs, which catered more to the needs of the different communities.

NOTES

1. British Library, Oriental and India Office Collections, London: Private Papers, Robert Montgomery, MSS Eur. D. 1019/5, letter no. 65. The original letter contains no initials but most likely it was written by the evangelical Henry Carre Tucker, who succeeded Montgomery as collector in Azamgarh and became a close friend. See Brian Montgomery, *Monty's Grandfather: A Life of Service for the Raj*, Poole: Blandford Press, 1984, pp. 18-19, 28; Peter Penner, *The Patronage Bureaucracy in North India: The Robert M. Bird and James Thomason School, 1820-1870*, New Delhi: Chanakya, 1986, p. 342.
2. Montgomery, *Monty's Grandfather*, p. 41.
3. Ibid., p. xvii.
4. John Beames, *Memoirs of a Bengal Civilian*, 1896, London: Eland, 1961, p. 103.
5. 'Queen Victoria's Proclamation 1 November 1858', in *The Evolution of India and Pakistan, 1858-1947: Select Documents*, ed. C.H. Philips, H.L. Singh and B.N. Pandey, London: Oxford University Press, 1962, pp. 10-11. The proclamation marked the dissolution of the East India Company, the abdication of the Mughal Emperor (who until that

time still had a court in Delhi) and the claim of sovereignty over the subcontinent by the Crown.

6. James Thomason officially declared himself neutral in religion but at the same time translated the Church of England prayer book into Hindustani for Indian converts. In R.C. Temple, *James Thomason*, Oxford: Clarendon Press, 1893, pp. 129-30.

7. Owen Chadwick, *The Secularization of the European Mind in the Nineteenth Century*, Cambridge: Cambridge University Press, 1975, p. 237.

8. John C.B. Webster, *The Christian Community and Change in North India*, New Delhi: Macmillan, 1976, p. 243.

9. Muhammad Husain Azad, Lala Lajpat Rai and Bhagat Lakshman Singh (more about them later) are three good examples among influential Punjabis. See Muhammad Husain Azad, *Ab-e Hayat: Shaping the Canon of Urdu*, tr./ed. Frances Pritchat and Shamsur Rahman Faruqi, 1880; repr. New Delhi: Oxford University Press, 2001, p. 91; Lala Lajpat Rai 'The Secret of the Greatness of Europeans', in *Selections for the Punjab Vernacular Press*, 1908, *The Arya Gazette*, 1 October, p. 610 and Ganda Singh's introduction about Bhagat Lakshman Singh in the latter's *Autobiography*, Calcutta: The Sikh Culture Centre, 1965, p. xii.

10. Judith M. Brown, *Modern India: Origins of An Asian Democracy*, New Delhi: Oxford University Press, 1984, pp. 148-9.

11. By 1890 there were more Christians than Sikhs in South Asia.

12. The latter was the elder brother of John Lawrence and already active in the Punjab for a long time. He had always opposed annexation, believing that the Punjab should remain a buffer state against the rowdy Pathans of the north-west frontier. As the permanent British resident in Lahore after the first Anglo-Sikh war of 1846, he was virtually ruler of the province. During early British rule, Henry was John's boss in the three-man board of administration set-up by Lord Dalhousie to govern the Punjab. While working together in Lahore, however, the Lawrence brothers disliked each other so much, that eventually they refused to meet, and communicated only through the third board member, Robert Montgomery. See further: Harold Lee, *Brothers in the Raj: The Lives of John and Henry Lawrence*, Karachi: Oxford University Press, 2004, p. 285.

13. Jeffrey Cox, *Imperial Fault Lines: Christianity and Colonial Power in India, 1818-1940*, Stanford: Stanford University Press, 2002, p. 53.

14. Antony Copley, *Religions in Conflict: Cultural Contact and Conversion in Late Colonial India*, New Delhi: Oxford University Press, 1997, p. xiii.

15. Ernest Trumpp, *The Adi Granth or the Holy Scriptures of the Sikhs Translated from the Original Gurmukhi with Introductory Essays*, London: Allen & Co., 1877, p. vii. Cf. Henry Martyn Clark, 'The

Decay of Sikhism', in *Punjab Notes and Queries*, 3, 1885; M.A. Macauliffe, 'The Sikh Religion', 1903, in *The Sikh Religion: A Symposium*, M.A. Macauliffe, H.H. Wilson, Frederic Pincott, John Malcolm and Sardar Kahn Singh, repr., Calcutta: Sushil Gupta, 1958, vol. I, p. lvii and R.C. Temple, *India in 1880*, London: John Murray, 1881, p. 120. Harjot Oberoi exposed this myth in *The Construction of Religious Boundaries: Culture, Identity and Diversity in the Sikh Tradition*, New Delhi: Oxford University Press, 1994, pp. 207-16 and I will discuss later how among the British this myth had much to do with their comparison between the Sikh tradition and their view of the European Reformation.

16. Edwin Arnold, *The Marquis of Dalhousie's Administration of British India*, London: Saunders Otley & Co., 1862, vol. I, p. 386 (translation mine).

17. G.R. Elsmie, *Thirty-Five Years in the Punjab 1858-1893*, Edinburgh: David Douglas, 1908, p. 48.

18. Robert Clark, *The Missions of the Church Missionary Society and the Church of England Zenana Missionary Society in the Punjab and Sindh, 1885*, ed. Robert Maconachie, London: Church Missionary Society, 1904, p. 16.

19. Ibid., pp. 242-3.

20. Copley, *Religions in Conflict*, p. 11.

21. Ibid., p. 13. Cf. Clive Dewey, *Anglo-Indian Attitudes: The Mind of the Indian Civil Service*, London: Hambledon Press, 1993, Chapter Two: 'The Making of an Evangelical'.

22. Kenneth W. Jones, *Socio-Religious Reform Movements in British India*, Cambridge: Cambridge University Press, 1989, p. 215.

23. Ibid.

24. Cox, *Imperial Fault Lines*, p. 7.

25. In the 1880s, in a response to racially charged rhetoric, the CMS changed the name of the Native Church Council to Indian Church Council.

26. Sayyid Ahmad Khan, *Asbab-e-Baghavat-e-Hind*, 1859; repr., Lahore: Sang-e-Meel, n.d., p. 42 (translations mine). At the time of writing this work, Sayyid Ahmad Khan already had been employed for twenty years in the judicial administration of the East India Company. Loyal to the British, he helped evacuate European residents from the town of Bijnor during the 1857 Revolt and, on behalf of the British, even took charge of the district.

27. Cox, *Imperial Fault Lines*, p. 7.

28. R.C. Temple, *Men and Events of My Time in India*, London: John Murray, 1882, pp. 498-9.

29. Thomas Babington Macaulay came to India as an inexperienced law member of the Legislative Council and was heavily involved in the creation of the body of Anglo-Indian law. Already in 1837 he made

a draft of the penal code, which survived remarkably unscathed twenty years of detailed criticism and was officially enacted in 1860. He became more famous, however, as an historian and especially because of two by now legendary statements. First, he declared that a single shelf of a good European library was worth the whole native literature of India and Arabia. Second, he believed that a thorough English education system to be introduced in India would create a class of persons, Indian in blood and colour, but English in taste, opinion, morals and intellect.

30. The term Anglo-vernacular education stresses the language skills that resulted from a public education combining knowledge of vernacular languages with English education. It was first imparted in mission and state schools and later in educational institutions set-up by indigenous elites.

31. G.W. Leitner, *History of Indigenous Education in the Punjab since Annexation and in 1882*, Gurgaon: Deepak, 1989, repr. Part I.

32. Stanley E. Brush, 'Protestants in the Punjab Religion and Social Change in an Indian Province in the Nineteenth Century', unpublished Ph.D. dissertation, Berkeley: University of California, p. 251.

33. Gauri Viswanathan, *Masks of Conquest: Literary Study and British Rule in India*, New York: Columbia University Press, 1989.

34. J.E. Walsh, *Growing Up in British India: Indian Autobiographers on Childhood and Education under the Raj*, New York: Holmes & Meier, 1983, p. 5.

35. Ibid., p. 6.

36. Ibid.

37. Sayyid Ahmad Khan, *Musafiran-e-Landan*, 1869, repr., Lahore: Majlis-e-Taraqqi-e Adab, n.d., pp. 183-4. On his return from London, Ahmad Khan started his reformist journal, *Tahzib ul-Akhlaq* or Refinement of morals, modelled on the *Spectator*.

38. Although many Europeans studied Indian Languages for their intrinsic value, the dominant impetus behind these reference works was to provide vernacular translations of the Bible.

39. Francis Robinson, 'Technology and Religious Change: Islam and the Impact of Print', *Modern Asian Studies*, 27, 1993, pp. 229-51 and Jones, *Socio-Religious Reform Movements in British India*, p. 213.

40. Frances W. Pritchett, *Nets of Awareness: Urdu Poetry and its Critics*, Berkeley: University of California Press, 1994, p. 143.

41. Azad, *Ab-e Hayat*, 91; Sudhir Chandra, *The Oppressive Present: Literature and Social Consciousness in Colonial India*, New Delhi: Oxford University Press, 1992.

42. *Imperial Gazetteer of India*, Provincial Series: Punjab, vol. 1, p. 144.

43. Barbara D. Metcalf, 'Imagining Community: Polemic Debates in Colonial India', in *Religious Controversy in British India: Dialogues*

in South Asian Languages, ed. Kenneth W. Jones, Albany: State University of New York Press, 1992, p. 234.

44. Barbara D. Metcalf, *Perfecting Women: Maulana Ashraf 'Ali Thanawi's Bihishti Zewar*, Berkeley: University of California Press, 1990, p. 26.

45. The 1891 Punjab census counted only 19,274 out of an approximate population of twenty-three million who could speak and write English.

46. Bhartendu Harishchandra, 'Dilli Darbar Darpan', in *Hindi and Urdu Since 1800: A Common Reader*, ed. Christopher Shackle and Rupert Snell, London: SOAS, 1990, p. 102.

47. Nazir Ahmad, *Ibn-ul-Vaqt*, 1889; repr., Lahore: Ferozsons, n.d., 8. Among many other things, Nazir Ahmad translated the Indian Penal Code into Urdu and wrote the first novels (which are in fact more reforming tales, written to illustrate a social or moral theme) in that same language.

48. H. Yule and A.C. Burnell, *Hobson-Jobson, a Glossary of Colloquial Anglo-Indian Words and Phrases* . . ., repr., Calcutta: Rupa & Co., 1990.

49. Lala Ruchi Ram Sahni, 'Self-Revelations of an Octogenarian', (unpublished manuscript). As cited in Kenneth W. Jones, *Arya Dharm: Hindu Consciousness in Nineteenth Century India*, 1976; repr., New Delhi: Manohar, 2006, p. 57.

50. Charles W. Dilke, *Greater Britain: A Record of Travels in English Speaking Countries during 1866 and 1867*, London: Macmillan, 1868, vol. 2, p. 288.

51. Ian Kerr, 'Urbanization and Colonial Rule in 19th-Century India: Lahore and Amritsar, 1849-1881', *Punjab Past and Present*, 14, 1980, p. 220.

52. *District Gazetteer*, Punjab: Lahore, 1883-84, p. 192; Amritsar, 1883-84, p. 72; *Imperial Gazetteer of India*, Provincial Series: Punjab, vol. 2, p. 19.

53. Prakash Tandon, *Punjabi Century*, London: Chatto & Windus, 1961, p. 192.

54. See for the term archival depth: C.A. Bayly, *Empire and Information: Intelligence Gathering and Social Communication in India*, Cambridge: Cambridge University Press, p. 349.

55. *Imperial Gazetteer of India*, Provincial Series: Punjab, vol. 1, p. 103.

56. John Strachey, *India: Its Administration & Progress*, London: Macmillan, 1911, p. 188.

57. Walsh, *Growing Up in British India*, ix.

58. Edward D. Churchill, 'Muslim Societies of the Punjab, 1860-1890', *Punjab Past and Present*, 8, 1974, p. 72.

59. Unitarians reject the doctrine of the Trinity and the divinity of Christ and instead believe that God is one person. As an organized Christian

church they date back to the Anabaptists at the time of the Reformation.

60. Donald McLeod was Robert Montgomery's son-in-law and succeeded the latter as Lieutenant-Governor. 'Beware of Donald McLeod's religious fanaticism', John Lawrence once wrote to Robert Montgomery. As cited in Montgomery, *Monty's Grandfather*, p. 119.

61. On Leitner: J.H. Stocqueler, *Review of the Life and Labours of Dr. G.W. Leitner*, Brighton: The Tower Press, 1875.

62. Leitner, *History of Indigenous Education*, p. v.

63. Born in a famous Sikh family, Dyal Singh Majithia became a Brahmo Samaji and besides establishing the *Tribune* as a mouthpiece primarily for Brahmo Samajis, he founded a school and library in Lahore.

64. Bhagat Lakshman Singh received Sikh baptism when he was 33 years old and afterwards was closely associated with many modern Sikh institutions, particularly as one of the founders and editor of the Sikh newspaper, *Khalsa* (Rawalpindi). In fact, generally he was not too happy with the new mode of higher learning, writing forty years later about his college experience in Lahore: 'my whole soul within me rebelled against the tyrannical control of the University and the College authorities in the choice of subjects to be learnt. And even at this long distance of time I cannot find words to give adequate expression to the absolute cussedness and fatuity which had led to the conception and adoption of one uniform scheme of studies for youngsters of different tastes and intellectual developments. . . . I can say that I have not benefited in the least from my study of the aforesaid subjects, with the exception of English and history, which I could have as well learnt privately with self effort' in *Autobiography*, pp. 71-2.

65. *Report by the Panjab Provincial Committee with Evidence Taken Before the Committee and Memorials Addressed to the Education Commission*, Calcutta: Government Printing, 1884, p. 369.

66. Ibid., p. 370.

67. J.P. Perrill, 'The Anjuman-i-Punjab as a Common Interest Association of Social Change in Nineteenth Century Punjab', *Punjab Past and Present*, 16, 1982, p. 347.

68. Pritchett, *Nets of Awareness*, 32-4.

69. Bhagat Lakshman Singh, *Autobiography*, pp. 40-1 (translation mine).

70. Ulrike Stark, 'Educating Women, Educating a Daughter: Babu Navincandra Rai, "Laksmi-Sarasvati Samvad" (1869) and Hemant Kumari Chaudhurani', in *Gurus and Their Followers: New Religious Reform Movements in Colonial India*, ed. Antony Copley, New Delhi: Oxford University Press, 2000, p. 33.

71. Lajpat Rai, 'The Story of My Life', in *The Collected Works of Lala Lajpat Rai*, ed. B.R. Nanda, vol. 5, New Delhi: Manohar, 2004, p. 294.

PART II

THE INTELLECTUAL TEXTURE

(The Singh Sabha, Arya Samaj and Ahmadiyah Moral Languages Stirring the Public Mind)

CHAPTER THREE

Tradition, Rationality and Reform

CRITICIZING TRADITION AND SOCIETY

A term such as moral languages clearly cannot do justice to the ideas of the Singh Sabha, Arya Samaj, Ahmadiyah and all other nineteenth century reform movements in British India, because each must be understood in terms of its own context, ideas and actions. I acknowledge many differences but believe that the underlying historical parallels, both in terms of the colonial interaction and world history, are much more interesting. So far, the Singh Sabhas, Arya Samaj and Ahmadiyahs more or less have been discussed separately and less in comparative terms.[1] Let us now compare the three movements as modern, rational and moral Punjabi initiatives coming out of one colonial culture. To criticize contemporary society has been common to all times through the world. As during the European Reformation, Indian reformers wanted clarity in community thought and behaviour. In the context of a fast changing society, the Singh Sabhaites, Arya Samajis and Ahmadiyahs argued that their respective traditions had degenerated and they propagated change for the better. The reformers not only referred to a pure past that was lost and needed to be revived but also, somewhat contradictorily, sought to construct a tradition in terms that would make sense to the late nineteenth century Punjabi. They reinterpreted their traditions on the basis of sacred texts and in the light of modern science and so often had to contend with the influence of Western Orientalism. Because of the fast changing intellectual culture the Punjabi social leadership stressed the importance of change in practical behaviour and rarely concerned themselves with theological questions. By propagating human will and a sense of moral duty, their message aimed at adaptation to social change through voluntary community practices.

Of the three movements discussed, only the Arya Samaj was established in Bombay (1875) instead of the Punjab. Yet, perhaps partly because of the minority status of Hindus in the Punjab, it was successful in that region. During its early Punjabi decades it went through some of its most important ideological and institutional developments and so provided, closely in the footsteps of the Christian missionaries and the Brahmo Samaj, a blueprint for reform. Influenced by the blind Guru Virjanand Saraswati, the founder of the Arya Samaj, Dayanand Saraswati (1824-83), challenged contemporary Hindu practices, especially the caste system and Brahmanical authority. He preached monotheism and rejected the justification of caste by birth, which instead should depend on a person's qualities and qualifications.[2] His inspiration mainly came from the Vedas, which according to him contained the pure religion to be revived. This gave broad scope for social reformation as all beliefs and customs sanctioned by later degenerate texts could be abandoned. Accordingly, in his most important work, *Satyarth Prakash* or Light of Truth (1875), Saraswati gave a list of traditional Hindu writings that should not be read for study.[3] Moreover, while believing in the total separation between God and the human soul, the Swami placed great emphasis on the freedom of human will and on the moral responsibility of man. He put the full burden of man's destiny on the shoulders of man.[4] Punjabi elites found this core message of activism and involvement most attractive. Dayanand was invited by Sikh and Hindu leaders, who were primarily Brahmo Samajis, to the 1877 Delhi *darbar*. In the Punjab, he preached and gave specific lectures on Islam, the Brahmo Samaj, the Sikhs and, indeed for the very first time, on Christianity. These led to passionate reactions from the different communities. Saraswati crisscrossed the province for more than a year and was very successful in the region.[5] In Lahore he attracted a group of dedicated disciples, most of whom were students and graduates of the local colleges. They established the Lahore Arya Samaj on 24 June 1877 and afterwards recasted the earlier long and detailed 28-point Bombay creed into the ten simple principles, which have been followed ever since.[6] According to R.B. Mulraj, close confidant of Saraswati and the first President of the Arya

Samaj, who was entrusted by Dayanand to frame these principles, the Swami did not approach them dogmatically. On the contrary, as Mulraj put it in a lecture at the sixteenth anniversary of the Lahore Arya Samaj on 25 November 1893, he 'purposely excluded doctrinal points and philosophical matters from the principles of the Arya Samaj'.[7]

The establishment of the first Singh Sabha in Amritsar (1873) was a complex response by Sikh elites, who had lost power and influence following British rule, to the fast changing circumstances in the Punjab. Significant were the Sikh conversions to Christianity that followed the conversion of Maharaja Duleep Singh, son of Ranjit Singh, in 1853.[8] With their community in danger, traditional Sikh leaders partially founded the Sabha in response. By the same token, however, following the 1872 Namdhari troubles, one of the founding principles of the Amritsar Singh Sabha was the propagation of loyalty to the British.[9] At first the Arya Samajis were regarded by the Sikhs as allies against the missionaries but soon it was seen that they too formed a threat to the community. Accordingly, while the elitist Amritsar Singh Sabha remained at ease with portraying Sikhism solely as an Hindu reformist element, subsequently lower caste and professional Singh Sabhaites led by the Lahore Singh Sabha (1879) were more radical in restoring the Sikh tradition to its supposed original purity, free from Hindu influences. This vision of Sikhism came to be known as Tat Khalsa: 'the word Tat denotes the unalloyed elements out of which the universe is created, and Khalsa in popular usage signifies "the pure"'.[10] Tat Khalsa followers began to attack Punjabi popular culture, preaching an end to the caste system (according to them, untouchables could enter the gurdwara any time) and the worship of Sufi *pirs* or descendants of the ten Gurus. While penetrating the Punjabi countryside more than other reformers, they were often banned from meeting in local gurdwaras (especially those dominated by Hindu priests) and subsequently erected gurdwaras served by Sikhs who accepted the Tat Khalsa ideology.

In 1880, the founder of the Ahmadiyah movement, Mirza Ghulam Ahmad, began the publication of his major work, *Barahin-i-Ahmadiyah* (Proofs of Ahmadiyah). In it, he stressed what he perceived as the true principles of Islam and the duties of all good Muslims. The work was well received by Muslims harassed by Christian missionaries and Arya Samajis. Like other Muslim reformers, Ghulam Ahmad was convinced that Islam had fallen to unprecedented depths. Agitated by the lethargy of the *ulema* (Islamic theologians) and the continuous Christian missionary criticism of the Prophet and Islam, he argued that the situation had reached such proportions that only a divinely inspired leader could halt the process of decline and restore Islam to its pristine purity. He himself of course was the one called upon to perform this task and soon afterwards the Mirza claimed he had received divine revelations telling him he was the renewer of faith (*mujaddid*), the Messiah (*masih mauwud*) and the rightly guided one (*mahdi*). Obviously, these claims were not accepted by the orthodox *ulema* and hence Ahmad became involved in many polemics with them.[11] As Yohanan Friedmann argued persuasively, Ghulam Ahmad's claims were adopted from medieval Islam but his interpretations transcended their earlier meaning.[12] The Mirza's most moderate claim was to be the renewer of Islam. Numerous Muslim leaders earlier had claimed or were awarded the title, and now Ghulam Ahmad claimed it for himself. He pointed out that the *hadith* predicted the appearance of the centennial *mujaddid* and they indeed appeared at the expected times. While the renewer of faith had appeared regularly since the emergence of Islam, nobody claimed the title on the eve of the fourteenth century AH (which started on 12 November 1882). His most controversial modification of the classical concept, however, was his idea that there was an affinity between the *mujaddid* and the Prophet.[13] Much more central to Ghulam Ahmad's world remains the idea of the Promised Messiah. Both the Christian and Islamic traditions followed the idea that Jesus is alive in heaven and will descend for another (final?) sojourn at the end of time. While the comparison between the living Jesus and the deceased Muhammad had been used in Christian polemics against Islam since medieval times, Ghulam Ahmad turned it all around (as he regularly did) to counter Christian arguments. Nearly the whole of his apologia is built up with the object of proving himself to be the fulfilment of the second coming of Christ. Thus he undermined the Christian view of Jesus and introduced substantial changes in some prevalent Muslim beliefs concerning him, like the claim to possess Jesus' spirit and power and to be Messiah for both Christians and Muslims. Moreover, Ghulam Ahmad reconciled the idea of resembling the Christian Messiah with that character of violence and blood, the *mahdi*, by declaring that traditions speaking of the *mahdi* as a man of violence were all forgeries and the 'rightly guided one' was to be a man of peace.[14]

What remains crucial in this criticism by Punjabi leaders towards the state of contemporary society is that it was similar to that made by missionaries of South Asian society: it included idol worship, priestly domination, child marriage, purdah and the degradation of widows. Furthermore, like the missionaries, Punjabi reformers for the first time organized themselves into voluntary movements, particularly for educational purposes. Goals were stated in purposive terms rather than in terms of creed. Reformers became preoccupied with technical and financial questions and rules were created to bring order into the patterns of behaviour for community members in and outside the modern institutions. It did not take long before Punjabi reformers began to establish their own schools and colleges wherein they could prepare their brethren for the future and make them aware of their past. Individuals (including women) were encouraged in speech and countless 'how to behave' manuals to cultivate personalities based on moderation and relentless self-control. Undoubtedly all this was boosted through a rapidly emerging print culture. Most Punjabi reformers set-up their own printing presses. This not only made possible the cheap production of texts but also furthered standardization. Alternatively, the wider availability of both indigenous and European texts encouraged the development of new intellectual combinations. Moreover, in line with what was taught at state and missionary schools, the reformers aimed at creating robust characters with a practical state of mind. Indeed, while the reformers remained rather indifferent to Western art and music, over time, they eagerly adopted Western sports in their educational institutions because they saw these as the special characteristics of the British rulers, embodying the values that they particularly prized: manliness, courage and physical endurance.

After the death of Dayanand Saraswati, the Arya Samaj went through some of its most important institutional developments. Arya Samajis sought to honour their departed teacher through the foundation of a school that would impart his Vedic Hinduism. Plans were drafted for its establishment and the Anglo-Vedic Trust and Management Society was set-up to raise funds. In 1886 the first Dayanand Anglo-Vedic School was opened in Lahore with Lala Hans Raj as the first headmaster of a high school under purely Indian management.[15] The School became a college affiliated to the Panjab University, where a curriculum was taught similar to that of the government schools but without government support or the participation of Englishmen on the faculty. Yet, as the Dayanand Anglo-Vedic College progressed from a set of ideals to their concrete expression, earlier organizational developments were followed (as in all three reform movements) by internal tensions and by 1893 the Arya Samaj was formally divided. Until his death, Pandit Guru Datta Vidyarthi (1864-90) led one faction and for him the movement first of all was a religious experience, i.e. Dayanand a *rishi* and his *Satyarth Prakash*—a text that had to be taken literally and could not be questioned.[16] Hence he wanted the College to focus on the study of Sanskrit and the Vedic scriptures. When this proved to be impossible, he and others such as Pandit Lekh Ram (1858-97) and Lala Munshi Ram (1856-1926), gained control over most of the local Arya Samajis, the provincial representative body (Punjab Arya Pratinidhi Sabha) and, importantly, started to emphasize proselytism and preaching. The other group of Arya Samajis, who saw Dayanand only as a great reformer, concentrated on the managing committee and the College. They established rival local organizations and in 1903 founded their own provincial representative body.[17] Overall, Anglo-vernacular education, safe from non-Hindu influence, but still relevant to government careers, remained their primary goal. Not that Pandit Guru Datta's followers neglected education. On the contrary, they founded an educational institution strictly for girls.

Moreover, Guru Datta's dream of a school system modelled after the ancient Hindu universities survived his death. In 1902, the Gurukul Kangri opened in Haridwar with Munshi Ram as its manager and moral guide.[18] The institution was established with the aim of 'making an experiment in truly national education'.[19] Founded, managed, staffed and financed by Indians, its students led a life of celibacy, discipline and Vedic learning. Unlike other educational institutions it took no notice of the official university courses or university examinations and its curriculum gave first place to Indian languages.[20] Even so, despite the prominence given to the study of Sanskrit, Hindi and the Vedas, it was equally decided that knowledge of English was indispensable.

[W]e cannot overlook the fact that for the study, to advantage, of modern sciences and of technical subjects, the study of English is, and will remain for some time to a come a *sine qua non*. The study of English, to limited extent, is also necessary for the preachers of the Vedic Dharm, who have not infrequently to preach to the English-educated classes.[21]

By 1912, the two wings of the Arya Samaj had founded one college, eight gurukuls, sixteen high schools, and a large number of middle and primary schools. Besides, Arya Samajis had become influential partners of Hindus and Sikhs in such public institutions as the Punjab National Bank and the Bharat Insurance Company.

The Amritsar Singh Sabha was from the beginning a modern voluntary association. It had a constitution and a managing committee and arranged regular elections. As it expanded, different kinds of functionaries were appointed. The Sabha came together regularly and produced income and expenditure records as well as annual reports. To provide a central organization for all Singh Sabhas, the Amritsar Khalsa Diwan was established in 1883. It included around thirty-six different Singh Sabhas, including the Lahore association. Yet even this effort at unity did not last long. In 1886 the Lahore Singh Sabha created its own Khalsa Diwan. Only the Sabhas of Faridkot, Amritsar, and Rawalpindi allied with the original Diwan, the rest turning to the more radical Lahori lay leaders. However, despite differences in membership, ideology, and programmes between the two

Diwans, they did cooperate (supported by the colonial government) in establishing a Sikh college. Meetings were organized telling Sikhs that the Arya Samaj had its institutions to teach Sanskrit and the Vedas, the Muslims had made the provision for the teaching of Arabic and the Koran in Aligarh, but the Sikhs had no institution for the study of Gurmukhi and the Granth Sahib. A decision was issued from the Golden Temple, requesting each Sikh to give a tenth of his income for the college project, though perhaps most support came from the Sikh rulers of Punjabi native states. In 1899, Khalsa College was established in Amritsar; it is still impressive today, being built, like many official buildings at that time, in Indo-Saracenic architectural style. One year later, there were almost a hundred Singh Sabhas and related societies scattered across the Punjab, most of them allied to the Lahore Diwan.[22] Meanwhile leadership shifted and Sikh leaders once again attempted to unite the diverse organizations through the foundation of the Amritsar Chief Khalsa Diwan in 1902. Only twenty-nine of the then existing 150 Singh Sabhas agreed to join this organization, but it became the major spokesman for the Sikhs. It mobilized financial and human resources and founded institutions. According to its ideology, Sikhism was a separate tradition with its own rituals and history. The Sikh identity was defined more strictly than ever before, as only Khalsa Sikhs could become members. The Chief Khalsa Diwan promised to cultivate loyalty to the Crown, to safeguard Sikh rights *vis-à-vis* other communities, and to fight for adequate representation of Sikhs in government services. Between 1890 and 1910, about a dozen Singh Sabha allied associations, ranging from publishing societies and orphanages to the Punjab and Sind Bank. Important also was the Sikh Education Conference (from 1908 onwards), which came together every year to take stock of the progress of literacy in the community and to collect money to build schools.

Though in reality each Arya Samaj and Singh Sabha tended to mirror the concerns and personalities of local lay leaders, at least in theory each regarded itself as the representative of its respective communities. What in spite of rivalries held these essentially different groups and institutions together was a developing sense of a distinct identity, including an image of the past and a vision of the future. As expected, these voluntary movements were characterized by enthusiastic participation, especially from those who joined them straight after college and were extremely willing to participate without asking too many questions. All this was part of the newly emerging modes of communication, expressing moral indignation on behalf of ideas that generally remained misty. So, for example, despite their criticism of the caste-system, both for Arya Samajis and Singh Sabhaites caste certainly mattered. In the case of the Singh Sabhaites Khatris and Aroras heavily influenced a Panth consisting largely of Jats. The Arya Samaj then consisted largely of Khatris and to a lesser degree Aroras. Otherwise, in general, one followed strategies of compromise and flexibility, as propagating specific rules or defending precise answers to controversial questions would have alienated both financial support and manpower. Accordingly, there were limits on the interpretation of the Hindu and Sikh traditions—a serious questioning of certain texts, rituals or values could mean ostracism, personal attack and the end of British patronage. For without doubt there was a shared view among Punjabi reformers of how personal or institutional struggles related to British authority. Accepting the official view of the government as a paternalistic source of justice and patronage (*ma-bap*), reformers emphasized their own 'loyalty and attachment to the Raj, while simultaneously tarring opponents as "seditious" or "trouble-making"'.[23] Supposedly, British allies would be protected and given aid (land, financial support, quotas and so on), 'whereas opponents would be injured by government fiat'.[24]

Compared to the Arya Samaj and the Singh Sabhas, the Ahmadiyah movement was much smaller and, initially, more locally based in the birthplace of Mirza Ghulam Ahmad, the little town of Qadian in rural Gurdaspur district.[25] Nonetheless it clearly showed the features of a modern voluntary association. Soon after its establishment a middle school was established in Qadian but education especially was vigorously pushed forward later, through the Anglo-vernacular high school. It contained about 400 students in all grades and was affiliated to the Panjab

University. Qadiyan also had a school (*madrasa*) for the study of Arabic and the Koran, which turned out missionaries (as was done until the Pakistan government forbade them to do so, after Partition, at the *madrasa* in Rabwah). Subsequently, primary schools were opened in other districts and to propagate their version of Islam, the movement started to publish its first periodicals: the Urdu weeklies *al-Hakam* (1897) and *Badr* (1902), and the *Review of Religions* (from 1902 in English and Urdu). Particularly important to the movement was Ghulam Ahmad's *al-Wasiyah* or The Will (1906) in which he made clear how the movement was to be organized after his death. Thus a specific association existing of leading Ahmadiyahs succeeded the founder after his death. Nur al-Din, one of Ahmad's earliest supporters and confidants, and the only name specifically mentioned by Ghulam Ahmad in *al-Wasiyah*, was elected by the association as Caliph.[26] Also the initiation ceremony or *baiat* was decentralized and no longer the exclusive prerogative of the leader.[27] To finance the goals of the movement taxes were imposed on Ahmadiyah members, who cheerfully paid up. Mirza Ghulam Ahmad made it obligatory for members of the community to donate a part of their income to the movement. He also pleaded for the establishment of a 'celestial cemetery' in Qadiyan. Those who wanted to be buried there had to pay a contribution and leave at least one-tenth of their property to a specific association. The graveyard became an instrument for long-term funding (it is still there, though financially the larger cemetery in Rabwah is more important now). The money collected was to be spent on spreading Islam, the teachings of the Koran, educating and sending out missionaries, building orphanages and giving financial assistance to members in need. Otherwise, of course, capital was to be invested in some profitable enterprise.[28] To take care of community dealings, two crucial associations were founded over time (the first by Ghulam Ahmad and the second by Caliph Nur al-Din). A central committee, with members appointed for life, looked after the executive and educational necessities of the community, while the Society for the Advancement of Islam took care mainly of missionary activities.

Though based in rural Qadiyan, the Ahmadiyah movement

did not differ much from the Arya Samaj and Singh Sabhas in terms of lay leadership. Like the other two movements, the Ahmadiyah community had a bipolar character from the beginning. The teachings of Ghulam Ahmad first appealed to affluent Muslims but especially later also attracted people among the illiterate poor. In the former category were doctors, attorneys, landowners and businessmen, who generally remained somewhat aloof from the growing number of poor rural members. Indeed, the leadership was always somewhat elitist and sensitive about the community's social standing. Ghulam Ahmad for example reacted fiercely to a passage included both in the 1891 *Gurdaspur District Gazetteer* and the 1901 Punjab census report which stated that he had 'a special mission to the sweepers'.[29] He replied that only 'the intelligent and noble-minded' were able to accept his principles and that among his followers there were numerous highly placed persons.[30] In many of his writings Ghulam Ahmad stressed the long-standing nobility of his family and its loyalty to the British during the 1857 Revolt.[31] Otherwise, comparable to what happened to the Arya Samaj and Singh Sabha movements, after the death of Nur al-Din, the Ahmadiyah movement was divided into two factions in 1914: the Qadiyani and the Lahori. The most crucial issues for this split were the idea of a Caliph as community leader and the fact that Lahori Ahmadiyahs took themselves as not so different as the Qadiyani faction from mainstream Sunni Islam. Undoubtedly of great importance in this context was an article published a few years earlier by the second Caliph, Mahmud Ahmad, in which he declared that all non-Ahmadiyah Muslims were *kafirs* (infidels).[32]

Criticism of traditional society propagated through modern institutions and practices were the distinct characteristics of leadership in the emerging liberal public sphere. No one took over traditional leadership overnight. On the contrary, that never happened and especially the early histories of the Singh Sabhas, Arya Samaj and Ahmadiyahs are replete with negotiations and confrontations between the old and new spokesmen. So it is interesting, for instance, that the Arya Samaj managed to achieve in barely fifteen months on several fronts (including a new ideology, organization and membership) what the Amritsar Singh

Sabha had failed to attain in six years: while the men behind the Amritsar Singh Sabha belonged to the traditional elite, the Arya Samaj attracted both Hindus and Sikhs who already felt comfortable in the newly emerging public sphere. The fast changing circumstances made clear to Punjabi reformers that rational choices were to be made. Alternatively, it seems that the educational institutions set-up by the reform movements suited the British racist politics of difference. In these institutions Indians spent time discussing the authenticity of their identities. The real trouble came from those who followed an entirely secular education and began to question the legitimacy of colonial rule.[33] In hindsight, the leading Arya Samaji, Lala Lajpat Rai (1865-1928),[34] therefore also concluded that, despite all the self-sacrifice and hard work of their personnel, all contemporary north Indian educational institutions unfortunately remained denominational and sectarian instead of truly 'national'.[35] Overall, the Singh Sabha, Arya Samaj and Ahmadiyah reformers proclaimed their loyalty to the British and through their educational institutions became vital in spreading their versions of the civilizing mission. Like the Christian missionaries they stressed the importance of education as a cure for all diseases; the masses needed material and moral improvement. Hence, during the period of social reform, rationality was particularly employed in defining a masculine self, which subsequently proved to be central to the moral and political identities that assertively stirred the Punjabi public mind. In these circumstances Singh Sabhaites, Arya Samajis and Ahmadiyahs retreated into their respective communities to redefine doctrine, conduct and ritual, creating moral languages that stressed the employment of human will in disciplining mind and body on the way.

DEFINING DOCTRINE, CONDUCT AND RITUAL

Although the understanding of faith as popularized since the Protestant Reformation through the idea of *sola fide* always has been a starting point within the Christian tradition, this notion never was essential to non-Western traditions. Instead, conduct in accordance with traditional law and ritual made up the most crucial aspect of the greater traditions of Islam, Hinduism and Sikhism. What is more, opposed to the Reformatory tradition of *sola scriptura*, this conduct did not necessarily have to be traceable in scripture. Nonetheless, many things changed in the non-Western world following the interaction with Western (Christian) thought. New ways of looking at one's own tradition were opened up transforming the texture of tradition in society. Increasingly, leading Singh Sabhaites, Arya Samajis and Ahmadiyahs appealed to tradition in a Reformatory way, by picking out concepts and changing their meanings into new contextual terminology. Sacred works were central to the project: the Granth Sahib for the Singh Sabhaites, the Vedas for Arya Samajis and the Koran for Ahmadiyahs. For indeed something new had happened in the nineteenth century: an increasing number of lay leaders claimed their public right to study and comment upon these works individually. While scriptural commentary earlier was regarded as an esoteric venture and intellectual subtlety, for the reformers conceptual clarity seemed to be the ultimate goal.

Following the establishment of the Amritsar Singh Sabha, some elite Sikhs began to perceive their tradition anew and, consequently, the codification of morality, which earlier had no definite shape, attained fixed form. They rationally construed the *rahit-namas* (manuals of *Rahit* principles) within a far narrower framework, eliminating Hindu elements and those of Punjabi popular culture.[36] The goal of the Singh Sabha reformers was to record once and for all the right way of conduct, supposedly restoring the *Rahit* to its pure form as delivered to the Panth by Guru Gobind Singh. Moreover, Singh Sabhaites turned to the important task of reinterpreting the Granth Sahib. It was argued that the latter contained the Sikh way of life and as such was authoritative. Hence, in hindsight, the Sikh tradition started with a human Guru, continued during a period of duality in which there were human Gurus and a collection of sacred writings, and with the Singh Sabha movement moved to a situation wherein the Granth Sahib is authoritative. Influenced by the studies of European scholars, commentaries on the scripture were written for the first time in the Sikh tradition. Singh

Sabhaites aimed to establish the strict moral meaning of scriptural word or phrase in terms that were principally Tat Khalsa. Especially it was stressed that these meanings were independent of Hindu learning.

While in theory (but not in practice) Singh Sabhaites rejected the caste system and rituals performed simply for the sake of spiritual purification, they produced a vast amount of polemical literature arguing that ritualism originated in Hinduism and was untrue to the Tat Khalsa. Liberation could not be reached merely through ceremonial acts. Instead, they argued that all the Sikhs should turn to the Granth Sahib, being a complete authoritative repository wherein each verse was endowed (like a *mantra* or incantation) with special power. This changing perception of the Granth is reflected for example in a novel by a leading Singh Sabhaite, the well-known Sikh author, Bhai Vir Singh (1872-1957).[37] In *Baba Naudh Singh* (first serialized from 1917 to 1921 and subtitled *A Study in Moral and Spiritual Awakening*), a reading from Sikh scripture can stop incessant rainfall.[38] In fact, Vir Singh's novels *Sundri* (1898), *Bijay Singh* (1900), *Satwant Kaur* (1900) and *Baba Naudh Singh* propagated Tat Khalsa ideals. These books were very popular during the first decades of the twentieth century and in them Sikhs could read about the right Sikh code of conduct. Repeated emphasis on the initiation rite and the five Ks in these novels and in Singh Sabha literature in general succeeded in turning initiation into the most salient of the Sikh *rites de passage*.[39] Indeed, against to what is commonly thought, it was only with the Singh Sabha movement that the five Ks became part of the *Rahit*.[40] This was a feature of the times, one could suggest, because something more or less similar took place among the Arya Samajis and Ahmadiyahs through the introduction of respectively the ten principles and the *baiat*. An all out campaign was launched to abolish the so-called Hindu customs and replace them with strictly defined Tat Khalsa *rites de passage*. Between 1884 and 1915 at least twenty-four manuals were produced to decide what sort of life-cycle rituals (most of them on marriage) should be performed.[41] To encourage acceptance they were published in the leading Sikh newspapers. What initially were changes introduced by a tiny minority, thus gradually came to be accepted by the Sikh public at large.

By this time, the question 'Are Sikhs Hindus?' already was firmly established and a public debate followed generating books, pamphlets and letters airing a wide variety of opinions on Sikh-Hindu relations. The fact that Singh Sabhaites were much involved in redefining a community different from Hindus particularly became clear with the publication of Kahn Singh Nabha's famous tract, *Ham Hindu Nahin* or We are not Hindus (1897).[42] It was first published in Hindi most likely because it was written for Hindus instead of Sikhs. Afterwards, it became famous in the Punjabi version which, on the contrary, in the first place addressed Sikhs who believed they were Hindus. The tract is written in the form of a dialogue (between a Hindu and a Sikh): a common practice in late nineteenth-century South Asia, presumably partly because of the example set by the Christian missionaries. Interesting remains Kahn Singh Nabha's comparison with the Semitic faiths 'in which Christianity emerged from Judaism, and Islam arose out of both'.[43] According to him, it was in a similar manner that the Sikh tradition had emerged from Hinduism and had become distinct. Most notable in the context of the definition of a distinct Sikh identity also was the death of Dyal Singh Majithia in 1898. He left his vast wealth to the Dyal Singh Trust but his widow and her cousin contested the will because according to them the Hindu law of inheritance did not apply because he was a Sikh instead of a Hindu:

The deceased was not a Hindu because (a) he was born a Sikh the connotations of which term exclude the notion of his being a Hindu, (b) he abandoned Sikhism and adopted Brahmoism which also similarly is a religion outside the pale of Hinduism and opposed to it and (c) he ate beef and food cooked by Mahomedans, Christians and others and in their company, contrary to the tenets of Hindu religion and the social usages of those who profess it and thereby was degraded from or lost his caste and thus at all events ceased to be a Hindu.[44]

Confronted with the most vital question of determining whether Sikhs were or were not Hindus, the High Court decided that Dyal Singh Majithia was a Hindu, with reference to the British Orientalists on Hinduism, it decided that 'Sikhism and Brahmoism are mere offshoots of the Hindu religion'.[45] Afterwards, Bhagat Lakshman Singh and others heavily debated the case in public meetings and the press.[46]

Undoubtedly, the discussions around Dyal Singh Majithia's Sikh identity boosted the acceptance by the government of the 1909 Anand Marriage Act. At the turn of the century a growing number of Sikhs performed their marriage ceremony according to the newly defined Singh Sabha norm. Yet it suddenly became clear to Singh Sabhaites that this mode of marriage had no legal recognition, as until then Sikhs officially were supposed to have Hindu weddings. This led to endless problems over the status of children, the distribution of wealth and inheritance. The government, however, was so impressed by the support that was given by the Sikh community to the Singh Sabha that in 1909 the Anand Marriage Act was passed in the legislative council.[47] It states that all Sikh marriages conducted according to the Anand marriage ceremony (requiring couples to walk round the Granth Sahib instead of a Hindu sacred fire) should be recognized as valid.[48] In 1925 the Tat Khalsa ideology gained somewhat more ground when the Gurdwara Act placed the management of Sikh shrines in the hands of the Shiromani Gurdwara Parbandhak Committee (SGPC). Then in 1931 a meeting was held at the Golden Temple where it was decided to draw up a code to regulate individual and community life. Lay leaders like Teja Singh, Bhai Vir Singh, Jodh Singh and Kahn Singh Nabha were present and influential. Ultimately, Sikh leaders agreed in 1945 upon one version, the Sikh *Rahit Maryada*, published in 1950 under the patronage of the SGPC. In it, a Sikh was strictly defined. It was prescribed how one should behave as individual and community member; what and where one should study and sing; what one should not say about the tradition in the gurdwara; which rituals should be followed; and (indeed like within the Arya Samaj and Ahmadiyah communities) what kind of community service should be dutifully performed.

Much more ardently than the Singh Sabhaites, Dayanand Saraswati opposed contemporary Hindu practices from within. His thinking took a crucial turn after his visit to Calcutta in 1872 when he gave up the dress of a mendicant and started to speak in Hindi instead of Sanskrit to reach a wider audience. Calcutta had confronted him with the world of reform. There he saw how the Brahmo Samajis propagated their ideas to the public through institutions, speeches and numerous writings. He saw how they compared Hindu practices with those of other traditions, with Western reason and Christianity. His main ideas were published for the first time in 1875 in the *Satyarth Prakash*. It has been argued these ideas are very similar to those propagated in *Brahmo Dharm* by Brahmo Samaj leader Debendranath Tagore.[49] In the *Satyarth Prakash*, Dayanand worked out his concept of true Vedic Hinduism and condemned all that he thought to be false: all non-Vedic versions of Hinduism, also Christianity, Islam, Buddhism, Jainism and Sikhism. The Punjab government temporarily banned the book because of its offensive reference to the Prophet Muhammad.

Like the Europeans of the eighteenth century, Dayanand argued that Sanskrit was the mother of all languages and stressed the importance of education. The Swami clearly was not a great theologian. His personal life reflected that he was more interested in the struggles of man than in the mysteries of God. Initially he was devoted to reaching salvation (*moksha*) but later devoted his life to the regeneration of *Arya Varta* (Aryan land).[50] In fact, the Swami (probably partly because of his Shaivite background) had imprinted on his mind the idea of a personal God, which after discussions with Christian missionaries and his stay in Calcutta developed into a clear doctrine of monotheism. Crucial also remain Dayanand's ideas about the Vedas and about God. He adopted the view that true religion must come directly from God in the form of a book, and combined this with the dogma of the superiority of Vedic Hinduism. He believed that God had revealed the truth in the Vedas, which therefore constituted the only real divine revelation. All other sacred Hindu books (as well as those of other traditions) were man's imperfect efforts. It was the first time in Hindu tradition that this concept of revelation was found. Dayanand's limited understanding of true religion, as of the final word, undoubtedly was inspired by the way Protestants viewed the Bible (and probably too a lesser extent, Muslims the Koran). Even so, he went further than any

Christian fundamentalist probably would dare and claimed that these ancient works contained the totality of all knowledge, including science and technology!

As said earlier, while he believed in the total separation of God and the human soul, Dayanand greatly emphasized the moral stature and responsibility of man, whose salvation was to be achieved by nothing else than his own works. Action on the basis of reason was the basic duty of anyone reaching out for salvation and, accordingly, Aryas stressed personal virtue and the performance of good works. All this then was to be regulated by the law of *karma*, an inexorably just law that man never escaped, not even in salvation! Although this law was to be executed by God, He never interfered with the laws of nature, for both these laws were perfect from the beginning.[51] For Dayanand, freedom, activity and involvement in the world constituted the basic pursuit of man as 'a free-agent who has the body, the vital forces, the senses and the mind subordinate to his will'.[52] No other Hindu theologian had elevated human will to such a rank in the scale of human effort, far above the powers of ritualism, the raptures of mysticism or the effectiveness of devotional love as common for example in the *bhakti* tradition.[53] Parallel to his ideas on the freedom of human will, Dayanand developed the concept of *dharm* or the duties man has to perform to achieve his worldly fulfilment. He elevated man to a position of complete freedom and responsibility. Stressing moral action (*dharmachar*), every individual had to live a morally good life, self-controlled, always active and in search of knowledge, governed by reason and duly assessed by the law of divine justice and reward. Although he argued that the state had to be the guardian of *dharm*, the state's effectiveness depended on the righteousness of all its members, from the ruler to the common man.[54] Compared to earlier interpretations, this earthly exposition of *dharm* no doubt brought Dayanand into confrontation with the caste system.[55]

To affirm their position within the larger Hindu tradition, Arya Samajis (like their Sikh counterparts) created their own rituals. To preach change meant little when no birth, death or marriage ceremony could be performed outside the world of orthodoxy. Accordingly, Saraswati's *Sanskar Vidhi* (1877) provided Aryas with the five principal sacred practices to be observed everyday and sixteen life-cycle rituals, beginning with conception and ending with cremation. This not only threatened existing beliefs, but also struck at the economic position of the Brahmans: Arya ceremonies did not employ the latter—they were conducted by Arya priests (*pandits*) or even, though not often, Samaj laymen instead. Generally Arya rituals were practical and could be performed without having to spend too much money, while emphasizing the pure and simple Vedic rites, without elaborate rituals common in the Hindu tradition or the fireworks and dancing girls found at more popular meetings. The marriage ritual in particular was to be less elaborate and expensive, pointing to a problem that still remains in contemporary Hindu life.[56]

By definition a good prophet is a bad theologian, as he speaks in inspiration and rapture without putting his ideas together in a clear system. Yet, though most of Mirza Ghulam Ahmad's ideas concern prophetology, he also had some thoughts on conduct or *adab*. This is crucial since in Islam conduct in accordance with the body of rules of the *shariat* (worked out through the discipline of *fiqh*) remains a *sine qua non* of salvation.[57] However, instead of following interpretations of the *hadith*, Ghulam Ahmad (resembling the Singh Sabhaites and Dayanand Saraswati) argued that this conduct had to be strictly traceable in the Koran.[58] Throughout the history of Islam, the Koran had proclaimed its moral authority on the basis of its being the very word of God (for in Islam God revealed himself not in any historical personage but in a book). Yet what Ghulam Ahmad did was to follow a specific mode of thought which would be increasingly common within modern Koran interpretation, whereby as J.M.S. Baljon put it, 'first and foremost we find the postulate of the Reformation that everybody is allowed to reflect on the purports of the Holy book'.[59] More than half of Ghulam Ahmad's *Islami Usul ki Falasafi* (1905) in fact is devoted to religious conduct. In it, he rationally interprets moral values in the Koran; he stresses the importance of human will by stating that 'faith without deeds is useless'.[60] Also he advocates the significance of gaining moral knowledge through the experience of 'sufferings and trials' in practice and that knowledge 'which never passes into the domain of the practical has no value'.[61] No doubt these ideas were central to the world of nineteenth century reform, both within Islamic and other traditions. Yet, Ghulam Ahmad's ideas have to be seen in the wider context of modern Muslim Koran interpretation. For example, the noun *'aql* was used with growing frequency in the sense of rationality in many places within the nineteenth century Islamic world.[62] Undoubtedly, as a result of the confrontation with the West, it referred to what came to be known as the greater *jihad* or the 'unceasing effort to discriminate the boundaries made clear in the Koran and relentless self-control in eschewing excess and living within them'.[63] One also finds this very same stress on *'aql* in such important contemporary books as Altaf Husain Hali's *Musaddas* (1879), Nazir Ahmad's moral tales, and Ashraf 'Ali Thanawi's *Bihisti Zewar* (1905) but I will deal with their influence in the Punjab later.

Even so, Ghulam Ahmad made clear that reason alone was not to be trusted, 'for its own existence is liable to pass away if revelation does not afford it nourishment'.[64] This is an important point as in the 1930s it made the famous Punjabi poet and philosopher, Muhammad Iqbal (1877-1938),[65] declare that Ahmadiyahs were non-Muslims. According to Iqbal 'in Islam prophecy reached its perfection in discovering the need for its own abolition' and hence man could develop an 'independent critical attitude towards mystic experience by generating the belief that all personal authority, claiming a supernatural origin, has come to an end in the history of man'.[66] Besides that the Ahmadiyahs damaged Islamic solidarity by their overall loyalty to the British (see Chapter Five), Iqbal was particularly furious about the fact that Ghulam Ahmad's claim to prophethood completely undermined his modern reconstruction of Islam.[67] Most critical here was the position of Mirza Ghulam Ahmad towards reason in relation to the Prophet Muhammad. Muhammad Iqbal stressed that the 'search for rational foundations in Islam may be regarded to have begun with the Prophet himself', the absence of the miraculous about him.[68] Though later Ahmadiyah leaders would be less aloof to reason, Ghulam

Ahmad did not champion Islam by praise of Islamic rationality. Instead, as a real prophet should, he believed that Islam was more truthful on the basis of revelation and divine assistance. Accordingly, Iqbal wrote that the real nature of Ahmadiyah thought remained 'hidden behind the mist of medieval mysticism and theology'.[69]

All in all, Singh Sabhaites, Arya Samajis and Ahmadiyahs defined themselves as followers of the Granth Sahib, Vedas and Koran. Most significant remains the inclination to rationality and the increasing number of commentaries by lay leaders on these works. These scriptures became an eternal referent of transcendence and so the colonial interaction (and that with Protestant evangelicals in particular) caused them to lose their implicit normative functions. The most authoritative text therefore, ironically, became the least living one.[70] On the basis of scripture reformers explicitly made clear what one had to do, where one was coming from and where one was heading. Nothing exceeded their ideas and experiences. They were utterly sovereign subjects who could define themselves while absorbing the other, even if this meant a denial of transcendence. For indeed, often not even God escaped the rationality of the reformers, while the moral imperative they followed existed less because God commanded it than because they willed it. Personal standards in ethics and worship were rationally enjoined, so that religious life became more congruent with a more mobile and urbanized society. Complex customary observations of funerals and marriages tied to specific times and places were de-emphasized and instead an internalized religion of individual responsibility was propagated.[71] Hence, similar to the worldly asceticism of the European Reformation as argued by Max Weber, the Singh Sabhaites, Arya Samajis and Ahmadiyahs sought to control the flux of the contemporary world with puritanism and restraint. The ultimate cause of the present was attributed to one's own individual moral corruption and therefore salvation was a personal and internal struggle, a feat of will.[72] Alternatively, the fact that more and more people claimed the right to participate in the redefinition of tradition brings us to the relationship between rationality and the growing authority of Western science.

INVOKING THE AUTHORITY OF SCIENCE

It may be difficult for us to visualize that in the second half of the nineteenth century the *Vedas* were a sealed book in India, and no one could even read them, much less quote them in open debate attended by all communities, Hindu and non-Hindus alike. At present the Vedas are being read, studied and commented upon by all classes and castes of Hindus. This is the greatest service rendered by Dayanand to the cause of religious and intellectual as well as social freedom in India, and this alone entitles him to be called the saviour of Hindu India.

LAJPAT RAI in *A History of the Arya Samaj* (1914)[73]

Over centuries the Vedas were transmitted orally by Brahmans on the basis of some scattered manuscripts. Hence when Europeans in eighteenth century South Asia found themselves wondering whether the Vedas really existed as no one seemed ever to have seen or known a copy of them, they were often told by Brahmans: 'Veda is whatever pertains to religion; Veda is not books'. In other words, knowledge of the Vedas was embodied knowledge and a centralized knowledge of them did not exist. The case of the Sikhs was somewhat more organized. They considered the Granth Sahib as their sacred book. Yet when in 1859 the Punjab government instituted a programme to preserve and translate an authentic version, finding copies of it was difficult. The Kartarpur Granth manuscript which is believed to be the original copy of the Granth Sahib was obtained after intense negotiations from Sadhu Singh Sodhi, who had previously refused to give the manuscript to Maharaja Ranjit Singh. Under the supervision of John Lawrence, the Granth was shipped to England and presented to the India Office Library. Certainly, much changed when Europeans began to translate and comment upon Indian sacred works. Their Protestant notion of scripture, as it were, set a precedent in replacing the scripture-tradition pair (Koran-*Sunnah*, *Sruti-Smriti*, Granth Sahib-Gurus) with a *sola scriptura* proposal. This was later followed, more or less, by many since Rammohun Roy, including as discussed above the Singh Sabhaites, Arya Samajis and Ahmadiyahs. Crucial to the process was the body of Western Orientalist knowledge of

Indian traditions, while in general science increasingly became authoritative.

The acceptance of the authority of science rested upon its functionalism: both mind and machine worked. Railways, telegraph, bridges and other features of modern times were to be seen everywhere and made for easy acceptance of the claims of science. Equally, science posed few problems for traditional Indian thinkers: 'if all truth rested in the scriptures or in the teachings of an inspired master, and if science was itself true, then no contradiction could possibly exist'.[74] For them, there was no conflict between science and tradition and accordingly they 'sought to prove the verity of their own sacred texts by showing that they were replete with scientific wisdom'.[75] If there was a moral problem, it was easy to overcome, in the case of the Arya Samaj through belief in the Hindu origin of science.[76] Nonetheless, there increasingly emerged a rational polemic through which Indians tried to counter Western scholarship. In the process ironically, Indians cited Western works as authorities. Or as leading Arya Samaji, Pandit Guru Datta Vidyarthi, explained,

If we have purposely avoided mentioning ancient eastern authorities on the subject, it is for the plain reason that India of the present day derives its intellectual activity, faith, belief and conviction mainly from civilized occidental England. Had we, in the very beginning, culled evidence from the ancient Sanskrit authors just to prove even these very positions literally, there is no doubt that these remarks would have been unhesitatingly pronounced as superstitions, whimsical, unscientific and old-grown; although, even after the best evidence from Western authors on the subject has been collected, there is not to be found that systematic, exhaustive enumeration of evidence which is the characteristic of a settled or decided opinion.[77]

Indeed, while science increasingly was taken as syntax for reform in order to establish firm identities, at the same time Indian reformers generally did not accept that it was more authoritative than traditional knowledge. In relation to the making of the Singh Sabha, Arya Samaj and Ahmadiyah moral languages, however, the main point is that traditional knowledge became more organized when the universal claims of science were represented, imposed, and, difficult enough, translated into vernacular terms.[78]

Punjabi traditions were described and explained by the British first in travelogues and later especially in the numerous ethnological descriptions formalized in the district gazetteers and census reports. Though John Malcolm for example already wrote his *Sketch of the Sikhs* in 1810, the writing of Sikh history really began with Joseph Davey Cunningham's *A History of the Sikhs* (1849).[79] Yet, as Max Arthur Macauliffe subsequently put it, these writings were essentially political and, because of their lack of knowledge of the Sikh sacred writings, they were restricted to 'some external observances of the Sikhs and to such details of their Gurus as are popularly mentioned'.[80] More relevant to the modern definition of the Sikh tradition were the two works by German missionary and linguist, Ernest Trumpp, and, more importantly, Max Arthur Macauliffe.[81] The India Office commissioned Trumpp to translate the (Kartarpur) Granth Sahib into English.[82] He completed the job but, as he stated in the introductory essays to *The Adi Granth* (1877), he found the Sikhs an uninteresting sect and their holy scripture badly written and boring to read. Obviously Trumpp did not endear himself to the Sikhs by insulting remarks like these and others prefacing his translation of the Granth Sahib. 'With an egotism reflecting his missionary background and rigorous training in linguistics, Trumpp felt he knew more about the meaning of the Sikh scriptures than those who revered them.'[83] Hence also he did not work together with Sikhs themselves but instead prepared his translations with the help of Hindu informants and sporadic advice from members of the Anjuman-i-Punjab. The point is that Trumpp's translation led to responses from the Sikh community and others (like the Arya Samaj) and hence opened up the modern discussion about the Sikh tradition.[84] In the wake of his translation, Sikh scholarship took upon itself the task of reinterpreting the Granth Sahib with vigour and devotion and so established the foundations of today's Granth Sahib studies. An early key work, later criticized by Singh Sabhaites, was the *Sri Granth Sahib ji Adi Satik* better known as the Faridkot Tika.[85] In 1877, Raja Bikram Singh, ruler of the princely state of Faridkot, commissioned a full-scale commentary on the Granth Sahib in Punjabi. The Faridkot Tika certainly marks a turning point in the history of the delineation of the Sikh tradition. Not only as a rebuttal of Trumpp's work but particularly also because through its publication earlier Sikh interpretations of the sacred scripture were categorically superseded. Before the four volumes were printed between 1898 and 1918, however, Lahori Singh Sabhaites already had criticised the interpretation and, instead, had become much involved in Max Arthur Macauliffe's translation project.

Opposed to Trumpp, Macauliffe thought it was not right to translate the Sikh scripture without asking the assistance of Sikhs themselves. In 1862, when he was twenty-five, he began his career in the Punjab administration where he served as a deputy commissioner (1882-4) and divisional judge (1884). During the 1870s, Macauliffe became interested in the traditions and history of the region. Hence, after his resignation from the administration in 1893, he worked on his monumental *The Sikh Religion: Its Gurus, Sacred Writings and Authors* (1909) with the help of Sikh lay leaders such as Kahn Singh Nabha, Bhai Ditt Singh and Bhai Vir Singh.[86] Completed sections were circulated for comment and eventually sent to a committee formed by the conservative Amritsar Singh Sabha. In essence, his work reflected the Tat Khalsa ideology and argued that Sikhism had been distinct from Hinduism since the time of Guru Nanak. Yet, to conservative Sikhs an English translation was an act of desecration, as it would be carried around like any other book and treated without respect. Bhagat Lakshman Singh was one of the Sikhs who helped Macauliffe and in his autobiography he wrote about the problems around the publication of *The Sikh Religion*. First, Macauliffe felt mistreated by the British government for not recognizing the importance of his work and the fact that, opposed to Trumpp, he earned the gratitude of the Sikhs. According to him, the reason behind it was that the India Office had invested much in Trumpp's work and, moreover, 'his insult to the Sikhs and their religion suited the Christian missionary policy of the Government'.[87] Second, Macauliffe had problems with the Amritsar Singh Sabha because it seems they also wanted to bring out a translation of the Sikh scriptures themselves and therefore 'looked upon Macauliffe with a feeling of jealousy'.[88] Thanks to Bhagat Lakshman Singh, however, at the 1912 Sikh Education Conference, though after some opposition, Macauliffe was offered an apology for past events and praise for his work. Two years later, after spending more than thirty years of his life on the study of the Sikhs, he died in London, indeed as Sikh and because of this, he told Lakshman Singh during a meeting in Rawalpindi, 'was treated as an outcaste by his countrymen, pointing with his finger at a group of Europeans who were then dining on the lawn outside'.[89] Yet, the Sikhs already had moved beyond trying to demonstrate the distinctiveness of their tradition through reference to doctrine, conduct and ritual and instead, were busy facing the troublesome task of defining the implications of being a Sikh in particular ways and in specific institutional settings. Interestingly, by this time, the editions of Kahn Singh Nabha's *Ham Hindu Nahin* also included references to European sources to give more authority to the argument.

Though Dayanand Saraswati had been traditionally educated, he often confronted Western reason and Christianity during his life. In fact, the first *Rigveda* he ever saw was the edition by Max Müller and shown to him by Reverend J. Robson in Ajmer in 1866. Until then Dayanand only knew the *Yajurveda*.[90] By now he regularly had discussions with Christian missionaries.[91] During this period he ordered Orientalist books from Germany.[92] In 1868, he met Reverend T.J. Scott, of the American Methodist Episcopal Church (more about him in Chapter Five), who gave him a copy of the Bible and influenced Dayanand's views of Christianity. Over time, the two developed an amicable relationship: Scott referred to him as 'my friend the fakir'.[93] In Calcutta, Saraswati came to know many Brahmo Samajis, visited the Royal Asiatic Society, and generally became familiar with modern educational institutions. On his way from Calcutta to Bombay, Dayanand met some British officials in Farrukhabad and Sayyid Ahmad Khan in Aligarh. In Bombay he had many discussions: both with the local elite, which led to the establishment of the Bombay Arya Samaj, and some European scholars. Shortly afterwards he started to learn English from a Bengali scholar in order to read Max Müller's translation of the

Vedas, but he soon gave up. Especially while in the Punjab, Dayanand did his best to be informed about what European scholars were publishing and most contemporary European (Vedic) scholars are mentioned in his writing during this period. Probably the best example of an Arya Samaji interacting with Western science during the early decades of the movement remains Pandit Guru Datta Vidyarthi. As leader of the Gurukul Aryas, he gave direction to Arya Samaj thinking between 1885 until his early death in 1890. Guru Datta became preoccupied with science and technology and eventually, in 1886, he was appointed Assistant Professor of Science at Lahore's Government College. The point is that in his writings and speeches, he infused Dayanand Saraswati's arguments with the authority of science and afterwards extended and popularized them. By doing so, he certainly defined a more sophisticated and elaborate world of thought than Dayanand, which at the same many Aryas did not follow because 'elaboration of meaning required increased commitment as implications became explicit, and thought followed its inner logic'.[94] Before he joined the Arya Samaj Guru Datta made clear in a lecture given in 1883, that his approach to 'religion' was scientific.[95] Particularly interesting remains his discussion of the redundancy of religious fanaticism because tolerance flourishes not so much by 'an increase in religious devotion, or religious sincerity' but by the secularization of knowledge.[96] Also Guru Datta questioned Max Müller's assumption that religion distinguishes man from animal and on the whole means a yearning for the infinite. Instead, calling upon the scientific authority of Charles Darwin, he argued that 'the difference in mind between man and the higher animals, great as it is, is certainly one of degree and not of kind'.[97] Elsewhere, in *Evidences of the Human Spirit* (1893), Guru Datta offers a scientific explanation (and cites scientists like Thomas Henry Huxley to authorize his case) for the term *atman* or human spirit as consciousness; when based on the intellect rather than prayer it provides inner tranquillity.[98]

Above all, Vidyarthi was irritated by the respect shown to such European scholars as Max Müller. According to him their interpretations of the Vedas not only were false but resulted in much misunderstanding in India itself.[99] When in 1895, for example, a public debate was held in a north Indian town between Arya Samajis and an orthodox Hindu priest on the rationality and legitimacy of the ritual of ancestor worship and the two could not come to an agreement, they forwarded their argument to Max Müller for arbitration.[100] In particular Vidyarthi argued that European Orientalists misunderstood Vedic Sanskrit grammar. According to Max Müller, certain terms mentioned in the Vedas still were in a fluid state: 'they never appear as appellations nor yet as proper names; they are organic, not yet broken or smoothed down'.[101] This made the Pandit furious and he made clear the difference between the East and the West by stating that Vedic terms could not be taken as nouns but instead had a derivative meaning. It was because of this absence of knowledge of Sanskrit grammar that European translations of the Vedas were wrong. Hence, to illustrate his point, he took the sentence translated by Max Müller as 'May Mitra, Varuna, Aryaman, Ayu, Indra, the Lord of Ribhus, and the Maruts not rebuke us, because we shall proclaim at the sacrifice the virtues of the swift horse sprung from god.'[102] According to Guru Datta, all this was mumbo-jumbo and instead he comes up with his own (no doubt creative) version:

We will describe the power-generating virtues of energetic horses endowed with brilliant properties, or virtues of the vigorous force of heat which learned or scientific men can evoke to work for purposes of appliances (not sacrifices). Let not philanthropists, noble men, judges, learned men, rulers, wise men and practical mechanics ever disregard these properties.[103]

Whether his translations provided the real meaning of the Sanskrit terms remains irrelevant. The point is that the Vedas were infused with the authority of science filtered through a vernacular idiom.

Guru Datta Vidyarthi also had many problems with the Orientalist writings of Monier Monier-Williams, who was the Boden Professor of Sanskrit at Oxford's Balliol College and a fanatic evangelical. As did Ernest Trumpp with Sikh scripture, Monier-Willaims in his works described the hymns of the Vedas as being 'too often marked by tedious repetitions, redundant epithets and far-fetched conceits', to which Guru Datta typically replied that he just lived 'in a climate too cold to admit of Oriental warmth of style'.[104] The refuting and ridiculing of opponents certainly was characteristic to the emerging mode of argumentation. When Monier-Williams, for example, argued that the Vedas were 'unwritten knowledge', as opposed to the revealed 'written knowledge' of the Bible and Koran, Guru Datta, like other Aryas, emphasized the revealed and infallible nature of the Vedas. Moreover, he started to attack the Monier-Williams by questioning the overall possibility of 'written knowledge', while any revelation always involves somebody and thus by definition is 'unwritten knowledge':

Thus, then, the Bible revelation is also an unwritten knowledge, and Professor Williams cannot in any way free himself from the dilemma that either Bible revelation itself is an unwritten knowledge and in that case does not differ in any way from the revelation of the Vedas which is also unwritten knowledge, or that the Bible is a mere record not felt in consciousness but made to descend just as the Quran descended to Mohammed, Mohammed himself became illiterate, not understanding it but only being specially directed and empowered by God to commit it to writing for the spread of the faith. In this case, the Bible is no more a revelation. It is a mere dead-letter book sent miraculously through people who themselves did not understand it. Can Professor Williams get rid of this difficulty?[105]

Today these are difficult discussions to read and understand. Nonetheless, their importance lies in the fact that through them Indian reformers defied Western scholarship and in the terms of the current rationality, defended their own tradition at the same time. Accordingly, the making of moral languages not only meant a re-organization of traditional knowledge but simultaneously led to assertive polemics that were defensive and moral rather than reasonable.

As for Mirza Ghulam Ahmad's interactions with Western thought, not much is known. His stay in Sialkot, however, seems to be the starting point. There he worked at the law court, most probably learned some English, met Christian missionaries, and became acquainted with the ideas of Sayyid Ahmad Khan.

Afterwards, Ghulam Ahmad refuted the pro-Western Aligarh position. Not only because of its adherence to natural philosophy (*nacheral filasafi*) but particularly because of its apologetic attitude: 'as if there were anything in Islam that could not hold its own in the face of modern knowledge and science'.[106] For his part Ahmad Khan found the Mirza to be a fraud. When, for instance, he was told that someone wanted to write a treatise against Ghulam Ahmad, the Sayyid replied that this 'preposterous movement' did not deserve a critique.[107]

Also crucial in terms of interaction with Western thought were the Mirza's meetings with Brahmo and Arya Samajis, who (more than the Christian missionaries) made clear to him the advantages of being organized as a voluntary association, the possibilities of modern printing techniques (his *Barahin-i-Ahmadiyah* was published by a Christian press in Amritsar), public lectures and educational institutions. Into the bargain, Ghulam Ahmad learned of course how tradition could be rationally reinterpreted and revived without succumbing completely, like Sayyid Ahmad Khan, to Western reason. Increasingly, the Mirza presented himself to Punjabi society through his lectures and writings. The titles of some of his tracts show that, probably more than other reformers, he constantly was in need to explain himself.[108] He not only criticized the ulama, Christianity and Hinduism, but in particular the Arya Samaj, employing the authority of science to validate an otherwise fundamentalist approach to the Koran. So indeed what took place in nineteenth century India was much in the spirit of what was happening simultaneously in Europe, where for example:

Historians of the later Enlightenment made themselves ridiculous by explaining wonder, by unquenchable prosiness, by 'rationalizing' the 'sandwiches' of five thousand or the walking on the water; reaching peak in the 'scientific' corrections of earlier hymns, as with the editor who was shocked by the hymn of Gerhardt '*Now all the woods are sleeping*' and to correspond with truth, amended it to the line '*Now half the woods are sleeping*'.[109]

Now, similarly, Mirza Ahmad argued that such a miracle as the rending of the moon in the Koran presented no real conflict with science, as 'no one has yet exhausted the knowledge of the working of nature'.[110] Otherwise, while reacting to Dayanand Saraswati's reviling writings about Sikhism (which surely echoed those of Trumpp and to which Sikhs themselves did not reply), Ghulam Ahmad wrote his *Sat Bachan* (1901) to protect the honour of Guru Nanak. For, as said earlier, Ghulam Ahmad believed that the latter was a Muslim saint and so now he only had to convince Sikhs that for them he was the Promised Messiah as well. Whatever the Mirza wanted, the point is that to state his case he used the works of Trumpp and Macauliffe. Likewise, besides many references to the Bible, Mirza Ghulam Ahmad cites authorities such as Monier-Williams and Max Müller, in one of his most important tracts, *Masih Hindustan Mein* or Jesus in India (1899), to prove his point that Jesus died in Kashmir instead of Jerusalem (see Chapter Five).[111]

CONCLUSION

The rational organization of knowledge lay at the basis of the Singh Sabha, Arya Samaj and Ahmadiyah moral languages. Criticism towards contemporary social circumstances common to all times and places became more widespread than ever because of the colonial encounter and the dominant presence of missionaries in particular. All this was part and parcel of the wider changes in society following the emergence of modern institutions and practices in the newly emerging liberal public sphere under the supervision of the Anglo-Indian colonial state. For the propagation of their message, reformers established their own educational, printing and other institutions through which they became voluntary participants in the public sphere. Their employment of the human will in disciplining mind and body undoubtedly was part of a dominant social consciousness comparable to the orderly and disciplined behaviour of British Christians preoccupied with public duty. Significant to the Singh Sabha, Arya Samaj and Ahmadiyah moral languages was an urge to revive past times to cope with present conditions. Obviously, rational criticism had been practised in South Asia long before the coming of the British. The point is that the elitist reformers now felt impelled to reinterpret their sacred texts and cast them in modern scientific language. South Asian sacred works became scriptures. Most significant in this context remains the emergence of lay leaders and the ability of community members to read and interpret the scriptures individually. Alternately, the reformist message was spread through educational institutions where the teachers saw it as their goal to create muscular students who would know their moral duty and strengthen the community for the future.

On the whole, science gained cultural authority. The more indigenous reformers became voluntarily active in the public sphere, the more they interacted with 'the authority and application of science as universal reason'.[112] Indian reformers not only regularly cited Western missionary and Orientalist studies as authoritative sources, they often did so to counter the claims of Western (Orientalist) science. Their argument was that their readings not only were equally scientific but often provided better knowledge than anything what Western authorities argued. Western ideas 'widely mingled with and were empowered by ideas derived from indigenous rationalistic and ethical traditions'.[113] Indian reformers simultaneously accepted the role of respondents within colonial culture. Besides the rational organization of knowledge, the relationship between Punjabi traditions and science therefore above all was about moral criticism. Accordingly, it should be stressed that the reformers, while thinking through the vernaculars or their interpretation of English, most probably did not see much difference between the traditional concepts of rationality and Western science. In the emerging forms of rationality, traditional concepts no doubt were imbued with Western reason to invoke the authority of science. Yet it remains unlikely that reformers conceived of these new forms of knowledge as an alternative truth arrived at through verification. According to Arya Samajis, for example, it remained unthinkable that science might produce a truth superior to Vedic revelation. On the contrary, 'the entire thrust of Dayanand's reaction to Western science and technology was to capture and incorporate it, not to refute it'.[114] Under the appearance of modern scholarship, the degree of interpretation of traditional sacred works which the reformist translators allowed themselves indicates that old habit of thought remained ingrained, namely the idea that any rendering in another language is more an explanation than a precise reproduction. On the whole, Indian elites 'may have operated within the confines of languages adopted from their rulers, but they did so to accomplish ends that were largely their own and they constantly reinterpreted the meanings of the concepts they employed.[115]

All in all, though British military and economic considerations incorporated the Punjab into the world of Empire, more important to this study remains the fact that by appealing to the authority of science Punjabis voluntarily expanded their intellectual horizons. Significantly, this incredibly complicated process took place interactively between the different communities as well as the British. This led to points of convergence as critical features of Punjabi colonial culture that acknowledge the internal dynamics of Indian society, not the instrumentality of the colonial state, as the ultimate cause for social change. The most crucial of those values and ideas that ruler and ruled more or less shared and which were fundamental to Anglo-Indian colonial state formation and the making of a liberal public sphere were the rational organization of knowledge; the authority of science; criticism of traditional society; education as most significant feature underlying both the British civilizing mission and Indian moral languages; the importance of the human will and a moral duty towards community and society; modern voluntary institutions and practices; and literal interpretation of scriptures. Otherwise, the definition of moral languages I discussed so far concerned a process of canonization and now it remains significant to see how these ideal types adapted to competitive political circumstances. This particularly because more than ever Punjabis gained access to rational forms of knowledge that underlined the functioning of the colonial state, the public sphere and the British civilizing mission at large. In this context, an important feature of the newly defined moral languages, remains the growing role of vernacular language politics and the discipline of history as identity markers.

NOTES

1. Kenneth W. Jones, *Arya Dharm: Hindu Consciousness in Nineteenth Century India*, 1976; repr., New Delhi: Manohar, 2006; Spencer Lavan, *The Ahmadiyah Movement: A History and Perspective*, New Delhi: Manohar, 1974 and Harjot Oberoi, *The Construction of Religious Boundaries: Culture, Identity and Diversity in the Sikh Tradition*, New Delhi: Oxford University Press, 1994.

2. J.T.F. Jordens, *Dayananda Sarasvati: His Life and Ideas*, New Delhi: Oxford University Press, 1979, p. 63.

3. Dayanand Saraswati, *Light of Truth*, tr. Dr. Charanjiva Bharadwaja, 1906; repr., New Delhi: Sarvadeshik Arya Pratinidhi Sabha, 1991, p. 733.

4. J.T.F. Jordens, *Dayananda Sarasvati: Essays on his Life and Ideas*, New Delhi: Manohar, 1998, pp. 61-2.

5. Peter van der Veer has argued that the Arya Samaj was successful in the Punjab because 'the attack on image worship fell on fertile soil, prepared by centuries of Sikh traditions of imageless devotion' in *Religious Nationalism: Hindus and Muslims in India*, Berkeley: University of California Press, 1994, p. 66 (and again in *Imperial Encounters: Religion and Modernity in India and Britain*, Princeton: Princeton University Press, 2001, p. 51). Here, he overlooks the importance of Punjabi popular culture. Sikh gurdwaras, for example, were often run by Hindu priests and more often than not contained images and not only in the countryside—anyone walking around the Golden Temple in Amritsar at the time would have come across miscellaneous idols near the steps of the sacred tank, representing non-Sikh deities. Hence one of the objectives of the Singh Sabhaites (as van der Veer also himself states, p. 74, *Religious Nationalism*, was to get rid of these images.

6. Jordens, *Dayananda Sarasvati: Essays on his Life and Ideas*, p. 62.

7. R.B. Mulraj, *Beginning of Punjabi Nationalism: Autobiography of R.B. Mulraj*, Hoshiarpur: V.V. Vedic Research Institute, 1975, p. 189.

8. Oberoi, *The Construction of Religious Boundaries*, pp. 222-3, 235.

9. Louis E. Fenech, 'Conversion and Sikh Tradition', in *Religious Conversion in India: Modes, Motivations and Meanings*, ed. Rowena Robinson and Sathianathan Clarke, New Delhi: Oxford University Press, 2003, p. 174.

10. Oberoi, *The Construction of Religious Boundaries*, p. 305.

11. On these polemics: Spencer Lavan, 'Polemics and Conflict in Ahmadiyah History: The Missionaries, the Ulama and the British', in *Essays in Honour of Dr. Ganda Singh*, ed. Harbans Singh and N. Gerald Barrier, Patiala: Punjabi University Press, 1976, pp. 454-74.

12. Yohanan Friedmann, *Prophecy Continues: Aspects of Ahmadi Religious Thought and its Medieval Background*, New Delhi: Oxford University Press, 1988, Chapter Four.

13. In a similar way, Ghulam Ahmad treated the less conventional claim to be a *muhaddath*, a person spoken to by Allah or an angel. The classical *hadith* was the authority that provided legitimacy for Ghulam Ahmad's use of the title but, like with his treatment of the concept of *mujaddid*, he transformed a personality of limited importance in classical thought into a recipient of divine revelation, entrusted with a crucial role hardly inferior to that of the Prophet.

14. And yet Ghulam Ahmad was not satisfied with the role he saw for himself in the world. Towards the end of his life he also claimed to be an incarnation of Vishnu, Krishna. The claim, however, was found so offensive even to his closest followers that they quietly dropped it. Also he had argued earlier that Sikh Guru Nanak was a Muslim saint on the basis of a cloak (embroidered with the Muslim creed and the opening chapter of the Koran) found in a village in Gurdaspur village and which supposedly belonged to the Guru. See further 'The Founder of Sikhism', in *Review of Religions*, January 1908, pp. 19-39 and 'Relations of Sikhism to Islam', in ibid., November 1908, pp. 425-42.

15. Still in 1886 Indian headmasters were few. For example the headmaster of the Anglo-Oriental Muslim School in Aligarh was British and hence the institution was, as Wilfred Cantwell Smith put it, 'distinguishable from a Christian missionary college only by the substitution of Islam for Christianity as the religious extra', in *Modern Islam in India*, repr., New Delhi: Usha, 1985, p. 14.

16. On Guru Datta Vidyarthi: Lajpat Rai, 'Life and Work of Pandit Guru Datta Vidyarthi', in *The Collected Works of Lala Lajpat Rai*, ed. B.R. Nanda, vol. 1, New Delhi: Manohar, 2003, pp. 143-246.

17. Kenneth W. Jones, *Socio-Religious Reform Movement in British India*, Cambridge: Cambridge University Press, 1989, pp. 98-9.

18. On Lala Munshi Ram, better known as Swami Shraddhanand: J.T.F. Jordens, *Swami Shraddhananda: His Life and Causes*, New Delhi: Oxford University Press, 1981.

19. *The Rules and the Scheme of Studies of the Proposed Gurukula Sanctioned by the Arya Pratinidhi Sabha, Punjab*, Lahore: Mufid-i-Am Press, 1899, p. 8.

20. Lajpat Rai, *The Problem of National Education in India*, London: George Allen & Unwin Ltd., 1920, pp. 23-4.

21. *The Rules and the Scheme of Studies of the Proposed Gurukula*, p. 16.

22. The Bhasaur Singh Sabha led by Teja Singh was the most fanatic in propagating the Tat Khalsa ideals. See N. Gerald Barrier, 'The

Formulation and Transmission of Sikh Tradition: Competing Organizations and Ideology, 1902-1925', in *The Transmission of Sikh Heritage in the Diaspora*, ed. Pashaura Singh and N. Gerald Barrier, New Delhi: Manohar, 1996, pp. 193-221.

23. N. Gerald Barrier, 'Sikh Politics in British Punjab prior to the Gurdwara Reform Movement', in *Sikh History and Religion in the Twentieth Century*, ed. Joseph T. O'Conell, et al., Toronto: University of Toronto Centre for South Asian Studies, 1988, p. 169.

24. Ibid.

25. Though Qadian was looted and sacked after Partition, a few hundred Ahmadiyahs remained there to take care of the former headquarters (now reduced to a small part of town). After Partition, many Ahmadiyahs settled down in Rabwah near Chiniot in Pakistani Punjab. Initially the influence of probably the most famous Ahmadiyah, Zafrullah Khan (Foreign Minister of Pakistan, President of the General Assembly of the United Nations and President of the International Court of Justice in The Hague, the Netherlands), postponed persecution of Ahmadiyahs. Yet, after the 1975 declaration in Mecca of Ahmadiyahs being non-Islamic, the Pakistani government started to persecute them. Subsequently, not only did many Ahmadiyahs drift back to Qadian but, more importantly, the Caliph moved to London which can be taken as the movement's headquarters ever since.

26. Mirza Ghulam Ahmad, *The Will*, repr., Qadian: Nazir Dawat-o-Tabligh, 1970, p. 41.

27. Ibid., p. 12. When Ghulam Ahmad decided to accept *baiat* in 1889 he meant it in the way it was done to a Caliph in Sunni Islam. Although he received revelations and won followers through his charismatic preaching and writing, he never claimed, as one perhaps would expect in the Punjab case, to be a *pir*.

28. Ibid., pp. 40-3.

29. *Gurdaspur District Gazetteer*, Punjab, 1891, p. 61; *Census of India*, Punjab, 1901, p. 143.

30. H.A. Walter, *The Ahmadiya Movement*, repr., New Delhi: Manohar, 1991, p. 98.

31. About Ghulam Ahmad's family: Lepel H. Griffin, *The Punjab Chiefs*, vol. 2, Lahore: Civil and Military Gazette Press, 1890, pp. 49-50.

32. Lavan, *The Ahmadiyah Movement*, p. 107.

33. Harald Fischer-Tiné, 'National Education Pulp Fiction and the Contradictions of Colonialism: Perceptions of an Educational Experiment in Early-Twentieth-Century India', in *Colonialism as Civilizing Mission: Cultural Ideology in British India*, ed. Herald Fisher-Tiné and Michael Mann, London: Anthem Press, 2005, p. 247.

34. Lajpat Rai was one of the pillars of both the emerging Punjabi public

sphere and the Indian nationalist movement at large. After his study at Lahore's Government College, he became a lawyer in several Punjabi towns. In 1882, he joined the Arya Samaj. He became a leading social worker, especially in the fields of famine relief, the organization of orphanages, the improvement of lower and outcastes and, above all, the promotion of modern education (for about twenty-five years he was closely associated with the Dayanand Anglo-Vedic College in Lahore). Likewise, he was the driving force behind several periodicals and newspapers as well as the founder of such public institutions as the Punjab National Bank and the Lakshmi Insurance Company.

35. Rai, *The Problem of National Education in India*, Chapter One.
36. The word *Rahit* derives from *rahana*, to live, and remains a crucial word within the Sikh tradition meaning the code of belief and discipline to be obeyed by *Khalsa* members. Since the eighteenth-century Sikhs often attempted to write down the *Khalsa* way of life in manuals called *rahit-namas*. See W.H. McLeod, *Sikhs of the Khalsa: A History of the Khalsa Rahit*, New Delhi: Oxford University Press, 2003.
37. Bhai Vir Singh went to the Church Mission High School in Amritsar. He started his career with the Khalsa Tract Society, which propagated Singh Sabha ideas, acquired a majority share in the publishing house Wazir-i-Hind (which published all his novels) and managed the journal, *Khalsa Samachar*.
38. Bhai Vir Singh, *Baba Naudh Singh*, repr., New Delhi: Bhai Vir Singh Sahitya Sadan, 1989, p. 39.
39. Oberoi, *The Construction of Religious Boundaries*, pp. 332-3. The five Ks are *Kesh* (uncut hair), *Kangha* (comb), *Kara* (steel bangle), *Kirpan* (sword or dagger) and *Kachh* (breeches).
40. McLeod, *Sikhs of the Khalsa*, p. 204.
41. Oberoi, *The Construction of Religious Boundaries*, p. 339.
42. More than Bhai Vir Singh, Kahn Singh Nabha (1867-1938), who unlike most Singh Sabhaites was a Jat, became the chief intellectual protagonist of the Tat Khalsa ideology, preparing studies which were to have an enduring influence on the Panth. From 1885 he developed a close relationship with Macauliffe and undoubtedly his *The Sikh Religion: Its Gurus, Sacred Writings and Authors* (repr. Bombay: Oxford University Press, 1963, 6 vols.) was as much written by him as by Kahn Singh. The latter is best remembered, however, as the compiler of the four volume encyclopedia, *Gurushabad Ratanakar Mahan Kosh* (1930).
43. J.S. Grewal, 'Nabha's "Ham Hindu Nahin": A Declaration of Sikh Ethnicity', in *Sikh Identity: Continuity and Change*, ed. Pashaura Singh and N. Gerald Barrier, New Delhi: Manohar, 1999, p. 233.
44. 'Sirdar Dyal Singh Will Case in the Chief Court of the Punjab, Probate

Case No. 4 of 1899', in *Brahmo Samaj and Dyal Singh Majithia*, ed. Madan Gopal, New Delhi: Uppal, 1998, p. 114.

45. Ibid., pp. 114, 120, 124.
46. Bhagat Lakshman Singh, *Autobiography*, Calcutta: The Sikh Cultural Centre, 1965, p. 154.
47. Harjot Oberoi, 'From Ritual to Counter-Ritual: Rethinking the Hindu-Sikh Question, 1884-1915', in *Sikh History and Religion in the Twentieth Century*, ed. Joseph T. O'Connell et al., Toronto: University of Toronto Centre for Asian Studies, 1988, pp. 152-3.
48. Earlier, the founder of the Nirankaris, Baba Dayal Das, revived the practice of marrying in the presence of the Granth Sahib.
49. Jordens, *Dayananda Sarasvati: His Life and Ideas*, pp. 79-81.
50. Ibid., p. 278.
51. Ibid., p. 282.
52. Saraswati, *Light of Truth*, 221.
53. Jordens, *Dayananda Sarasvati: His Life and Ideas*, p. 282.
54. Ibid., p. 284.
55. Cf. Philip Lutgendorf, *The Life of a Text: Performing the Ramcaritmanas of Tulsidas*, Berkeley: University of California Press, 1991, pp. 380, 389-92.
56. Jones, *Arya Dharm*, 94-103.
57. J.M.S. Baljon, *Modern Muslim Koran Interpretation, 1880-1960*, Leiden: Brill, 1961, p. 83.
58. Mirza Ghulam Ahmad, *The Philosophy of Islam*, 1905; repr., New Delhi: Inter-India, 1978, p. 13. It was first read in December 1896 as a paper entitled The Sources of Divine Knowledge by one of Ghulam Ahmad's followers at the Conference of religions in Lahore and later often reprinted in English under the above title and *The Teachings of Islam* (subtitled A Solution of Five Fundamental Religious Problems from the Muslim Point of View).
59. Baljon, *Modern Muslim Koran Interpretation*, p. 16.
60. Ahmad, *The Philosophy of Islam*, p. 113.
61. Ibid., p. 188.
62. Baljon, *Modern Muslim Koran Interpretation*, p. 21.
63. Barbara D. Metcalf, 'Introduction', in *Moral Conduct and Authority: The Place of Adab in South Asian Islam*, ed. Barbara D. Metcalf, Berkeley: University of California Press, 1984, p. 10.
64. Ahmad, *The Philosophy of Islam*, p. 167.
65. Muhammad Iqbal was born in Sialkot. He taught philosophy in Lahore, studied law in England and was knighted in 1923. He wrote poems in Urdu and Persian which are full of a compelling mysticism and nationalism which turned him into almost a prophet for Muslims. His *The Reconstruction of Religious Thought in Islam*, 1934; repr., Lahore: Muhammad Ashraf, 1954 in particular, was significant for

its modern assessment of Islam. Crucial was his idea of a (Punjabi) Muslim state within India (based on the Muslim majority provinces of the Punjab, North-West Frontier Province, Sind and Baluchistan) which he expressed at the all India Muslim League's annual session in 1930 and was dismissed as mere poetics by the Muslim leaders from the minority provinces that dominated the League.

66. Iqbal, *The Reconstruction*, pp. 126-7.
67. Iqbal, *Islam and Ahmadism*, Lahore: Anjuman-i-Khuddam ud-Din, 1936.
68. Iqbal, *The Reconstruction*, p. 3.
69. Iqbal, *Islam and Ahmadism*, pp. 18, 27.
70. Cf. Lutgendorf, *The Life of a Text*, pp. 434-5.
71. Barbara D. Metcalf, 'Imagining Community: Polemic Debates in Colonial India', in *Religious Controversy in British India: Diologues in South Asian Languages*, ed. Kenneth W. Jones, Albany: State University of New York Press, 1992, p. 240.
72. Francis Robinson, 'Islam and Muslim Separatism', in *Political Identity in South Asia*, ed. David Taylor and Malcolm Yapp, London: Curzon Press, 1979, p. 99.
73. Lajpat Rai, *A History of the Arya Samaj: An Account of its Origin, Doctrines and Activities with a Biographical Sketch of the Founder*, repr., New Delhi: Munshiram Manoharlal, 1992, pp. 54-5.
74. Jones, *Socio-Religious Reform Movement in British India*, p. 212.
75. C.A. Bayly, *The Birth of the Modern World 1780-1914*, London: Blackwell, 2004, p. 363.
76. Gyan Prakash, *Another Reason: Science and the Imagination of Modern India*, Princeton: Princeton University Press, 1999, Chapter Four.
77. Guru Datta Vidyarthi, 'Evidences of the Human Spirit' as reprinted in *Works of Late Pandit Guru Datta Vidyarthi M.A.*, Lahore: Punjab Economical Press, 1897, p. 90.
78. Prakash, *Another Reason*, Chapter One.
79. John Malcolm, 'A Sketch of the Sikhs', in *The Sikh Religion: A Symposium*, M.A. Macauliffe, H.H. Wilson, Frederic Pincott, John Malcolm and Sardar Kahn Singh; repr., Calcutta: Sushil Gupta, 1958, pp. 84-145; Joseph Davy Cunningham, *A History of the Sikhs from the Origin of the Nation to the Battles of the Sutlej*, ed. H.L.O. Garrett, repr. New Delhi: S. Chand, 1966.
80. M.A. Macauliffe, 'The Sikh Religion', in *The Sikh Religion: A Symposium*, M.A. Macauliffe, H.H. Wilson, Frederic Pincott, John Malcolm and Sardar Kahn Singh; repr., Calcutta: Sushil Gupta, 1958, p. 1.
81. Ernest Trumpp, *The Adi Granth or the Holy Scriptures of the Sikhs Translated from the Original Gurmukhi with Introductory Essays*, London: Allen & Co., 1877; M.A. Macauliffe, *The Sikh Religion: Its*

Gurus, Sacred Writings and Authors, 6 vols., 1909; repr. Bombay: Oxford University Press, 1963.

82. Ernest Trumpp was born in 1828. He received a degree in language and linguistics from Tubingen (Germany) and afterwards passed theological exams. In 1854 he went to Karachi, where he did research sponsored by the CMS and learned several languages. When the India Office contacted him he was lecturing in Oriental languages at Tubingen.

83. N. Gerald Barrier, 'In Search of Identity: Scholarship and Authority among Sikhs in Nineteenth Century Punjab', in *Language and Society in Modern India*, ed. R.I. Crane and B. Spangenberg, New Delhi: Heritage, 1981, p. 5.

84. Indeed, what is often forgotten is that at the time 'many Sikhs agreed with Trumpp's conclusions', ibid., p. 7.

85. Oberoi, *The Construction of Religious Boundaries*, p. 241.

86. Bhai Hazara Singh was one of the Sikh scholars who helped Macauliffe. He was the maternal grandfather of Bhai Vir Singh, belonged to an illustrious lineage of Amritsar *gianis* and was a founding member of the Amritsar Singh Sabha. More importantly, he wrote the Granth Sahib dictionary Macauliffe used and further was commissioned by the colonial government to translate school textbooks from Urdu into Punjabi. See further: Ibid., pp. 250-1.

87. Bhagat Lakshman Singh, *Autobiography*, p. 124.

88. Ibid.

89. Ibid., p. 294.

90. J. Robson, *Hinduism and its Relation to Christianity*, London: Oliphant, Andersen & Ferrier, 1893, pp. 218-19. Max Müller, who never visited India and still is much (more than ever in Europe) referred to in South Asia, was a German philologist and Orientalist. Commissioned by the East India Company he examined and edited the MS of the *Rigveda* in London for publication, his most important scholarly work. He was appointed Taylorian Professor of Modern language at Oxford (1854) and Professor of Comparative Philology (1868), a subject he did more than anyone else to promote in Britain.

91. See about some of these meetings: ibid.; T.J. Scott, *Missionary Life Among the Villages in India*, Cincinnati: Hitchcock and Walden, 1876 and A.F.R. Hoernle's article (from the *Church Missionary Intelligencer* of March 1870) reprinted in Rai, *A History of the Arya Samaj*, pp. 28-39.

92. Jordens, *Dayanand Sarasvati: His Life and Ideas*, p. 51.

93. Scott, *Missionary Life*, pp. 162-8.

94. Jones, *Arya Dharm*, p. 161.

95. Vidyarthi, 'On Religion in 1883', in *Works of Late Pandit Guru Datta*, p. 211.

96. Ibid., p. 212.
97. Ibid., p. 215.
98. As reprinted in ibid.
99. The Terminology of the Vedas and European Scholars (1893) as reprinted in ibid., p. 16.
100. Anon., *Controversy Between the Arya Samaj of Wazirabad and Pandit Ganesh Datta Shastri on the Shraddha Ceremony, with the Opinions of F. Max Müller,* Lahore, 1896.
101. Vidyarthi, 'The Terminology of the Vedas and European Scholars' (1893) as reprinted in *Works of Pandit Guru Datta*, p. 23.
102. Ibid., p. 33.
103. Ibid., p. 35.
104. Guru Datta Vidyarthi, *Fragments of Pandit Guru Datta Vidyarthi M.A.'s Criticism on Monier William's Indian Wisdom,* Lahore: Virajanand Press, 1892, p. 1.
105. Ibid., pp. 7-8.
106. As cited in Lavan, *The Ahmadiyah Movement*, p. 31.
107. Altaf Husain Hali, *Hayat-i-Javed*, repr., Lahore, 1901, p. 536.
108. See for example: Mirza Ghulam Ahmad, *A Clarification*, repr., Lahore: Ahmadiyya Anjuman Isha'at Islam, 1966 and *A Misunderstanding Removed*, repr., Qadian: Nazir Dawat-o-Tabligh, 1974.
109. Owen Chadwick, *The Secularization of the European Mind in the Nineteenth Century*, Cambridge: Cambridge University Press, 1975, p. 190.
110. As cited in Spencer Lavan, 'Communalism in the Punjab: The Ahmadiyahs versus the Arya Samaj During the Lifetime of Mirza Ghulam Ahmad', *Punjab Past and Present*, 5, 1971, pp. 325-6.
111. Mirza Ghulam Ahmad, *Jesus in India*, repr., Qadian: Nazarat Nashr-o-Ishaat, 1991.
112. Prakash, *Another Reason*, p. 4.
113. Bayly, *The Birth of the Modern World*, p. 285.
114. Jones, *Arya Dharm*, p. 141.
115. Douglas Haynes, *Rhetoric and Ritual in Colonial India: The Shaping of the Public Sphere in Surat City, 1852-1928*, New Delhi: Oxford University Press, 1992, p. ix.

CHAPTER FOUR

Strengthening Identity through Language, History and Patriarchy

VERNACULAR LANGUAGE POLITICS

Indian reformers followed the Christian missionaries in stressing the importance of vernacular education and often used missionary study and reference materials. The modern development of the vernaculars, therefore, is directly related to the creation of moral languages, as the choice of a vernacular and the cultural meanings embedded in that choice became themes in the writings of reform. While reformers articulated and disseminated new textual standards of tradition among a growing audience, 'the use of one specific vernacular became a claim to the legitimacy of that language for a particular group at the expense of other languages'.[1] Best known remains the Hindi-Urdu controversy in north India. In many ways a surprising one, for example, because ordinary Muslims and Hindus largely spoke the same language at least more or less from Lahore to Delhi. Hence, Sayyid Ahmad Khan, being most cynical about the claims for increased British recognition of Hindi, sneered at the Allahabad Association, which lobbied for the recognition of Hindi, stating that he could converse in Urdu while travelling all the way from Allahabad to Bombay.[2] Moreover, despite the many dialects spoken, Hindus, Muslims, and often Sikhs generally used the Persian-Arabic Nastaliq script and so did not perceive clear boundaries between Hindi and Urdu.

As literacy, education, and employment became increasingly important in the newly emerging public sphere, the choice of a specific language became a matter of anxiety for the elite. Again the role of the British was critical because they patronized Urdu as the language of administration. Though Hindus began to claim recognition for Hindi and gradually induced the British to repeal the privileged status of Urdu, the latter continued to favour it. Hindustani (i.e. simplified Urdu) was the language into which government recruits fresh from England were immediately pitched. John Platts' *Dictionary of Urdu, Classical Hindi and English* (1884) reflected this preference which was taken over in most subsequent dictionaries, including the monumental monolingual *Hindi Shabd-Sagar* (1929) edited by Syamsundardas.[3] The Hindi-Urdu divide remains all the more surprising as before the coming of the colonial public education system, 'Urdu was not used in its written form as a medium of instruction in traditional Islamic schools'.[4] Traditionally, Muslim children were taught Persian and Arabic because Muslim elites generally condemned Urdu. It was only when the latter and the British decided that in relation to Hindus, Muslims were backward in education and therefore should be encouraged to attend government schools, that it was felt necessary to offer Urdu in Nastaliq as a carrot to Muslims to attend schools.[5] After more and more government schools were set up, Hindi and Urdu spokesmen increasingly insisted that Hindus had the right to be taught in Devanagari and Muslims in Nastaliq. Subsequently they set out to separate the two languages by referring to Sanskrit or Persian as distinct sources from the past and for the future, emphasizing linguistic differences instead of commonalities. Thus, while much less an issue during former times, the rivalry between Hindi and Urdu centred on its most obvious and graphic manifestation, that of script—here it should be mentioned that it was comparatively easier for Muslims to learn the Devanagari script, than for Hindus to learn the Persian-Arabic script of Urdu.[6] One of the main themes of the controversy between Hindi and Urdu speakers as expressed by the supporters of Hindi, was that Urdu and the Nastaliq script promoted fraud and deceit whereas Hindi and the Devanagari script enhanced truth and honesty. Ironically, much of the polemic with which the Hindi-Urdu debate was fought 'was heavily influenced by English in its syntax and its rhetoric'.[7]

So how do the Singh Sabha, Arya Samaj and Ahmadiyah movements fit in? Again the Arya Samaj was at the vanguard when putting up Hindi as a symbolic identity marker and, in this way, once more functioned as a catalyst. Swami Dayanand replaced Sanskrit with Hindi to spread his teachings among a wider audience. Afterwards he encouraged the Aryas to use Hindi in Devanagari as *Arya Bhasha* or the heavily Sanskritized form of Hindi that the Samaj came to cherish (but which few but themselves could understand).[8] Also the Swami was the first to translate the Vedas into Hindi. More important steps, however, were taken after his death, when Hindi was made obligatory in the educational institutions of the Arya Samaj and its members increasingly propagated its importance in public. For example, while R.B. Mulraj argued, in reply to the 1882 Sir William Hunter Education Commission, that Devanagari was the most scientific script because of the direct relationship between sound and writing,[9] Lala Dwarka Dass stressed that Devanagari types were much more durable and moreover took less space in writing and printing:

Everybody who has seen Urdu types must have perceived that their fine points wear off very soon. Moreover, Hindi printing is much more beautiful than Urdu pri]\nting. In this respect there is no difference between Hindi and English. Urdu letters are not adapted to printing, and hence they are more illegible when printed than when lithographed.[10]

Lala Lajpat Rai stated that the Hindi-Urdu controversy taught him his first lesson in Hindu nationalism. His father was a teacher of Persian and Urdu in government schools. Particularly interesting about his case is the fact that one would logically expect that because of his education and parental language he would have taken the side of Urdu. Though he did not even know the Hindi alphabet, he 'became convinced that political solidarity demanded the spread of Hindi and Devanagari' and hence 'brushed aside all personal considerations and started propaganda for Hindi'.[11]

Even so, Hindi was not so important in the Punjab. Urdu was the dominant language in the press and it slowly replaced Persian as a literary language.[12] Moreover, the language was used by the Punjab Education Department for official notices and for major translations from Arabic, Persian and English.

And yet, though Urdu (using the Prophet's script) subsequently became a symbol of Muslim identity second only to Islam itself, Mirza Ghulam Ahmad definitely was not one of its champions. Being the son of a prosperous Punjabi landowner, he knew Arabic and Persian well. His Urdu writings however were not of a high literary standard and difficult to follow even for the native speaker, in part because these included revelatory passages in Arabic, Persian and English terms written in Nastaliq. In accordance with the times, nonetheless, he stressed Urdu was as suitable as Arabic for a thorough understanding of the Koran (which like the Bible by that time already was translated several times into Urdu, by Nazir Ahmad among others). Furthermore, he claimed to receive his revelations in Urdu rather than in Arabic! The focus on Urdu was further strengthened after Partition when Urdu was made the national language of Pakistan and, until they were declared non-Muslims in 1975 and persecuted afterwards, many Ahmadiyahs had high jobs in the government and the army.

The fact that the British privileged Urdu (over Persian) as the language of administration and Muslims furthermore made it in one of the main symbols of identification, obviously led to a less important role for Punjabi, which because of Muslim rulers generally was written in the Nastaliq script. While earlier Muslim poets had contributed much to Punjabi literature, Muhammad Iqbal for example never wrote in his mother tongue. Even so, it was the language of the Punjab, used not so much by the cultural elites but in verse for more popular literature, i.e. *qissas*, street songs, folk legends, and works related to *pir* worship and shrine rituals. Hence there were no textbooks in Punjabi even for primary education at Panjab University College.[13] In fact, because of the dominance of the Nastaliq script, it was only in the beginning of the twentieth century that (thanks to the teachers of the Gurukul Kangri) Hindi textbooks were written and marketed.[14] Linguistically, Punjabi was not as developed as both Hindi and Urdu. Yet according to Baba Buddh Singh (1878-1931) this was not something to worry about, as the language was only in a formative stage and eventually would be like any other language.

Born in Lahore, Buddh Singh studied at both the Lahore

Mission high school and college. Afterwards he graduated in 1902 at the Roorki College and worked at the Punjab Public Works Department. In his spare time he was a prolific writer, passionately devoted to the cause of Punjabi literature. At his own expense, he wrote books which included essays and several full length plays, besides collections of translated and original verse. In fact, Buddh Singh was the author of the first moral drama in Punjabi, *Chandar Hari* (1909), which, like most of Bhai Vir Singh's writings, became part of the educational curriculum of the Chief Khalsa Diwan. Like many contemporary plays written in Indian languages, it owed more, as Christopher Shackle put it, 'to a perceived need to match up to the Shakespearian profile of the English literary canon than to any living local theatrical tradition'.[15] More important to this study however remains the fact that it became increasingly common for Indian theatrical plays to spread the message of social reform, if only because they were increasingly criticized by reformers when not doing so.[16] Even so, in order 'to reach the largest numbers of readers', in *Chandar Hari*, Buddh Singh 'added the spice of sex and love to his concern for social reform'.[17] Otherwise, he argued that the development of the language had to be seen as a contribution to the Punjab as a whole and that its association with religion would be its doom.[18] By that time, however, Singh Sabhaites already had turned Punjabi written in Gurmukhi into the sacred language of the Sikhs instead of that of the region and had become its most zealous crusaders. A process which ultimately resulted in the standardization of the Granth Sahib, i.e. page length, numbering and the use of Gurmukhi irrespective of whether the original hymn was composed in medieval Hindi, Punjabi or some other language. Likewise, as discussed earlier, Bhai Vir Singh stressed the relevance of drawing the value and ideal of Sikh life from the Granth Sahib in his writings. Hence, while Baba Buddh Singh wrote for the people of the Punjab country (*des*), Bhai Vir Singh stressed he always wrote for the Sikh community (*qaum*), while India was his country.[19] Interestingly, from the very beginning he recognized the necessity of doing all this in simple and direct Punjabi.

The simplicity of Bhai Vir Singh's style of writing reflected trends in the evolution of contemporary Urdu prose as in the cases of Sayyid Ahmad Khan, Nazir Ahmad and Muhammad Husain Azad. A most interesting propagator of writing in a colloquial vernacular remains the famous literary figure of the Aligarh movement, Altaf Husain of Panipat (1837-1914), better known as Hali, his pen name meaning modern or up to date.[20] In Lahore, he had worked in the Punjab government book depot, revising the style of textbooks that had been translated from English into Urdu for the Education Department. Hence, without knowing English, Hali became familiar with a wide range of English literature. His *Majalis-un-Nissa* or Assemblies of Women (1874), written in the form of conversations between upper-class Muslim women, is an excellent source of social history that includes descriptions of women's daily life, their education and training in household management, childrearing practices, customs, and beliefs. Even so, like all contemporary books on female reform the *Majalis-un-Nissa* was just a pedagogical work created by a man to reform Muslim women in the dialect of Urdu spoken by them (*Begamati zaban*). Though the very earthy and colloquial dialect, with very few Persian and Arabic loan words, was often regarded as low status, the Director of Public Instruction Colonel W.R.M. Holroyd recommended it for a literary prize and Viceroy Lord Northbrooke awarded Hali Rs. 400. Afterwards it was adopted as a textbook for girls' schools in the Punjab. Interestingly S.W. Falcon included the vocabulary of women (here called *rekhti* or *zanani boli*) as part of the colloquial vernacular in his 1879 *Hindustani-English Dictionary*. For according to him, 'the seclusion of native females in India has been the asylum of the true vernaculars, as pure and simple as it is unaffected by the pedantries of word-makers'.[21] More significant in terms of literary history remains the fact that Altaf Husain Hali (like Muhammad Husain Azad) advocated a natural (*necharal*) style as the only possible medium for serious and relevant poetry.[22] In a most important piece of literary criticism in Urdu, *Muqaddama-e-Si'r-o-Sairi* or Introduction to Poetry and Poetics (1893), he 'mercilessly criticized the traditional poets because he felt that neither high-soaring mystical dreams nor complicated rhetorical devices could help Muslims face their basic duties and lead them to towards a more glorious future'.[23] Through developments like these, Urdu heavily influenced modern Hindi and Punjabi literary history. As R.S. McGregor put it in relation to the case of Hindi:

Factors retarding the progress of Hindi were the relative infancy and consequent restricted range of the new style, its continuing dependence into the twentieth century on Urdu for models and also for some of its authors in the field of prose, and the natural difficulties in the way of a wholesale exchange of one set of language habits for another.[24]

Similarly, since knowledge of Urdu was so widely disseminated by the Punjab educational system, Christopher Shackle argued that early attempts at constructing modern Punjabi literary history were much indebted to both Muhammad Husain Azad's *Ab-e Hayat* (1880) and Hali's *Muqaddama*.[25] As Baba Buddh Singh put it in *Koil Ku* (1916), in which he discusses the *qissa* poets of the Mughal period and subsequently offers an elementary theory of poetry:

These verses are stuffed full of Persian images, and the custom started by these masters has continued down to the present. Even the poetry of today simply clings to the example of Fazl Shah. Those same Persian images which infuriated Azad and Hali and to which they said 'Enough!' have today found a home in Punjabi poetry. . . . But they are after all quite alien, and hardly pleasing to the Punjabi ear.[26]

All in all, both the growing organization of knowledge among Punjabis and the introduction of print culture meant that the colonial presence had decisive consequences for the standardization of the vernaculars. Not only were several editions of a work brought out on the market, but these often also came out with revisions. Works increasingly had prefaces and/or introductions, in which authors explained the message they wanted to spread. In the Preface to the *Mir'at-ul-Urus* or The Bride's Mirror, for example, a self-satisfied Nazir Ahmad stated that his moral tale proved to be useful for women, as 'they took the greatest interest in reading it or hearing it read'.[27] Alternately, (sub-) headings were increasingly used to lead the separate parts of a work more smoothly into each other and generally make the organization of a work more rational for better communication of the message. Interestingly, while making no concessions to traditional elegant forms of rhyme, rational headings often make clear the newly emerged social consciousness. Probably one of the best examples is Dayanand's *Satyarth Prakash*, where one finds such subject headings as: 'On Edu-cation', 'An Examination of the Different Religions prevailing in *Arya Varta*' and 'An Examination of the Doctrines of Christianity'. Likewise, as discussed in the previous chapter, in their urge to counter Western knowledge while simultaneously reviving their traditions, some Punjabis began citing Western authorities on the subject and referring to them in footnotes, organized by number and content, partly to invoke the authority of science. Singh Sabhaites, Arya Samajis and Ahmadiyahs kept a close watch on what was written about their own and other traditions and referred to them. Hence their reinterpretations and writings often came to be embedded in and entangled with the wider world of Western Orientalism.

In Chapter Two, I have referred to the complications involved in learning English in nineteenth century South Asia as well as the interpretation of an accumulating amount of texts. Translation from one vernacular into another and especially from English was crucial to what concerned Indian social consciousness under colonial rule. In relation to this are some vernacular terms (a few of which still are to come): *unnati, seva, dharmachar, 'aql, Arya Varta, Arya Bhasha, desh, qaum, swadeshi, swaraj, shuddhi, niyog, yaugika* and *sangathan*. Most of these words existed earlier but the point is that they were presented as part of a new powerful and authoritative rational language in the public sphere and therefore attained a different meaning. In the same way, though few of them knew English well, the authors often retained English words they felt were impossible to translate but nonetheless crucial to be maintained.[28] In contemporary tracts English words such as civilization, science, society, liberal, public, moral, natural philosophy and poetry, political crop up in careful transliteration.[29] These words complete, as it were, the full circle which in the Introduction began with Bhartendu Harishchandra's Ballia speech, *Bharatvarsh ki unnati kaise ho sakti hai?* (How can India progress?). Otherwise, because of their grammars, dictionaries and teaching materials, Christian missionaries were crucial to the creation of modern Hindi, Urdu and Punjabi.[30] Indeed, the growing importance of these vernaculars, besides their centrality in conveying the reformist meaning to a larger public, can be compared with what happened during the Reformation in Europe, i.e. the translation of the word of God into the vernaculars. Punjabi elites increasingly took care of their language in practice. All new literary forms (novel, drama, poems, etc.) had a strong moral content and so were definitely part of the dominant contemporary social consciousness. Equally crucial in terms of moral strengthening of the Singh Sabha, Arya Samaj and Ahmadiyah identities remains the modern scientific discipline of history. The latter not only made it possible to define moral languages in time and space, it particularly was excellent for use in polemic. Being continuously confronted with Western missionary and historical writings moulded by the ever recurring theme of Indians being uncivilized and backward compared to the West, reformers set out on countering these by writing their own history. For indeed, how could it be that the British would know more about Indian history than Indians themselves? Moreover, though belonging to the world of science, the writing of history was different from the scientific experiments held in the laboratories and could easily suit a moral purpose.

WRITING MORAL HISTORIES

Since the second half of the eighteenth century the British were engrossed with the writing of Indian history. Everywhere they went in the subcontinent they searched for ancient documents. Often they expressed their surprise that Hindus had no sense of history, but the British obsession with the past perhaps remains even more surprising.[31] The discovery and recreation of India's past was very largely a British achievement and one that was largely done by gifted amateurs. In their spare time, and almost as a hobby, civil servants translated works from Sanskrit and Persian, deciphered inscriptions, and worked out a chronology of India's past. Others wrote grammars and compiled dictionaries. In 1861, the second younger brother of Joseph Davy Cunningham, Alexander, was appointed the first Director-

General of Archaeology, after he had bothered the government into giving him a small staff to catalogue India's monuments.[32] He or most of his immediate successors were not a trained archaeologist but they succeeded in saving and recording some movements. Indeed, it is one of the many ironies of the colonial encounter that it was the curiosity of these early British archaeologists that provided the material framework for the version of the past that infused Indian nationalism. Elitist Indians became fascinated with the discipline and started to historicize their traditions in time, if only to counter the earlier historical claim made by the British. As still today, the search for history became one for legitimacy, especially because the Anglo-Indian colonial state often acknowledged the so-called historical facts brought forward or even gave authority to them in the first place (like stressing Muslims as being a foreign element). A growing number of historical works were written (involving consulting original sources, asking different kinds of questions, collecting different kinds of information and coming to new kinds of conclusions) which heavily influenced the redefinition of traditions.

As in Europe, perhaps the great question was whether the study of history could affect the meaning of religion by probing the moments of time associated with it. Ernest Renan's biographical study, *The Life of Jesus* (1863), for instance, not only excluded the supernatural but at the same time was written for the general reader who wanted an understandable Christ without simultaneously having to accept magical stories.[33] Interestingly, Mirza Ghulam Ahmad quotes this book to prove that Jesus did not die upon the cross.[34] Earlier in 1861, the publication of *Life of Mohamet* by William Muir provoked a new Muslim orientation towards the study of the life of the Prophet. From 1868 to 1874 Muir was Lieutenant-Governor of the North-West Provinces (modern Uttar Pradesh) and it was his official position in particular which aroused great interest in the book. Already during the time of the 1857 Revolt he promoted the myth of Muslims as religious fanatics and warmongers: 'all the ancient feelings of warring for the Faith, reminding one of the days of the first Caliphs, were re-suscitated'.[35] Now that Muir pointed the finger at the Prophet's sincerity, Muslim leaders like Sayyid Ahmad Khan were 'horrified to see how the picture of their Prophet was distorted in Western publications' and especially disappointed by such ideas because instead they at least 'could claim to have always paid due respect to Jesus the Prophet and his virgin mother'.[36] Yet, while Ahmad Khan argued that *Life of Mohamet* contained numerous distortions and lies, young English-educated Muslims who were unaware of their traditional literature asked them-selves: 'if Muir's book was a perversion of the truth, what was the real story?'. Hence one of the reasons behind Ahmad Khan's seventeen-month trip to England in 1868-70 was to study the original source material in the British Museum and the library of the India Office for a refutation of Muir's book, the result of which was his famous *Essays on the Life of Mohammad* (1870).[37] In this book he aimed at giving a rational and historical account of the life of the Prophet and so laid the basis for a new field of study. Like in the case of Jesus, Muhammad more than ever before was taken as the true guide, equally indeed for both men and women. To know more about Muhammad and to see him as the model, not only for details of ritual but rather for the whole approach to life, was the duty of Muslims. The *Life and Teachings of Mohammad or the Spirit of Islam* (1891) by a Shia Muslim, Sayyid Amir Ali (1849-1928) had a great impact on the mind of English educated Muslims.[38] In this popular work, he asserted in an Aligarh mode of thought that Muhammad's essential and primary role was that of a moral teacher who understood the unity and harmony between God and nature. Muhammad's mind was essentially modern because he taught that man could not exist without constant effort. The world was 'a well-ordered Creation, regulated and guided by a Supreme Intelligence overshadowing the Universe', wherein 'human will was free to work for its own salvation'.[39]

A crucial landmark in historiography is Sayyid Ahmad Khan's *Asbab-e-Baghavat-e-Hind* (1859) in which he tried to explain the causes of the 1857 Revolt by laying the blame upon both sides: the government had ignored the conditions of its subjects,[40] while Indians misunderstood British rule. While finding mutual misunderstanding to be at the root of what happened, Ahmad

Khan began to strive for means to bring about a rapproachment. Convinced that Muslims ought to know more about the faith of their rulers, he came up in 1862 with his *Tabyin-al-Kalam*, the first commentary on the Bible written by a Muslim anywhere. Though incomplete this work remains the first attempt to take seriously the claims of Christianity (it may be viewed as a follow up to Rammohun Roy's contribution in 1820 to the theology of Christian Unitarianism, *The Precept of Jesus*). Interestingly, as Wilfred Cantwell Smith pointed out, in this work: 'he arrived at the key unit concept of "religion" itself, as that which is common to all, a practical morality'.[41] Yet, as will be discussed further, while Ahmad Khan's commentary was not negative towards the Bible, other reformers in their writings and speeches denied the supremacy of Christian doctrines (indeed not so much its practice or morality). Among others, works by Muir, Ahmad Khan and Amir Ali were dispersed by the Punjab Education Department throughout the province. This organization was seminal in the dispersal of the earliest Indian works indebted to Western historiography and for which people like Dr. Leitner prepared history texts.[42] Also there was a sudden and voluminous production in the 1880s of short eulogistic accounts of historical charismatic figures (besides that of the Prophet Muhammad), to set a moral example and generally to create pride in the tradition. Though these were mostly uncritical accounts, through them one slowly but surely adopted a new way of writing about individuals in history. Until that time in the Indian tradition biographies generally focused on the sublimation of individuals (kings and other heroes) to broader historical forces. The new writing was more about the development of personality and the unique place of individuals in history. Altaf Husain Hali's *Hayat-i-Javed* (1901) despite its adulatory tone (for Altaf Husain was one of Sayyid Ahmad Khan's most devoted disciples), is still one of the best available biographies on the Muslim reformer.[43]

By the end of the nineteenth century, at least two Singh Sabhas sponsored historical research. Besides examining sources, one important aim of these societies was to prevent the publication of what they perceived as writings untrue to the Sikh tradition. Scholars such as Professor Gurmukh Singh and Bhai Kahn Singh

Nabha toured the Punjab in search of old texts. They discovered, for example, a number of previously unknown traditional biographies of Guru Nanak (*janam sakhis*), which generated a debate on the nature and reliability of sources.[44] The work of Ernest Trumpp remains crucial because of its negative conclusions about the historicity of Bhai Bala (a cherished figure in the tradition of the time), today widely accepted. Trumpp based his conclusions on the then oldest extant *janam sakhi*; the so-called Colebrooke manuscript, now in the British Library.[45] Overall publication of glossaries and studies of the Granth Sahib intensified concern with historical problems, while alternatively individuals such as Bhai Ditt Singh and Bhai Vir Singh reflected on the tradition in historical novels and short biographies on the lives of the Gurus. Fascinating is the case of the Raja Rasalu cycle, one of the most famous folk tales collected in the Punjab by Richard Temple among others. Baba Buddh Singh became extremely interested in proving the historical existence of Raja Rasalu. Accordingly, in 1931 he published, believe it or not, a transliteration into Gurmukhi of Richard Temple's romanized recordings of Punjabi oral texts in *The Legends of the Punjab* (1884-6).[46]

Also interesting remain the parallels drawn by Mirza Ghulam Ahmad between Jesus Christ and himself to prove the rightful cause of their missions (on earth at least). According to him Indians under the British were in very much the same corrupt situation as the Jews under the Romans and in need of similar divinely appointed mediators. Otherwise the Ahmadiyah periodical, *Review of Religions*, clearly fitted in with the times. Being an outlet for propaganda, it featured many articles discussing the different faiths in a comparative historical manner. Christian missionary H.A. Walter wrote a book on the Ahmadiyah movement mainly on the basis of the periodical and by and large was enthusiastic about its contents (not so much about Mirza Ghulam Ahmad's claims).[47] Mirza Ghulam Ahmad also became the moral example and guiding light for many Ahmadiyahs. Soon biographical accounts of his life and teachings were written by himself and his followers. Alternatively, second generation Ahmadiyah women 'could benefit from biographical accounts of wives and mothers written by males belonging to prominent families within the movement, who often had close relationships, through marriage and service, with the founder's family'.[48] Also the Ahmadiyahs appointed an historian to give the official account of the movement in time and space.[49]

Since the beginning of the twentieth century, Arya Samajis began with the writing of the history of their movement. Most important were Lajpat Rai's *A History of the Arya Samaj* (1914) and the three volumes of *Bharatvarsh ka Itihas* (1910-33) written by the then headmaster of the Gurukul Kangri, Ramdev. The latter work became one of the most widely distributed publications of the Gurukul and was used as history textbook in that same institution until the 1970s. Importantly, as Harald Fischer-Tiné put it:

The book was a corrective to Western representations of Indian history, hence its aggressively assertive character throughout. Almost every page contains a quotation from or a reference to the statements of historians and indologists like W. Jones, H.H. Wilson, J. Todd, F.M. Muller, V.A. Smith et al. which are subsequently debunked.[50]

Then, despite the scarcity of sources, the exemplary lives of important Arya Samajis were described in several biographies, first of course of their leader. Among the earliest were those by Lekh Ram (1897) and Lajpat Rai (1898). Earlier, in 1891, the latter also wrote his first ever book, the only biography of Guru ·Datta Vidyarthi in English so far.[51] Incontestably important in this context also were *shahid* or martyrdom writings. The ideal of martyrdom was first formulated by Jews in the mid-second century BC. The Christian sense of the term martyr originally applied to those apostles who were eyewitnesses to the life and death of Christ. Following the model of Christ's own sacrifice, one of the Fathers of the Latin Church, Tertullian (*c.* 160–220), proclaimed: 'the blood of the martyrs is the seed of the church'. However, as Christianity underwent persecution by the Roman authorities, the term was applied to those who witnessed for their faith by undergoing suffering and death. Probably it was through contact with Christians (and not Jews) that early Islam picked up its analogous language and theology for those who die for the faith. Ever since, in many traditions martyrs are revered, occupying a high place in heaven and acting as heroic figures of inspiration for the faithful. As immediate travellers to paradise, martyrs were a unique point of contact between heaven and earth. Thus it does not come as a surprise that martyrs were institutionalized into history by Punjabi reformers and the masculine Christian British alike.[52] After his death, Swami Dayanand more or less became a martyr, but the assassinations of Pandit Lekh Ram and Swami Shraddhanand (both by a Muslim) led to a series of biographies and eulogic poetry. By this time, both Arya Samajis (like Lajpat Rai) and Singh Sabhaites (like Lakshman Singh) increasingly began to adhere to Tertullian's saying in their writings.[53]

Though Mirza Ghulam Ahmad made clear that his interpretation of *jihad* differed completely from that of other Muslims (see the next chapter), in 1903 he wrote a tract in which he reflected on the martyrdom of two of his followers who were stoned to death in Kabul.[54] Ghulam Ahmad became after his death a martyr whose prophecy continues to be a source of inspiration up to today. Even so, Ahmadiyah ideas on martyrdom should be seen in terms of strengthening the community, inspiring missionaries by example rather than societal confrontation. This was in contrast to the Singh Sabhaites who made the Sikh martyr an important symbol of the Tat Khalsa identity in numerous martyrologies that eventually proved inspirational to militant Sikhs. According to the standard Tat Khalsa narrative, Guru Arjan, Guru Tegh Bahadur, 'martial' Guru Gobind Singh, 'protector of the early Khalsa' Guru Banda Singh Bahadur and numerous other Sikhs who chose to die during Mughal times rather than disavow their faith were exemplary martyrs.[55] During the late nineteenth century, then, 'the undaunted bravery and unflinching devotion to duty' of the Sikh soldiers in the British Indian army who died while defending the fort of Saragarhi in the Samana hills at the Afghan border in 1897 'passed into a proverb'.[56] Yet, the ultimate Tat Khalsa martyrs emerged during the so-called Gurdwara Reform Movement (better known as Akali movement), when some radical Singh Sabhaites wanted the control of gurdwaras to be taken out of private, hereditary ownership.[57] The recruitment of *nihangs*, men dressed in blue robes with yellow sashes and blue turbans, heavily armed and sworn to defend gurdwaras to the death, increased. Hence, individuals who had been overlooked since the eighteenth century once more assumed relevance as martyrs for a secular cause.[58]

Surprisingly, Bhagat Lakshman Singh's most important contribution to the canonization of martyrs, *Sikh Martyrs* (1923), was published at the time but did not pay attention to these Tat Khalsa martyrs. Instead, it consists of anecdotes about Sikhs who died for the truth of their faith in the face of Mughal oppression and so gave an example for the Panth. Likewise, Bhai Vir Singh's novels as well as the memory of Sikh heroes and martyrs were a source of inspiration for Sikh ghadarites to live or die heroically. The Ghadar movement was founded by Sikhs and Hindus living on the Pacific coast of America. There they suffered from racism and during the First World War ghadarites returned to the Punjab from Canada, the United States, Hong Kong and Shanghai, to provoke a rebellion (*ghadar*) against the British in India.[59] The loyal Chief Khalsa Diwan, however, sided with the British against the ghadarites and instead considerably aided the war effort by spreading Tat Khalsa writings on sacrifice and martyrdom with the aim of recruiting martial Sikhs.[60] Disillusioned with the Indian people, the ghadarites, who earlier had escaped the police at the Indian ports, surrendered to the British-Indian army in the beginning of 1915.

Clearly the idea of martyrdom lay deep in Punjabi popular culture. Similar to such saints as Pir Sakhi Sarvar, Baba Farid and Hazrat Datta Ganj Bakhsh, martyrs of any tradition were supernatural beings and venerated by all communities.[61] The point is that the Singh Sabha, Arya Samaj and Ahmadiyah moral languages could unleash militancy on the basis of ideas about martyrdom. Martyrs now were canonically defined in history and turned into a powerful source of moral inspiration to enter the public sphere in the name of truth and for a secular cause. The notion of martyrdom brought together ideas about the importance of human will and sacrifice for the honour of the community. By invoking the memory of past heroes traditional leaders could convince community members to show moral muscle or, worse, legitimize violence. The martyr was one on whom one could focus to strengthen one's own identity. As communities had to progress both in order to keep up with the times and in competition with others, martyrs thus increasingly became another point of symbolic reference for Indian moral languages, the ultimate embodiment of heroism, defiance, endurance, loyalty, fearlessness and altruism. Martyrdom was especially called upon when the community was in danger. While the state commanded the British Indian army, traditions had their volunteers that were willing to die for the faith and become martyrs. Important examples remain the cases of the Akalis, ghadarites, the Khilafat movement (featuring Indian Hindu-Muslim sympathies for the Ottoman Caliph following the defeat of Turkey during the First World War),[62] as well as the patriotic actions initiated by such Arya Samajis as Pandit Lekh Ram, Lala Lajpat Rai and Swami Shraddhanand (to whom I will return in the next chapter). Certainly the language of sacrifice with its rhetoric of warfare and martial metaphors is part of all modern traditions. Hence, for example, Indian ideas about martyrdom were more or less convergent with those of British Protestant preachers encouraging their flocks to wage war against the forces of evil. It was through the heroic acts of past and present martyrs that contemporaries became more involved with their own community and, moreover, familiar with the newly constructed histories by the Singh Sabha, Arya Samaj, and Ahmadiyah reformers.

Through their writings these reformers increasingly engaged with history because the discipline proved politically useful, especially when authorized by the state. The writing of history determined the processes of Indian identity formation. For if the British could choose the ancient Greeks as their ancestors rather than the less philosophically engaged people of the British Isles, were Indians not equally right to reveal, for example, that they were incontrovertible descendants of the writers of the Vedas? Indeed they were. The point however is that by locating themselves in history they engaged in a dialogue with such

Orientalist works as those by James Mill's *History of British India* (1818) and H.M. Eliot's *The History of India as told by its own Historians* (1867-77). Particularly in these two works ancient India was condemned as a despotic and immoral civilization, fortunately conquered by the slightly more civilized Muslims and then the far superior British. Such an interpretation not only laid the foundation for a communal interpretation of Indian history but also led for example to Arya Samajis defending the supposedly Golden Age of the Vedas. In fact, compared to the Singh Sabhas and Ahmadiyahs (and indeed perhaps most other reform movements), Aryas extensively used the so-called facts of history in their polemic to legitimate their positions. All the same, whatever the ideology, in the end one generally referred to the authority of history as a science. Increasingly historical facts counted in debates, to defeat opponents or convince the government to bring in support. Modern science as well as their functioning within a liberal public sphere made Punjabi reformers think more rationally than ever before. To be with the times, one had to position oneself and take steps urgently, before falling behind competitors within one's own community or another. But were the reformers liberal enough also to encourage the view that women ought to be treated as rational creatures and commit themselves to the general emancipation of women as men's equals?

DIRECTING THE IDEAL PUNJABI WOMAN

I then tried to find some kind of book—well stored of course with moral instruction, and which should improve their ideas and correct their habits in respect of those affairs which a woman encounters in her daily life—and in which, by reason of their romantic notions, or through ignorance or perseverity, so many women are overtaken by disaster and sorrow—and yet which should be in a form sufficiently attractive to prevent their being discouraged or dismayed by its perusal. But though I searched and searched for such a book through a whole library of volumes, not a trace of one could I find.

NAZIR AHMAD in *Mir'at-ul-Urus* (1869).[63]

Though Indian women traditionally were prohibited from being introduced to bookish learning in South Asia, during the nineteenth century the education and hence supposedly moral growth of women became a crucial focus of reform movements through the subcontinent. Women became central to the newly defined moral languages as guardians of morality against a supposedly encroaching and dangerous outside world. The American Presbyterian Mission in Ludhiana set-up its first elementary school for females in 1836. The British soon followed after their annexation of the region because they were strongly in favour of educating and unveiling Indian women. Except in the central districts, however, female education hardly took root in the next few decades. As one Punjabi schoolmaster put it:

Female education in this country is purely and simply a forced thing, and almost a farce, because girls cannot stay long on account of early marriage; because some instruction in their own religion is of necessity to be given them in the school hours, otherwise they would not attend; and because efficient teachers (females) cannot be readily had for them.[64]

Clearly the majority of women still were given, if at all, an almost exclusively religious education privately at home. The tradition of purdah (seclusion) also kept most women out of the reach of Christian preaching until it was decided about 1870 to send female missionaries to the Punjabi women's quarters (*zanana*). These missionaries gained access to a small but important number of secluded women, while visiting during the day when men (who overall resented the missionaries for tampering with their womenfolk) were in the fields, to discuss health, education and sanitation. Soon Punjabi reformers followed the British example and established the first girls' schools, but the lack of qualified women teachers remained an obstacle for some time. Central to the whole process was the development of educative literature and teaching materials in the vernaculars. Reformers argued that through education women got a chance to stand on their own feet. Female education was meant to inculcate in women the virtues of orderliness, thrift, cleanliness and a personal sense of responsibility as well as the practical skills of literacy, accounting, hygiene and the ability to run the household efficiently. In this way, the activities of women came to be newly defined by male reformers. This patriarchy combined coercive authority with the subtle force of persuasion, expressed most generally in the inverted ideological form of the relation of power between the sexes, indeed much like in the Indian tradition through the hypocrisy of woman as goddess or mother.[65]

Nazir Ahmad published his first three novels *Mir'at-ul-Urus* (1869), *Banat-an-Na'sh* (1872) and *Taubat an Nussooh* (1874), as a syllabus for the instruction of women and for the propagation of the reformist message. Generally appreciative of British culture, the three novels earned rewards from the government. This in part because the new patron of learning had earlier declared that books suitable for the women of India would be accepted and rewarded.[66] Ahmad's books were successfully disseminated through state educational institutions as their idiomatic style made them 'suitable for use as textbooks for the examinations in Urdu taken by British civil and military officers, for whom a number of annotated editions and translations were prepared'.[67] Some major concerns in Nazir Ahmad's fiction that evidently belonged to the times were the uplift and problems of women, proper upbringing and the importance of the family for the improvement of society. Unlike Sayyid Ahmad Khan and most Europeans at the time, Nazir Ahmad saw women as equal to men and argued that the solution to the remaining differences was education:

Hence, except reading and writing, there is positively no method by which you can develop your intellects. Indeed, if you compare them with men, the need of education for women is even greater. For since men admittedly live an out-of-door life, they will pick up the experience they want by associating with other people. But you, who sit at home all day long—what will you do? Will you fish out a little packet of common-sense from your sewing-bag, or fetch a napkin full of experience out of the grain closet? Learn to read; and while you are seated behind the purdah you may make a tour of the whole world. Get knowledge; and without going outside the house you may become acquainted with what has happened in all ages.[68]

Some decades later, the famous Deobandi Maulana Ashraf 'Ali Thanawi (1863-1943), listed Nazir Ahmad's three novels as harmful books in his influential *Bihisti Zewar* (Heavenly

Jewels). Unsupported by the British, Thanawi rivaled Nazir Ahmad in spreading the reformist message among women. He was aware of the strong temptation facing the Muslim to ape the powerful European and prepared to allow a place for science in man's acquisitive life. Even so, Thanawi saw no danger for Islam in the assumptions of science, as European virtues were borrowed from Islam earlier and anyway a bad Muslim was always better than a good unbeliever.[69] Though his *Bihisti Zewar* also treats women and men as essentially the same, the work was directed towards Muslim women and, in fact, was often given to girls as part of their dowry. First published in 1905 but still read by Muslims through the world, it may be the first book of its kind in Islamic *adab* literature and definitely played a significant role in disseminating modern female Muslim self-consciousness in South Asia. It was written when female education already had made some progress and Muslim women themselves increasingly were playing an active role in that process. This is worth mentioning, as the Singh Sabha, Arya Samaj and Ahmadiyah attitudes towards female education more or less paralleled Thanawi's. Nazir Ahmad had followed a too broad-based *adab* for most reformers, who were critical of Western morality (not of science) and instead glorified their own traditions through their moral languages. Though one preached the uplift of women, the advocated reforms were justified only in terms of women's traditional roles. There was no talk of a Western style curriculum, higher education or of tearing down the curtains of purdah. According to the newly defined moral languages, women had to stay at home. The inclusion of women in the newly defined teachings thus simultaneously meant the constricting of cultural behaviour in formerly female domains by male standards, though equally it should be stressed that the reforms sometimes could be progressive. Earlier, for example, it was not considered proper for Punjabi girls to learn how to write, since if a woman in purdah learned how to write letters, she might communicate with men beyond the permissible circle of kin.

In *Satyarth Prakash* Dayanand Saraswati was not concerned with women as independent individuals. Above all, he stressed the importance of marriage and the woman's role to serve her man.[70] Opposed to what was written in the traditional scriptures, nonetheless, he was in favour of female education, if only because it would create less tension in the home and produce teachers for the girls' schools.[71] In accordance with the ideas of their leader, Arya Samajis began to advocate female education. To create the daughters of *Arya Varta*, several girls' schools were founded where a limited curriculum in Hindi of reading and arithmetic was taught but also the useful arts of sewing and knitting. In fact, because of female education in Hindi there emerged some humorous situations between Punjabi Hindu men and women because 'there were many women who could not communicate with their husbands when they were away from each other, as they could only write in Hindi and their husbands only in Urdu or English'.[72] Yet as female education advanced, some male Arya Samajis found themselves caught between the desire to reform women and the fear of the possible impact education might have on women and their relationship with men. 'The education we give our girls should not unsex them', wrote one of them.[73] Subsequently, the Arya Samaj published journals addressed to women. These focused on diffusing rational knowledge authorized by the invocation of the Vedas with articles on health, diet, cleanliness and hygiene, education, child care and the follies of astrology. Around the same time, women's societies were established, as well as homes for widows, and more and more women missionaries began to travel around the province.

Most interesting was the Arya Samaj's controversial propagation of widow remarriage (*niyog*). To what extent was this a reaction to the specific circumstances in the Punjab? In 1881, a quarter of Punjabi women over 15 years of age in all communities were widows. In many cases these women were abandoned by their families and afterwards often became prostitutes, lived on charity in a pilgrimage centre or converted to Christianity.[74] In one contemporary tract in the form of a dialogue between two widows, one of them argues that she would rather commit *sati* than to suffer the taunts of relatives.[75] Arya Samajis thought widow remarriage was a respectable way of reintegrating widows into society and harnessing their reproductive potential and sexuality at the same time. However, as Dayanand Saraswati made clear, there was a difference between *niyog* and remarriage, as the former was to be performed solely by widows and widowers and not by 'bachelors and virgins'.[76] In practice the widow permitted to be a mother had no choice of a sexual partner and the custom therefore solely amounted to levirate. Importantly, because Punjabi reformers and Christian missionaries simultaneously recognized the marginal position of widows, particularly in high caste society, *niyog* became crucial to public debate. Mirza Ghulam Ahmad too attacked the custom in his tract *Radd-i-Niyog* or Rejection of Niyog (1895). According to him, *niyog* was nothing more than an excuse for transgressing exactly what the Vedas forbid, remarriage (though he was willing to offer Rs. 500 to anyone who could disprove his position).[77] Even so, in reality, *niyog* was never widely practised by Arya Samajis. Probably because it was discussed in the *Satyarth Prakash*, most were not prepared to publicly abandon the idea however—though over time it 'was quietly dropped and widows who were virgins were advised to devote themselves to social service'.[78] Moreover, important in terms of continuity of tradition, remains the fact that the exit of *niyog* at the same time meant a renewed glorification of *sati* in Arya Samaj writings.

Singh Sabhaites were alarmed by the progress in female education made by both Christian missionaries and Arya Samajis and soon came up with their own programme. In particular the girls' school (Kanya Mahavidyalaya) set-up in Ferozepur in 1892 by Bhai Thakat Singh and his wife Harnam Kaur was crucial. The curriculum was largely made up of instruction in Gurmukhi, readings from the Granth Sahib, and lessons in embroidery and cooking. All this was to create the ideal Sikh woman, who could read and write, was knowledgeable about the scripture, able to perform all household duties, respectful and obedient to the wishes of her husband, and able to bring up children in accordance with the Tat Khalsa ideology. The rising popularity of the school attracted students from as far as Agra and Rawalpindi (during 1908-14, a staff of 45 persons taught a total of 1608 students) and it became a model for later schools, turning out women stamped with a distinctive Tat Khalsa image. Yet, it should be stressed that the ideals preached at the Kanya Mahavidyalaya were not uniquely Sikh. On the contrary, because Harnam Kaur was educated in an Arya Samaj school, the Kanya Mahavidyalaya largely was run on the basis of Arya principles.[79] Like Dayanand Saraswati, Harnam Kaur argued that 'education would also lead to happier conjugal relations and peace in the home'.[80] All in all, despite the lack of originality, with the Ferozepur girls' school, Singh Sabha men possessed a powerful resource to discipline women, whom they always considered more open to the influence of popular as well as Hindu and Muslim cultures. It was with this purpose in mind that they started papers focusing on female education. Otherwise, the main characters in Bhai Vir Singh's pseudo-historical novels are women of heroism and piety in search of the Sikh truth, who in the end nonetheless remain much within the greater Indian tradition in which female protagonists always find their ultimate consolation in complete devotion to their men. Even so, Sikh reformers turned these women into moral examples who had fully imbibed the Sikh duty of service towards husband and community. It was in this context also that Harnam Kaur later attained martyrdom because of her educational service to the community.[81]

In the *Rahit* literature it is stated, 'Women should never be trusted. They should be regarded as inherently deceitful, and *Khalsa* Sikhs must never confide in them nor rely on them'.[82] Yet, as in most (if not all) modern traditions, equality was never officially denied to Sikh women and hence the *Rahit Maryada* states there are no functions that women cannot perform. Nonetheless the position of women remains problematic because practice rarely conformed with ideal. Most probably there never has been a female *granthi* (one who reads the Granth Sahib, though nowadays also custodian of gurdwara). On the whole, women in the gurdwara had to be content with singing hymns from the Granth Sahib (*gurbani*) and serving food (*langar*).[83] Similarly, as in the Hindu tradition, to this day neither the dowry system nor female infanticide (which both were condemned by the Gurus), have been completely eradicated among the Sikhs.

In traditional Punjabi (and Hindu) culture a girl remains the property of others. More than her husband, her father is responsible for her. She is never her own person but a costly expense to her parents, as a dowry will be expected, and after they have spent everything on her, the benefit is enjoyed by the family she marries into. The rest of her life will be spent with them! Though today broader views are emerging, until pension schemes replace the dependence of parents upon their sons for security in old age, change is likely to be slow and limited.

After his visit to Qadian, H.A. Walter noted that among the Ahmadiyahs 'a beginning has been made in the education of women' and their status 'on the whole, seems to be above the standard obtaining in Islam generally'.[84] Mirza Ghulam Ahmad preached to change the social position of women and accordingly they were educated within the community at purdah schools. Seeing that women's inferior status was caused particularly by their economic dependence on men, Ghulam Ahmad argued that women should be given their dowry as 'a free gift' and that women's property should not be taken out of their hands by their husbands.[85] Thus the Ahmadiyah case fitted in the pattern common throughout the Islamic world, wherein modern reformers advocated women's rights provided in Koranic teachings in some specific legal areas (especially property and marriage). At the same time, however, the Ahmadiyahs clearly were on the puritanical side as defenders of purdah and polygamy. According to Ghulam Ahmad, the latter two were closely linked, for although the Koran states that both sexes should restrain their sexual passions, he stresses that the male has a 'natural propensity' to fulfil his sexual appetite, unless temptation is removed from his vicinity.[86] Hence, he continues, female purdah is 'conducive to the good of both sexes' and did not mean 'shutting up women like prisoners in gaol'.[87] Likewise he was clear about polygamy: Ahmadiyah men could marry a number of women as long as they acted 'equitably towards them in all respects'.[88] If they could not, however, he stressed, 'then marry only one (though you may need more)'.[89] Until his death, Mirza Ghulam Ahmad personally allowed brides from outside into the movement, provided they followed appropriate Ahmadiyah education after marriage.[90] After 1915, nonetheless, the community refused to marry its womenfolk to other Muslims 'for wives are generally influenced by their husbands'.[91] As for the Arya Samajis and Singh Sabhaites, here too marriage was crucial to the expansion and control of community membership. While there was a strong emphasis on female literacy within the movement, strict moral conduct (*adab*) was expected from women within the Ahmadiyah marriage relationship. Ahmadiyah girls received religious education at home: correct understanding of the Koran, Arabic and didactic literature for moral lessons. This female education in fact differed little from Sunni reformist instruction elsewhere in northern India and included Nazir Ahmad's writings and Thanawi's *Bihisti Zewar*. Even so, as Avril A. Powell perceptively argues,

What was different, however, was the widespread availability of Ahmadiyah schools at village level as well as in the towns of the Punjab, with the result that education for girls seems to have acted as one of the factors which, during its early decades, began to reduce the distance between the urban and rural poles of recruitment to this new religious movement.[92]

Thus women in the Singh Sabha, Arya Samaj and Ahmadiyah communities accepted male ideologies that inhibited them by taking away many choices. But what was the alternative? Obviously, the few female activists that existed 'wished to be accepted within a system that professed as one of its foremost objectives women's reform'.[93] Reform movements provided women the option to do their duty and become more active in the community than ever before but simultaneously required them to live in purdah.

Though followed more among Muslims than Sikhs and Hindus, purdah was part of Punjabi culture at large. During the end of the nineteenth century, however, it became closely connected with the changing hierarchies in society.[94] The more strictly a family confined its women, the higher its status and honour (*izzat*). Hence, as a marker of the influence of moral languages, a Muslim Punjabi captain born in 1857 told Malcolm Darling how during his youth women had enjoyed much more freedom to move around the countryside but that since then a lot had changed·

The children are better cared for, the house is better run, and needlework is done instead of cutting grass. There is modesty, too. Before they could be seen by anyone of their own tribe, but now only by those of their own village. When they go farther, they wear *burqa* unknown in the old days. . . . Before we did not know the world, but we went forth serving in the army and we saw other countries. Now we have civilization: (we do) what the Quran orders.[95]

Even if women enjoyed less freedom, perhaps partly also it was their own choice. Otherwise it remains difficult to understand how half of the population could have been confined (with many recruited men away) without their consent. Obviously, in a rural, violent and poor society like that of nineteenth century Punjab, seclusion had its attractions, as a woman's segregation from unrelated men entitled her to a much higher degree of protection from the men to whom she was related. The alternative, for example, as in the Muslim districts in the south (which produced no recruits), was to be as liberated as the most ardent feminist:

Here women could come back to their ostensible husbands after an absence of a few years, present them with a couple of strange children, and say 'God has increased your honour'. But they could also be bought and sold; they were expected to redeem bad debts by extending their favours to moneylenders; 'no girl was safe' from the local landlords; and they were constantly abandoned in ill-health and old age.[96]

Malcolm Darling was told by different informants that ever since men joined the army and saw the world, the position of women had improved. As indeed stressed also by male Singh Sabha, Arya Samaj and Ahmadiyah reformers, marriages had become more companionable. Likewise Darling was told that there was less wife beating: true, childless wives continued to be beaten, but the tyranny of the mother-in-law was coming to an end since young wives 'took their mothers-in-law by the ears' while their soldier husbands looked on.[97] Though today generally taken as a sign of medieval obscurantism, according to C.A. Bayly, since the end of the nineteenth century full body covering (*burqah*) grew in popularity throughout the Islamic world as a modern dress that 'allowed women to come out of the seclusion of their homes and participate to a limited degree in public and commercial affairs'.[98]

Undeniably, the notion of the ideal Punjabi woman remains much similar to the Victorian ideal of the domesticated Christian wife and mother. Except in the Cambridge mission, male missionaries in the Punjab 'were meant to be married'.[99] Though it is often said that by emphasizing the significance of marriage, Protestants raised the status of women, it can equally be said to have narrowed the choice of acceptable female identities. For example, 'the choice of an independent and celibate religious vocation in which a woman might develop her own talents was removed' when it was replaced by 'the ideal of the pastor's wife'.[100] Within this patriarchal world, the wife further of course had the Christian duty to fulfil her husband's (carnal) demands, 'for otherwise he might fall into sin'.[101] Interestingly, the colonial context also opened up new possibilities for British women. Not only did missionary wives carry out 'their own partly autonomous professional responsibilities to a far greater extent than clergymen's wives at home', but, more importantly, at the beginning of the twentieth century 'unmarried women, appointed as independent missionaries, would outnumber ordained males'.[102] Missionary wives, independent female missionaries, and European and Indian female staff 'transformed almost every mission in the Punjab into a predominantly female organization'.[103] Female missionaries were freed of clerical professionalism and therefore became particularly important as teachers and medical workers for Indian women in hospitals and local medical posts. So while earlier they encountered Indians as fellows within the mission or as social equals during *zanana* work, as the missions growingly institutionalized, female missionaries largely encountered them as students, patients and employees 'to be managed, disciplined, or discharged'.[104]

All things considered, female reform should be situated in the context of a society that became increasingly rational, disciplined and masculine. Empire sharpened gender distinctions. It brought into prominence the hard masculine values central to a world of duty and grit and lessened the importance of the softer, supposedly feminine, virtues of tenderness and feeling (female intuition!). Punjabi men wanted their women to stay at home to retain the status (*izzat*) of the family and the community.

This perhaps partly because there was a growing psychological need among them for a refuge to gain strength after doing their public duty and to some extent, as Anshu Malhotra argues, because women in the shaping of a new middle-class identity among male Punjabi Hindus and Muslims were seen as 'hallmarks of caste status'.[105] Otherwise, Punjabi men (and especially Muslims) often wanted to hide away their women from the British (and some Westernized upper-class Punjabis), shocked as they were by these eaters of pork and drinkers of wine with badly behaving women baring their shoulders and freely dancing at social events.[106] Or were Punjabi men afraid of the overwhelming sensuality of feminine sexuality? In India, prostitutes were not regarded as degraded, as in Britain.[107] Yet, nineteenth-century Indian male poets and moralists constantly lamented that men were made weak by women and therefore had to avoid and resent them. Simultaneously in Britain and India reformers aimed to control sexual permissiveness. This is the context of the Arya Samaj propagation of widow remarriage (*niyog*)—a society wherein male moralists continued to be haunted by the fear of a widow's sexuality, 'even as they idealized the ascetic widow who had managed to suppress her sexual self'.[108] Widows had to devote their life to public service, at best become teachers or nurses.

CONCLUSION

In the Introduction I wrote that fundamental to this study and the nature of intellectual history is the relationship between social and intellectual change. I have situated the Singh Sabha, Arya Samaj and Ahmadiyah moral languages squarely within the complex world of opportunities, constraints and motivations they shared in different degrees with other groups within non-Western secularizing traditions. I repeat these statements to stress the point that in the end I believe no causal answers are possible concerning the relationship between social and intellectual change. Besides my emphasis on imperial context in the making of modern Punjabi identities, therefore, I emphasize equally the internal dynamics of Punjabi society in the making of history.

As stated in the Introduction, because the nature and mode of what happened remains almost inconceivably complex, if not actually incomprehensible, instead of implying historical causality I take the social process and the intellectual texture as part of a complex configuration of change.

Within this configuration then European knowledge may have been hegemonic but it was never absolute. On the contrary, the colonial culture that created the identities of both colonizer and colonized was a diffuse and open process. The moral languages of the three groups resulted from a polyphonic intellectual dialogue that included debates within the respective greater traditions as well as discussion with reformers of other traditions, Christian missionaries and British officials. Because of the growth of public knowledge, Punjabi reformers became increasingly aware of the wide range of arguments that they were responding to and the different audiences they were dealing with. This polyphonic intellectual dialogue existed because Punjabis were incorporated into the wider world of the British Empire which, 'as a system of mobility, where certain ideas, commodities and people circulated', certainly worked as a catalyst for change.[109]

While Chapter Three largely concerned the definition of the moral languages, this chapter discussed how the corresponding emerging identities were strenghtened by the choice for a specific vernacular language and the writing of the history of one's own community. Punjabi in Gurmukhi, Hindi in Devanagari and Urdu in Nastaliq, were the languages chosen for the writing and spread of the moral languages concerned among the populace. Numerous historical books, (auto)biographies and works on martyrdom were published that positioned the communities in time and for debate in the public sphere. Crucial to the whole process was the growing presence of print culture as the midwife to intellectual change. Most important also were the linguistic demands of the Anglo-Indian colonial state and the community politics inherent to the liberal public sphere. Language politics and the discipline of history certainly belong to the modern political world wherein science is taken as universal reason. Though Punjabi reformers saw their choice of language and history as sacred and symbolic to their traditional identities, simultaneously they legitimized their choice in the name of science in order to attain a secular goal. Underlying the emerging moral languages was an understanding of what constituted a good society. Hence, as a point of convergence, the notion of masculinity became central to a modern public culture, for example in terms of doing one's duty, maintaining one's honour and being disciplined by education. No doubt this already existed in a region which, before the coming of the British, had been the overland gateway to the subcontinent. The point is that Punjabis (and in this case the Sikhs in particular) made use of the timely importance of masculine behaviour and by doing so gained cultural recognition and economic benefit from the colonial authorities. Alternately, the British by acknowledging such values only strengthened their imperial power. So Anglo-Indian colonial culture constructed and affirmed societal values more or less shared by both colonizer and colonized that, equally, 'rested on the identification and marginalization of other groups who lacked those qualities'.[110] Even so, the colonial situation was one of inequality and therefore elitist Punjabi reformers were respondent to the psychological limits set by what Ashis Nandy has labelled the 'second colonization'. They had to find ways to cope with Western hegemony, which in fact they perceived to be morally grounded, and, simultaneously, as moral and political leaders they had to guide their fellow Punjabis in the public sphere. In the next chapter I shall discuss how reformers propagated their moral languages that incorporated traditional sacred symbols and patriotisms in a rhetorical fashion to mobilize followers through identity politics.

NOTES

1. Barbara D. Metcalf, 'Imagining Community: Polemic Debates in Colonial India', in *Religious Controversy in British India: Dialogues in South Asian Languages*, ed. Kenneth W. Jones, Albany: State University of New York Press, 1992, p. 234.
2. Sayyid Ahmad Khan, *Musafiran-e-Landan*, 1869, repr. Lahore: Majlis-e-Taraqqi-e-Adab, n.d., p. 184.
3. W.H. McGregor, *The Oxford Hindi-English Dictionary*, New Delhi: Oxford University Press, 1995, p. v.

4. Paul R. Brass, 'Elite Groups, Symbols Manipulations and Ethnic Identity Among the Muslims of South Asia', in *Political Identity in South Asia*, ed. David Taylor and Malcolm Yapp, London: Curzon Press, 1979, p. 49.

5. Ibid.

6. Ibid., p. 50.

7. Christopher Shackle and Rupert Snell, *Hindi and Urdu Since 1800: A Common Reader*, London, SOAS, 1990, p. 44.

8. In 1920 Hindi and the Devanagari script were adopted as the official language in the constitution drawn up by the Indian National Congress. In fact, the so-called *sarkari* Hindi or government Hindi adopted by the Congress-led government of independent India is clearly Sanskrit biased and very close to the ideal of *Arya Bhasha*.

9. R.B. Mulraj, *Beginning of Punjabi Nationalism: Autobiography of R.B. Mulraj*, Hoshiarpur: V.V. Vedic Research Institute, 1975, pp. 133-5.

10. Lala Dwarka Dass, *Hindi versus Urdu*, Lahore: Arya Press, 1882, p. 11. Lala Dwarka Dass worked in the Chief Court in Lahore and served as Vice-President of the Arya Samaj managing committee in 1906 and as President from 1907 to 1909. He was closely related to Lala Hans Raj, Lajpat Rai and Guru Datta Vidyarthi.

11. Lajpat Rai, 'The Story of My Life', in *The Collected Works of Lala Lajpat Rai*, vol. 5, ed. B.R. Nanda, New Delhi: Manohar, 2004, p. 332.

12. The fact that Persian gave way to the lay language of Urdu explains the absence of periodicals in the former language, while on the whole print culture further encouraged the dissemination of Urdu (as generally still today, by lithographic reproduction of calligraphic originals rather than by typesetting). Otherwise, though the Muslim elite turned to the cultivation of Urdu as a worthy successor to Persian poetry, the shift was somewhat lurchingly realized in prose instead of poetry.

13. *The Tribune*, 16 February 1881, p. 8.

14. J.T.F. Jordens, *Swami Shraddhananda: His Life and Causes*, New Delhi: Oxford University Press, 1981, p. 71.

15. Christopher Shackle, 'Making Punjabi Literary History', in *Sikh Religion, Culture and Ethnicity*, ed. Christopher Shackle, Gurharpal Singh and Arvind-Pal Mandair, Richmond: Curzon Press, 2001, p. 114.

16. *Regenerator of Arya Varta*, vol. 1, 27 August 1883, pp. 1-2.

17. J.S. Grewal, *The Emergence of Punjabi Drama: A Cultural Response to Colonial Rule*, Amritsar: Guru Nanak Dev University, 1986, p. 7.

18. Ibid.

19. Ibid., p. 15.

20. Hali replaced *khastah* or the exhausted, distressed or heartbroken and, hence, this change in pen name can be taken as symbolically imperative to the change in South Asian social consciousness under colonial rule.
21. S.W. Falcon, *A New Hindustani-English Dictionary*, London: Trübner, 1879, p. iii.
22. As Frances W. Pritchett argued, Hali got much of the inspiration for his natural style from an understanding of English poetics, mostly those articulated by Wordsworth. In *Nets of Awareness: Urdu Poetry and its Critics*, Berkeley: University of California Press, 1994, pp. 166-7. Like Azad, Hali gave presentations at the *mushairah* meetings organized by the Anjuman-i-Punjab in Lahore.
23. Annemarie Schimmel, *Islam in the Indian Subcontinent*, Leiden: Brill, 1980, p. 200.
24. R.S. McGregor, *Urdu Study Materials*, New Delhi: Oxford University Press, 1992. p. xi.
25. Shackle, 'Making Punjabi Literary History', p. 102.
26. Ibid., p. 113.
27. Nazir Ahmad, *The Bride's Mirror*, tr. G.E. Ward, London: Henry Frowde, 1903, p. 186.
28. Fortunately, English words were transliterated through South Asian sound systems and hence the Western translator regularly is confronted with amusing findings (*maijik lentarn, necharal poitri*). Similarly, because of the peculiar combination of consonants in English, one can often recognize transliterated English words beforehand in vernacular texts.
29. I refer to texts by such authors as Bhartendu Harishchandra, Altaf Husain Hali, Muhammad Husain Azad, Nazir Ahmad, Sayyid Ahmad Khan, Bhai Vir Singh, Bhagat Lakshman Singh, Baba Buddh Singh, Pandit Guru Datta Vidyarthi, and Lala Lajpat Rai. They were at the vanguard in terms of late nineteenth century social consciousness, as it were, for obviously one finds these terms not so much in the writings of for example Mirza Ghulam Ahmad or Dayanand Saraswati, if only because their lack of (first hand) knowledge of the English language.
30. In the Punjab, for example, the Ludhiana Mission Press for many years was the proud owner of the only Gurmukhi typefaces in India. In 1851, American Presbyterian, John Newton, published the first Punjabi grammar to be followed by the *Punjabi Dictionary* (1854) written by him and his cousin Levi Janvier.
31. Compared to Hindus, Muslims were more consciousness of the past. Following their own Islamic calendar that started on 16 July 622 with the holy flight (*hijrat*) from Mecca to Medina by Muhammad and his followers, at least there were numerous biographies of the Prophet's life.

32. Joseph Davy Cunningham, *A History of the Sikhs from the Origin of the Nation to the Battles of the Sutlej*, ed. H.L.O. Garrett, New Delhi: S. Chand, 1966, A Note on the Cunningham Family.

33. Owen Chadwick, *The Secularization of the European Mind in the Nineteenth Century*, Cambridge: Cambridge University Press, 1975, Chapter Eight.

34. Mirza Ghulam Ahmad, *A Review of Christianity from a New Point of View*, repr., Qadian: Nazir Dawat-o-Tabligh, n.d., pp. 25-6.

35. William Muir, *Records of the Intelligence Department of the North-West Provinces of India during the Mutiny of 1857*, Edinburgh: Clark, 1902, vol. 1, p. 46.

36. Schimmel, *Islam in the Indian Subcontinent*, p. 206.

37. Sayyid Ahmad Khan did not know English and his two sons acted as interpreters and research assistants. See further on his journey to London: Ahmad Khan, *Musafiran*.

38. This was a revised version of his *A Critical Examination of the Life and Teachings of Mohammad* published earlier in 1873.

39. Sayyid Amir Ali, *The Spirit of Islam*, repr., London: Christophers, 1953, p. 121.

40. The 1857 Revolt overturned the dominant British belief that Indians did not care who ruled them, as long as they were well ruled. Afterwards, they concluded that they had made errors in ruling the subcontinent and hence the structure of the administration was to be changed, the army reorganized and, in general, the direction of government policy re-examined. While Indians did not care who governed them or even how they were governed, 1857 proved that they cared about their traditions and society.

41. Wilfred Cantwell Smith, *Modern Islam in India*, repr., New Delhi: Usha, 1985, p. 11.

42. Important also was the increase in Punjab regional history books. Best known probably remain those by Muhammad Latif, originally published in Urdu but afterwards translated into English: *History of the Punjab from the Remotest Antiquity to the Present Time*, Calcutta: Central Press, 1891 and *Lahore: Its History, Architectural Remains and Antiquities*, Lahore: The New Imperial Press, 1892.

43. Edward D. Churchill, 'Printed Literature of the Punjabi Muslims, 1860-1900', in W. Eric Gustafson and Kenneth W. Jones, eds., *Sources on Punjab History*, New Delhi: Manohar, 1975, pp. 319-20.

44. N. Gerald Barrier, *The Sikhs and their Literature: A Guide to Books, Tracts and Periodicals (1849-1919)*, New Delhi: Manohar, 1970, p. xxi.

45. Ernest Trumpp, *The Adi Granth or the Holy Scriptures of the Sikhs Translated from the Original Gurmukhi with Introductory Essays*, London: Allen & Co., 1877, p. v.

46. Christopher Shackle, 'Making Punjabi Literary History', in *Sikh Religion, Culture and Ethnicity*, ed. Christopher Shackle, Gurharpal Singh and Arvind-Pal Mandair, Richmond: Curzon Press, 2001, p. 114.

47. H.A. Walter, *The Ahmadiya Movement*, 1948; repr. New Delhi: Manohar, 1991, pp. 7, 17. Walter was educated at Princeton and Hartford theological seminaries and served in Lahore with the YMCA.

48. Avril A. Powell, '"Duties of Ahmadi Women"': Educative Processes in the Early Stages of the Ahmadiyya Movement', in *Gurus and Their Followers: New Religious Reforms Movements in Colonial India*, ed. Antony Copley, New Delhi: Oxford University Press, 2000, pp. 137-8.

49. The post still exists and hence in 1996 I was kindly received in Rabwah by Dost Muhammad Shahid, historian of the Ahmadiyah community and author/editor of the *Tarikh-i-Ahmadiyah*, 9 vols., Rabwah, n.d.

50. Harald Fischer-Tiné, '"The Only Hope for Fallen India": The Gurukul Kangri as an Experiment in National Education (1902-1922)', in *Explorations in the History of South Asia: Essays in Honour of Dietmar Rothermund*, ed. Georg Berkemer et al., New Delhi: Manohar, 2001, p. 287.

51. Lajpat Rai, 'Life and Work of Pandit Guru Datta Vidyarathi' in *The Collected Works of Lala Lajpat Rai*, vol. 1, ed. B.R. Nanda, New Delhi: Manohar, 2003, pp. 143-264.

52. The latter particularly after 1857, when in numerous writings Indian brutality and cruelty were juxtaposed with British heroism and endurance. Henry Lawrence for example reached the status of martyr after his death in Lucknow.

53. Lajpat Rai, 'The Arya Samaj and the Present Crisis', in *Selections from the Punjab Vernacular Press*, 1908, *Prakash*, 1 September 554; *Young India*, 324 and Bhagat Lakshman Singh, *Sikh Martyrs*, repr., Ludhiana: Lahore Book Shop, 1989, p. 8.

54. Spencer Lavan, *The Ahmadiyah Movement: A History and Perspective*, New Delhi: Manohar, 1974, pp. 73-4.

55. For a discussion of the standard Tat Khalsa narrative on martyrdom: Louis E. Fenech, *Martyrdom in the Sikh Tradition: Playing the 'Game of Love'*, New Delhi: Oxford University Press, 2000, Chapter Three.

56. Bhagat Lakshman Singh, *Autobiography*, ed. Ganda Singh, Calcutta: The Sikh Cultural Centre, 1965, p. 116.

57. J.S. Grewal, *The Sikhs of the Punjab*, Cambridge: Cambridge University Press, 1990, pp. 157-63.

58. *Nihangs* served valiantly in the forces of Guru Gobind Singh and in the eighteenth-century they formed horseback units to harass Mughal and Afghan forces in the Punjab. *Nihang* means carefree and ac-

cordingly the *Nihangs* lead a relatively non-materialistic life in their desire to serve the Sikh cause. Organizing themselves into an 'army' they live in encampments, have few belongings and upto today travel around the Punjab often on horseback.

59. Grewal, *The Sikhs of the Punjab*, pp. 153-6.

60. N. Gerald Barrier, 'Vernacular Publishing and Sikh Public Life in the Punjab, 1880-1910', in *Religious Controversy in British India: Dialogues in South Asian Languages*, ed. Kenneth W. Jones, Albany: State University of New York Press, 1992, p. 287 and 'Sikh Politics in British Punjab prior to the Gurdwara Reform Movement', in *Sikh History and Religion in the Twentieth Century*, ed. Joseph T. O'Conell et al., Toronto: University of Toronto Center for South Asian Studies, 1988, pp. 186-7.

61. Fenech, *Martyrdom in the Sikh Tradition*, p. 157.

62. As Caliph of Islam, the Sultan of the Ottoman Empire had both a temporal and religious role. He was the central figure of the Islamic world, whose duties still included the responsibility of declaring a holy war (*jihad*), which all true Muslims were bound to obey. This religious sanction gave the Sultan a theoretical though limited authority even beyond the borders of the Empire, and among his Muslim subjects, made him an object of veneration. Hitherto angered by the apparent Hindu pre-emption of the all India national movement, Indian Muslims were themselves pan-Islamically provoked because Britain was at war with Turkey. The surrender of a British Army to Turkish troops near Baghdad in 1916 therefore brought satisfaction to nationalist Indian Hindus and Muslims alike.

63. Ahmad, *The Bride's Mirror*, p. 186.

64. As cited in G.W. Leitner, *History of Indigenous Education in the Punjab Since Annexation and in 1882*; repr., Gurgaon: Deepak, 1989, p. 105.

65. Partha Chatterjee, *The Nation and its Fragments: Colonial and Post-Colonial Histories*, New Delhi: Oxford University Press, 1993, Chapter Six.

66. See further: C.M. Naim, 'Prize-winning Adab: A Study of Five Urdu Books Written in Response to the Allahabad Gazette Notification', in *Moral Conduct and Authority: The Place of Adab in South Asian Islam*, ed. Barbara D. Metcalf, Berkeley: University of California Press, 1984, pp. 290-314.

67. D.J. Matthews, C. Shackle and Shahrukh Husain, *Urdu Literature*, London: Gora, 1985, p. 104. The Director of Public Instruction, M. Kempson, personally translated Nazir Ahmad's *Taubat an Nussooh* or *Repentance of Nussooh*, London: W.H. Allen & Co., 1894.

68. Ahmad, *The Bride's Mirror*, p. 200.

69. See further: Barbara D. Metcalf, *Perfecting Women: Maulana Ashraf 'Ali Thanawi's Bihishti Zewar*, Berkeley: University of California Press, 1990.
70. Dayanand Saraswati, *Light of Truth*, tr. Dr. Charanjiva Bharadwaja, 1906; repr., New Delhi: Sarvadeshik Arya Pratinidhi Sabha, 1991, Chapter Four.
71. Ibid., p. 79.
72. Prakash Tandon, *Punjabi Century*, London: Chatto & Windus, 1961, p. 67.
73. *The Tribune*, 11 April 1894, p. 5.
74. Madhu Kishwar, 'The Daughters of Aryavarta', in *Women in Colonial India: Essays of Survival Work and the State*, ed. J. Krishnamurty, New Delhi: Oxford University Press, 1989, pp. 82-4.
75. Lala Jivan Das, *Do Hindu Beva Auraton ki Baatchit*, Lahore: Arya Pustakalaya, 1891.
76. Saraswati, *Light of Truth*, pp. 130-42.
77. As cited in Spencer Lavan, 'Communalism in the Punjab: The Ahmadiyahs versus the Arya Samaj During the Lifetime of Mirza Ghulam Ahmad', *Punjab Past and Present*, 5, 1971, p. 330.
78. Kishwar, 'The Daughters of Aryavarta', p. 111.
79. Doris R. Jakobsh, *Relocating Gender in Sikh History: Transformation, Meaning and Identity*, New Delhi: Oxford University Press, 2003, p. 146.
80. Ibid., p. 147.
81. Ibid., pp. 155-7.
82. W.H. McLeod, *Sikhs of the Khalsa: A History of the Khalsa Rahit*, New Delhi: Oxford University Press, 2003, p. 243.
83. Only recently have women singers performed daily inside Amritsar's Golden Temple and, after many years of unsuccessful petitioning, Sikh women seeking equal position and status in the performances of rituals finally found a champion in Bibi Jagir Kaur, who became the first woman to be appointed president of the SGPC (to be deposed in November 2000). Ibid., p. 253.
84. Walter, *The Ahmadiya Movement*, p. 117.
85. Ahmad, *The Philosophy of Islam*, repr., New Delhi: Inter-India, 1978, pp. 30-4.
86. Ibid., pp. 43-4.
87. Ibid.
88. Ibid., p. 33.
89. Ibid.
90. Powell, 'Duties of Ahmadi Women', p. 136.
91. Lavan, *The Ahmadiyah Movement*, p. 114.
92. Powell, 'Duties of Ahmadi Women', p. 152.

93. Jakobsh, *Relocating Gender in Sikh History*, p. 242.

94. Ibid., p. 152 and Anshu Malhotra, *Gender, Caste, and Religious Identities: Restructuring Class in Colonial Punjab*, New Delhi: Oxford University Press, 2002.

95. As cited in Clive Dewey, 'Some Consequences of Military Expenditure in British India: The Case of the Upper Sind Sagar Doab, 1849-1947', in *Arrested Development in India: The Historical Dimension*, ed. Clive Dewey, New Delhi: Manohar, 1988, p. 111.

96. Ibid., pp. 152-4.

97. Ibid.

98. C.A. Bayly, *The Birth of the Modern World 1780-1914*, London: Blackwell, 2004, p. 15.

99. Jeffrey Cox, *Imperial Fault Lines: Christianity and Colonial Power in India, 1818-1940*, Stanford: Stanford University Press, 2002, p. 78.

100. R.W. Scribner, *The German Reformation*, Basingstoke: Macmillan, 1992, p. 60.

101. Ibid.

102. Cox, *Imperial Fault Lines*, pp. 41, 48.

103. Ibid., pp. 5, 153.

104. Ibid., pp. 181-2.

105. Malhotra, *Gender, Caste, and Religious Identities*.

106. Likewise the British were often irritated by the fact that Indians almost never brought their women along.

107. Jakobsh, *Relocating Gender in Sikh History*, p. 105.

108. Ibid., p. 83.

109. Tony Ballantyne, 'Looking Back, Looking Forward: The Historiography of Sikhism', *New Zealand Journal of Asian Studies*, 4, 2002, pp. 23-4.

110. Ibid., 20.

CHAPTER FIVE

Community, Government and Social Consciousness

COMPARATIVE MORAL POLEMICS

In pre-colonial Punjab the followers of different traditions were frequently in conflict with each other. This was predominantly about the control of buildings and land, though festivals regularly were also accompanied by violence. However, while conflict seemed accidental and implicit in pre-colonial society, since the 1880s redefined traditional identities and their moral languages received more loyalty than ever before, especially among urban Punjabis. Activities that in the past had incidentally resulted in violence, were now consciously practised and in public. Moreover, by this time Arya Samajis for example also would march like the Salvation Army, though without uniforms and brass band, through the Lahore Anarkali market and other Punjabi city centres, singing devotional songs and preaching against Christianity on the way.[1] Otherwise, Swami Dayanand Saraswati's *Satyarth Prakash*, with its violent attack on adversary traditions (including Christianity), 'represents not a solitary peak but a large and crowded plateau'.[2] Strife grew within a polemical atmosphere, as members of different communities sought to project their own truths against that of others, both within their own tradition in rivalry for internal leadership and beyond. It seems as if polemics satisfied those involved. In most writings one senses an element of enjoyment of 'the position of being unique, of being misunderstood, of being wronged by the whole world but knowing what is morally right, morally superior'.[3] Propaganda surely played a part in arousing militancy. It incited people to action on behalf of one or the other community, depicting with approval those who took violent steps against one's own tradition and those of other communities. Lay leaders themselves often gave the example. Sometimes they did this through militancy in public speeches and print, at other times, by inciting their followers to militant actions through provocation. The latter could mean, for example, disruption of others' meetings, ceremonies, processions, personal abuse of members of other communities, and attacks on individuals and their property. Certainly the unprecedented socio-political changes under the Pax Britannica played a vital role. Now at least one had the right to differ in public because officially the government gave universal protection by law to all, even minorities. Accordingly, appeals often were made in terms of narrowly defined numerical strength, while ideals and values were generally seen within a limited scope, serving the well-being of the community and those trying to break away from existing societal norms.

Most significantly, as a crucial feature of the colonial interaction, reformers took a comparative moral standpoint with regard to other traditions beginning with Christianity and its moralizing towards Indian society. As always, Arya Samajis were at the vanguard and many of their arguments were drawn from the *Satyarth Prakash*. In this seminal work, Dayanand discussed Christianity and its errors in response to Christian missionaries who had rejected his form of Vedic Hinduism.[4] Many concepts were unknown to the Swami, like for example the making of the universe; God's creation of man in his own image; and the concepts of inherited sin and immaculate conception. No doubt one of the most repugnant Biblical customs to Saraswati and upper caste Hindus in general was the eating of meat (i.e. the Cain and Abel story). Often Dayanand responded with a degree of pragmatism to these unfamiliar ideas. This certainly was a practice all communities, including Christian missionaries, followed towards each other. Hence a description of circumcision again demonstrated to him that the Christian God lacked foresight. Why otherwise would he first create foreskins and afterwards declare them unnecessary and to be removed? Also Saraswati could not understand why Christians depended on such a powerless figure as Jesus Christ who failed to protect himself or others; the Last Supper was most repugnant to him: disciples do not eat their Gurus![5]

A disputation was held at the 1877 Chandapur fair. There, the Swami took part in a public discussion together with two Christian Reverends, including his friend T.J. Scott, and some learned Muslims, among whom was Maulana Muhammad Qasim Nanawatani, the founder of the Deoband theological academy. For two days they discussed topics such as the creation of the universe and salvation. As always, Saraswati's main method of attack consisted of a simplistic literal interpretation of Biblical passages. This was in sheer contrast to the rules of interpretation he suggested in the introduction of the *Satyarth Prakash*.[6] To give one characteristic example. Reverend Scott replied to Dayanand's definition of salvation (*mukti*) as emancipation from pain that this also was possible for Hindus during the contemporary era of sin and corruption (*Kali Yuga*) 'if they will only put their faith in Jesus'.[7] Naturally Saraswati had heard the key Christian doctrine of redemption (faith in Christ as the only means of securing salvation) before and criticized it in turn, especially because of the (for him) unacceptable idea of sin. Also he detested the idea of Satan as the tempter: 'If Satan is everybody's tempter, who was Satan's tempter? If you reply, that he was tempted by himself, then I say that the same could be said with equal force in respect of human beings. In such case, it is useless to believe in Satan as the tempter.'[8]

Furthermore, the Swami continued, if Satan was tempted by someone else (i.e. God), then who would be the saviour? Such a thing is 'against the divine nature, for God is just and true, and his actions are always just, and he can never be a tempter'.[9] As part of the newly emerging dominant social consciousness and modes of communication, disputes such as these were crucial to the spread of moral languages. One experimented with ideas, which being sharpened, often were put into print (newspapers in particular) and, what should be stressed, read in public to spark the public consciousness.[10] In this way, reformers not only consciously defined themselves and others, but also created specific forms of rationality, if only because these were constrained by thinking in the vernacular language and by traditional morality. More often than not, communication meant firmly making a point (i.e. to be biased but strong instead of open and amenable), not to communicate but to gain authority and influence. This situation especially seemed to be the case in the dialogues between Indians and British missionaries because of language barriers and completely different cultural back-grounds. No doubt the missionaries knew what they stood for and wanted for the 'improvement' of India.

Interestingly, while Christianity and Islam have a long history of disputations, Mirza Ghulam Ahmad not only used many of the arguments against Christianity as put forward by Dayanand Saraswati in the *Satyarth Prakash*, but, for his reinterpretation of Islam, went one step further than other Muslim polemicists by accepting and revising parts of the Christian tradition. Probably the best example remains the one about the death of Jesus in Kashmir in connection with the second coming of Christ, and Ghulam Ahmad's claim to be the Promised Messiah. Ahmad argued that Jesus did not die on the cross, or rise from the death and ascend to heaven. According to him the Gospels were corrupt: Jesus was taken down from the cross seemingly dead but in reality in a swoon, recovered from his wounds, and after a long journey arrived in Kashmir where he led a normal life until his death. The Mirza identified the tomb of Yus Asaf in Srinagar as the place where Jesus was buried.[11] Otherwise, Mirza Ghulam Ahmad kept to discussions characteristic of the times. In *How to get rid of the Bondage of Sin*, for example, he straight-forwardly bashed Christian Europe:

Nineteen hundred years have elapsed since the blood of Jesus was first introduced into the world as a patent sin-healing remedy, but instead of doing any good it has proved harmful to society and intensified the evil which it affected to mitigate. Are we still to believe that faith in the blood of Jesus delivers man from the bondage of sin. . . . The two great vices in which grow up all carnal passions are drinking and prostitution, and it is in Christian nations that we find their worst development. The majority of the inhabitants of Europe are involved in these two vices, and there is no exaggeration in the assertion that in drunkenness Europe beats all the vastly populated countries of Asia, and a single city of Europe has a larger number of public-houses than the total number of shops of all sorts in an Asiatic town.[12]

It was about time for Christians to grow up and leave behind their archaic doctrines, Ghulam Ahmad continued, because 'the suicide of a Messiah has no conceivable relation to the remission of another man's sins'.[13] Likewise he argued in relation to Christian salvation that it was amazing that 'in this age of reason' the missionaries preached the 'childish doctrines' of Jesus' freedom from sin and atonement through his blood which 'on account of their absurdity are rejected by every sensible person'.[14]

On the whole, there were few disputes between Singh Sabhaites and the British. A relationship between Sikhs and Christian missionaries had existed before the firm establishment of British rule. Maharaja Ranjit Singh had invited Christian missionaries to his court. After annexation, the British treated the former rulers of the Punjab with respect. In the words of the contemporary Punjabi historian, Muhammad Latif, 'the British government did all it consistently could to mitigate the reverses of the feudal nobility of the defunct Sikh realm. They received handsome pensions, their hereditary claims were recognized, and they were treated with consideration and regard by the officers of Government.'[15] Generally the British believed that the martial Sikhs were people who knew their duty, like themselves: Sikhs were hard workers, and good farmers and soldiers, loyal during the 1857 Revolt. Otherwise, most members of the Amritsar Singh Sabha received missionary education and Lahori Singh Sabhaites worked closely together with Macauliffe in the making of *The Sikh Religion*. Because of this close and loyal relationship with both the government and the missionaries, Singh Sabhaites were not involved in arguments against Christianity. Instead, they aimed at strengthening and intensifying the loyalty of Sikhs to the Tat Khalsa in opposition to Punjabi popular culture, Hinduism (the Arya Samaj) and non-Khalsa Sikh traditions—not at all against their traditional enemies, the Muslims! All the same, in the novels of Bhai Vir Singh the Sikh tradition is always portrayed as superior and Christians, Hindus and Muslims inevitably end up embracing the Sikh faith.

In addition to that of the Christian missionaries, the presence of the Arya Samaj boosted comparative argumentation. Their writing and preaching against Islam led to much antagonism among Hindus against Muslims and Christians. Most important in this context was the cow protection movement begun by Dayanand Saraswati in 1882 in the Punjab.[16] It followed his famous statement on cow protection, *Gokarunanidhi* (1880), which interestingly was based on economic rather than spiritual grounds. A sacred animal in the Hindu tradition, officially the cow is treated with reverence and is not killed, though as everyone in South Asia can see, generally walking around more dead than alive. The five products of the cow (milk, clarified butter, curds, urine and dung) are regarded as purifying and small quantities of these products might be ingested in a ritual context. In *Gokarunanidhi*, nonetheless, Dayanand Saraswati particularly stressed the economic value of milk, clarified butter and curds to the Hindu diet, cow urine as a cleansing agent and dried cow dung as fuel.[17] In many north Indian towns societies for the protection of cows (*Gauraksha Sabhas*) by Aryas and other Hindus were established. In 1888, however, the North-Western Provincial High Court at Allahabad made clear that the cow was not a sacred object and hence was not protected by the colonial state. Increasingly, both Muslims and Europeans were described as barbarian cow eaters by Arya Samajis in particular and the slaughtering of cows became a burning issue often accompanied by violence. Although the main targets of Swami Dayanand Saraswati initially were orthodox Hindu practices and Christianity, he gave more space in his *Satyarth Prakash* to attacks on Islam. Like Christianity, Dayanand argued, Islam knew a greater God, sin, judgement, salvation and miracles and both therefore were superstitious faiths unfit for modern man. Unlike later Arya Samajis and Hindu patriots, however, Dayanand did not mention the historic confrontation between Islam and Hinduism in negative terms. Characteristically, he limited himself to the literal interpretation of the scriptures.

Likewise, large portions of Mirza Ghulam Ahmad's *Barahin-i-Ahmadiyah* argued systematically against the statements of the Arya Samaj, especially as proclaimed by Dayanand in the *Satyarth Prakash*. In fact, he even wrote a letter to Saraswati

offering him a copy of the *Barahin-i-Ahmadiyah* to debate over
the truth of Islam and its superiority over Hinduism. Dayanand
did not respond, and some time later Ghulam Ahmad reported
a dream (as he regularly did) in which he saw Dayanand dying
(as happened soon afterwards). Before that time, nonetheless,
the Ahmadiyahs were already considered major enemies of the
Punjabi Aryas, resulting in fierce disputation between Pandit
Lekh Ram and Mirza Ghulam Ahmad.[18]

In 1885 Lekh Ram first wrote to Ahmad from Amritsar saying
he would like to come to Qadiyan to see Ahmad perform
heavenly signs. Afterwards confrontations started between the
two, ending in the murder of one of them twelve years later.
Born a Brahman in the Jhelum district, Lekh Ram was educated
in Urdu and Persian by Muslims and subsequently used his
knowledge of these languages and Islam to condemn everything
Islamic. Lekh Ram became an important Arya Samaj spokesman
and wrote numerous books and pamphlets on such issues as
cow protection, the need of *niyog*, salvation and the promotion
of Hindi. Yet his real struggle was with Islam and Ghulam
Ahmad in particular. In 1887 he attacked the latter for the first
time in 'Refutation of Ahmadiyah Proofs' with the provoca-tive
subtitle 'A Gunfire to Break the Flanks and Tyranny of
Mohammad's Islam'. Subsequently a tract warfare followed
between the two reformers in which each subsequent tract led
to a counter attack. Lekh Ram's most famous polemic tract,
nonetheless, was against Islam in general: 'The Epistle of *Jihad*
or the Foundation of the Muhammadan Religion', published in
Lahore in 1892. In it, he incorporated paragraphs of the *Satyarth
Prakash* charging Islam with violence, slaughter and liking of
loot. Unlike Dayanand, Lekh Ram also turned to history for
ammunition, blaming all India's ills on the devastation of the
early Muslim invader, Mahmud of Ghazni.[19] While the Pandit's
controversies with Ghulam Ahmad had only limited effects
outside Ahmadiyah circles, his 'The Epistle of *Jihad*' irritated a
wide section of the Muslim community. Overall Lekh Ram's
activities contributed greatly to the growth of confrontation in
the Punjab and soon he was attacked in Muslim, Sikh and
Christian newspapers. Finally it was violence that brought an
end to his career: he was assassinated on the 6 March 1897.

Immediately a debate followed between the different communities, as Aryas celebrated him as a martyr whose crusade had to be continued. Ghulam Ahmad put some coal on the fire by thanking God for the fulfilment of his prophecy ten years earlier that Lekh Ram would die a violent death.[20] Several newspapers angrily suggested Ghulam Ahmad's complicity in the event because of his prophecy and the rumour spread that he had asked the government (instead of God) for protection because he feared an Arya plot against his life. Riots followed as throughout the province it was said that all leading Aryas would be assassinated, Muslims were conspiring to kill Sikh and Hindu leaders and the latter would seek revenge in return. Within three months, nonetheless, life returned to its normal pace, though controversy between the Ahmadiyahs and the Arya Samaj continued during the lifetime of Ghulam Ahmad and after.

Compared to Christians and Muslims Dayanand Saraswati was much less interested in Sikhism, and in a few pages of the *Satyarth Prakash* dismissed the tradition as being just one of the many Hindu cults. But not all Aryas thought as Dayanand. Instead, they saw the tradition in comparative terms as paralleling the Samaj in its aim to purify the Hindu tradition of idolatry, caste and the evils of Brahmanical dominance. Other young educated Sikhs reacted to the Samaj with interest. This changed however when from 1887 onwards, Aryas started to interfere directly in internal Sikh affairs. Not only did they want to have a voice in the location of Khalsa College but they also started to convert Sikhs in public ceremonies which included the cutting of hair.[21] Boundaries between the communities began to be clearly drawn when Arya Samajis unleashed a campaign of criticism questioning the validity of the Granth Sahib and spreading abuse of the Gurus. The whole process was boosted by the critical speech Guru Datta Vidyarthi gave on Sikhism to the assembly at the Lahore Arya Samaj anniversary celebration on 25 November 1888. Sikhs who earlier had been sympathetic to the Arya Samaj turned their backs on the movement and joined the Lahore Singh Sabha, becoming fanatic defenders of the Tat Khalsa. Singh Sabhaites held a large protest meeting, condemning the Arya Samajis and specifically Pandit Guru Datta. Soon afterwards the controversy moved to the press, where Sikh and non-Sikh papers denounced the Samaj for its habit of aggressively condemning other traditional leaders and doctrines.[22]

Ever more, Singh Sabhaites, Arya Samajis, and Ahmadiyahs asserted themselves in public, creating and stressing stereotypes of the other at the same time. Leading Muslims and Sikhs came to emphasize more what distinguished them from other communities than what they shared with them because they wondered how they could sustain their communities now that they no longer wielded state power. The fact that reformers more and more said what they thought, once more makes clear that certain forms of rational knowledge increasingly defined a social consciousness crucial to the emergence of a liberal public sphere. Because the Raj exercised such tight control over access to state institutions, it seems Indians were increasingly inclined to step forward into the public sphere through voluntary activities involving discussions about sacred space, conduct and ceremonies.

Whatever the full case, no doubt decisive were the activities and polemics of Christian missionaries, heightened by those of the Arya Samaj. Once again, protestant evangelicalism was provocative and disruptive. Under the banner of the civilizing mission, local traditions were attacked and the Christian word spread. This had profound consequences, as Punjabi reformers reacted in turn. Above all, the position of the Arya Samaj remains pivotal because in its need for self-legitimacy within the orthodox Hindu tradition, its leading members directly attacked Muslims, the Ahmadiyahs in particular, who found themselves in a similar isolated position within Islam. As a result, as Harald Fischer-Tiné puts it, the martyrdom of Pandit Lekh Ram 'earned the reformers more sympathy than any other of their activities till then' and anti-Islamic bias became 'a constant feature of the Arya Samaj policy'.[23]

Arguments heated up in the print media with the growing tendency to rationality among reformers. In general, one knew more about each other. An ever increasing amount of information became available, circulated faster than before because of new modes of communication and was officially made public by state authorities. Though this drew more people in, simultaneously the growth and style of disputations showed communities becoming more inward looking. In many instances open books indeed led to closed minds. Scriptures of other traditions were read literally, with no desire to discover positive qualities in them nor to discuss points of mutual concern or elements of similarity. For how could the other be right, if one had clear images of how the world ought to be and knew what constituted a good society? Indeed surprising in relation to this adherence to scriptural literalism, remains the fact that it never occurred to the protagonists that 'those most thoroughly committed to their faith would be the least likely to abandon it'.[24]

Contemporary Punjabi polemics certainly have been discussed comprehensively elsewhere.[25] Here it is solely my aim to stress some crucial underlying features of the dominant contemporary social consciousness through which debates became increasingly rational, comparative and competitive. The emergence of a liberal public sphere under the supervision of the colonial power accelerated an atmosphere of growing fervour, impatience, militancy and turbulence. Punjabi leaders consciously took a respondent position not only towards the British and Western ideas but, it cannot be stressed enough, also towards one another. For the game of politics of difference could yield rewards in terms of representation or acts of positive discrimination. All of course only if the game was played fairly and for that purpose obviously loyalty to the British was favourable.

LOYALTY TO THE GOVERNMENT AND BEYOND

The British government defined a territorial space for interaction between itself and numerous Indian communities, and for the latter among themselves. In line with the idea that 'nations do not make states and nationalisms but the other way around',[26] this led to a growth of a territorial patriotism among Indians from a specific region and community. These politics of belonging were novel, directly encouraged by the administration, and by representative politics in particular. Yet, the British were foreign rulers: how did they gain the loyalty of their Indian subjects in the first place? Most Indians barely thought about the legitimacy of British rule: 'it was accepted because it was there and apparently successful', while alternately the Mughals had lost credibility as they lost power.[27] The reverence for the Mughal ruler was transferred to Queen Victoria when she became Empress of India, and in a sense replaced the Mughal Emperor at the apex of the existing hierarchical structure in which many Indians lived.[28] Crucial to this process then was that from the very beginning the British, who obsessively wanted to reorder the societies they ruled according to an image of their own class hierarchies, had been sensitive to the problem of their public image; of the visible demonstration of authority, with their insistence on status, and meticulous attention to rank and precedence and its public display.[29] Furthermore, while prominent local men participated in the colonial state bureaucracy 'the British could assume that the clients and social inferiors of such men would follow suit'.[30] By and large, the British received loyalty from the Indian elite because they unconsciously participated in the public sphere, over time especially through representative politics. Now that the state had made political arrangements that gave its subjects a voice, one had to step forward and claim the rights of the community in order to be authoritative and influential. In result, Indians often accepted the uniform and bureaucratically useful categories of difference as defined by the British. One was either Hindu, Muslim or Sikh and had to be loyal both to the community and to the political structures supervised by the state. Political participation helped to solve the problem of how the Anglo-Indian colonial state could acquire legitimacy in the eyes of its subjects, even if these were disaffected. Yet, because traditions and old patriotisms often found each other in a moral attitude,[31] there simultaneously emerged alternative forces in South Asia that proved equally able to mobilize people and so increasingly compete for the loyalty of which the state claimed to be the only legitimate repository.

During the period of social reform, nonetheless, the political spirit in South Asia still was very much that of loyalty to the British. This is critical because it provides a sign of the Indian involvement in the making of a public sphere. Some general ideas among the Indian elite for example were that the colonial state provided security and justice, would take care of its subjects (through public health and in times of famine), guarantee equal access to education and eliminate the inequalities of the caste system. The civilizing mission was particularly accepted in the idea that it was education that fostered a true community spirit and guaranteed improvement. This resulted in a social consciousness of being independent and strong of will as individual and community. Illustrative is the case of Altaf Husain Hali, who in his most famous work, *Musaddas* (1879), straightforwardly praised British rule for opening up the roads to progress.[32] Therefore also, he continued, 'there is no condition worse than the community becoming a complete burden upon the Empire, and its subjects being in its hands like a corpse in the grasp of a body-washer'.[33] Thus, partly in the footsteps of the Christian missionaries, many Indians devoted themselves to the service of their community (called *seva* by Hindus and Sikhs), while being conscious that the community also was supporting them. Likewise, social work became a competitive exercise. Practices such as orphan and famine relief were connected with the desire to contest the conversion activities of other communities (especially of the Christian missionaries of course). Much of the moral polemic of the *Musaddas* indeed stresses those very virtues which promulgated the contemporary spirit of the civilizing mission. While the *shariat* and *hadith* are seen to prefigure significant aspects of the European liberal rhetoric of improvement, values such as self-help are seen to be foreshadowed by the morality of the Prophet's message, i.e. 'legitimized and re-deployed in the figure of the Prophet'.[34] At least in this case, therefore, the *Musaddas* appears to be rebutting the stereotype of Orientals lacking that individual and community virtue of self-discipline which the British so prided themselves on, by re-inscribing that virtue as part of the Prophet's original message. The final message of the poem, nonetheless, remains that the ultimate solution to the community's problems lay not so much in education and industrious self-help as in a renewal of the Islamic faith through passionate devotion to the Prophet.[35]

Many Indian reformers and politicians ultimately accepted British moral superiority and took the values of the civilizing mission as a point of reference. Altaf Husain Hali's notion of self-help therefore was much similar to the ideas of *swadeshi* and *swaraj* that were increasingly propagated by Arya Samajis and by members of the Indian National Congress under the leadership of Mahatma Gandhi.[36] In *Hind Swaraj* (1909), for example, Gandhi presented a double concept of *swaraj* whereby moral self-discipline is seen as seminal to Indian independence. More interesting to this study remains the similar position taken by the leading Arya Samaji Swami Shraddhanand, who in fact throughout north India was widely respected as a Mahatma (great soul) before this title was given to Gandhi, with whom during 1919-22 he worked together in the Satyagraha movement:

We advocate *swaraj* or self-government but not in the lower sense. True *swaraj* is dominion over the self, self-conquest, the thorough control of concupiscence and the lower passions. If the individuals composing a nation are devoid of this kind of *swaraj*, political *swaraj* becomes a curse instead of a blessing and brings in its train widespread misery and corruption instead of social happiness, material gains and intellectual tranquility.[37]

What remains most crucial in relation to these cases of moral self pre-occupation (and for example the greater *jihad* among Muslims mentioned in Chapter Three) is that most authors are more concerned with locating the sources of weakness in the Indian self than with putting the blame on British avarice or deceit.[38] So Mahatma Gandhi for example argued that Indian moral failure was responsible for the British conquest of the subcontinent:

The English have not taken India; we have given it to them. They are not in India because of their strength, but because we keep them. . . . Recall the Company *Bahadur*. Who made it *Bahadur*? They had not the slightest intention at the time of establishing a kingdom. Who assisted the Company's officers? Who was tempted at the sight of their silver? Who bought their goods? History testifies that we did all this. . . . When our Princes fought among themselves, they sought assistance of Company *Bahadur*. That corporation was versed alike in commerce and war. It was unhampered by questions of morality. . . . It is not then useless to blame the English for what we did at the time? . . . it is truer to say that we gave India to the English than that India was lost.[39]

Indian social consciousness during the period of social reform certainly was ambivalent. On the one hand, traditional identities were more firmly defined than ever in reaction to a fast changing society and increasingly out of protest against British rule. On the other, one's own moral stature was negatively perceived and instead the moral values of the British civilizing mission were highly admired and often adopted. This ambivalence was most vital to the making of a liberal public sphere and state formation. It confirms the important point made by Ashis Nandy that within a colonial culture 'the ruled are constantly tempted to fight their rulers within the psychological limits set by the latter'.[40] This partly because, as Dirk Kolff rightly stressed, it is difficult not to speak the language of power when one wants to retain some control over one's own future.[41]

By this time, the public sphere in British India not only epitomized moral values such as self-help, duty, *seva*, and improvement but, above all, became dominated by scientific rationality. This was exemplified in the ever increasing adherence to numbers. In relation to the latter, the census operations of the colonial ruler in the Punjab since 1853 were decisive.[42] Although a normal function of any modern government, mostly to make taxation more effective, what needs to be stressed is that the Indian census was dominated by the category religion. This was not the case in Europe for example, where the focus was on language. Accordingly, the decennial census became a crucial reference point for Indian reformers, as it recorded and showed the progress or decline of each community, and was eagerly awaited, closely read and cited.[43] In fact, Indians not only used these British defined categories; they also played a central role in the further definition and spread of them. Gurukul Aryas such as Pandit Lekh Ram rejected the name Hindu, feeling that it was a derogative label given to them by the followers of Islam. Instead they wished to be known as Arya and hence instructed their followers to write Arya instead of Hindu in the 1891 census questionnaires.[44] In the same way, after the 1891 census reported the numbers of Ahl-i-Hadiths and Wahhabis for the Punjab but did not mention the Ahmadiyahs in spite of their description in the *Gurdaspur District Gazetteer*, Ghulam Ahmad wanted his followers to be enumerated separately (as happened) under the category of Ahmadiyah in the next census. Otherwise changes in census definitions often boosted animosity. Until the 1901 census, for example, in line with the Tat Khalsa ideology, only Khalsa Sikhs were defined as Sikhs.[45] When the government expanded this definition with the 1911 census, it not only led to a considerable expansion of the number of Sikhs at the expense of Hindus but, more importantly, vehement reactions from Hindus (under Arya Samaj leadership) as well.

Significantly, because of political representation, the Punjab bureaucracy became a focus of antagonism from the 1880s onwards. Anglo-vernacular education was crucial to government work. Yet, as each community increasingly offered English and local-language education in their own institutions, this not only strengthened awareness of community boundaries but, importantly, contributed to an oversupply of candidates for government employment. Clearly Muslims lagged behind in the race for education and employment and accordingly they hoped that the 1882 Hunter Education Commission would lead to scholarships and other favours for their community. The reaction of the 'neutral' government nonetheless was the same as always: every Punjabi had equal opportunities and if Muslims could not compete they must 'go to the wall'.[46] As riots heated up the situation, some Punjab officers suggested that more qualified Muslims should be brought into the administration to prevent total Hindu domination, reduce Muslim militancy, and create circumstances in which Hindus and Muslims could constantly observe and check each other's actions. In 1899, a scheme was created to raise the number of Muslims in several government posts until it equalled that of Hindus.

On the whole, the Punjab government gradually furthered political representation through the introduction of separate electorates: first in the municipal committees and in 1909 in the Punjab legislative council (the scope of which was extended by the 1919 and 1935 Government of India Acts). Interestingly, in the Punjab the British always rejected the introduction of separate electorates for the rural district boards, because stability of the rural areas from where recruits for the British Indian army were drawn was too important. This refers to the protection by the

British of tribal identities mentioned in Chapter One, whereby the 1900 Alienation of Land Act 'formed the basis for a rural political hierarchy in which religious solidarity was relegated to a secondary role'.[47] Moreover, following the 1935 Government of India Act the borders of the constituencies in the countryside were redrawn 'so that they coincided with *tahsils* strengthening the importance of the "tribal" idiom of politics'.[48] Still, during the first decade of the twentieth century, British officials noted that throughout the Punjab there was a lack of interest in the elections for the district boards: 'both candidates and voters appear to be equally apathetic' and 'generally speaking, appointment is considered more honourable than canvassing for voters'.[49]

The Indian Councils Act of 1909, better known as the Morley-Minto reforms, was announced on the fiftieth anniversary of Queen Victoria's Proclamation. Sixty Indian representatives were to be elected to the Viceroy's executive councils and between thirty and fifty to the provincial legislative councils, where they believed they could work for the interests of their countrymen. Electoral procedures were deliberately designed to achieve a balance of all minority interests. This much to the regret of the members of the Indian National Congress, who argued that representation should not be based on differences in religion. Instead, they wanted a representative government with the will of the numerical majority being the will of the people. Yet, political unity, law and order, were the result of the Pax Britannica, the British argued, and India was not a nation but a subcontinent full of nations. As John Strachey put it:

This is the first and most essential thing to learn about India, that there is not, and never was an India, or even any country of India possessing, according to European ideas, any sort of unity, physical, political, social or religious; no Indian nation, no 'people of India,' of which we hear so much.[50]

With the Morley-Minto reforms, the government openly declared that it was determined to help Muslims by providing them with more seats in the constituencies than they were entitled to by population. A crucial decision because it not only gave Muslims the status of an all India political category but simultaneously condemned them to being a perpetual minority in any scheme of constitutional reform. It meant the establishment of majority rule ever since. Moreover, as Muslim leaders expected favouritism and protection up to Partition, Hindus became increasingly embittered by official efforts to maintain equal representation.

The creation of separate electorates has been widely discussed,[51] but the fact that they were vital to the relationship between the seemingly discordant idioms of moral languages and politics of belonging remains understudied. In the opinion of David Gilmartin, 'the election process was, in fact, critical to the re-conceptualization of community that made the merging of religious and national visions of community possible'.[52] Elections formed a new public arena to be exploited through new forms of political rhetoric to get people in line. Not only were they important as a straightforward political act but particularly also for their ritual and ceremonial aspects. Divisive overtones gained strength as communities came to see each other in the terminology of majority and minority. Accordingly, there emerged a distinctive image of the relationship between the individual and community in terms of loyalty, duty and sacrifice.[53] What should be emphasized is that in such cases as the calls for *swadeshi* and *swaraj*, the Sikh-Akali and Hindu-Muslim Khilafat movements, this moral appeal opposed the supposedly objective morality propagated by the British through state institutions. As a result, in the context of a liberal public sphere, the earlier discussed comparative moral polemics simultaneously often came to dispute state power in foreign hands.

More and more, Indian elites saw the colonial state as a backer of rights, privileges and claims on resources. This meant that when claims were not delivered, these were demanded vociferously. Consequently, the British authorities received an increasing stream of petitions for arbitration from the different communities. These ranged from issues such as representation and rights, the establishment and management of educational, publishing and other societies, procession routes, killing of cows, playing of music anywhere at any time (Hindus in front of the mosque on a sacred Islamic day for example) and the language to be used in school. Petitions were crucial to the routinization of the liberal public sphere in South Asia. Through them one could be critical of the government, as long as the language was polite and loyal. By petitioning one accepted justice from the government and correspondence reached a wider audience when published in newspapers. Though the Punjab government remained officially neutral, it obviously became involved after taking decisions on all kind of issues. In the eyes of the government the most constant danger to law and order over time, however, did not come from the Indian National Congress, whose members did their best to cooperate on liberal terms. Problematic instead were the communal controversies that often led to so-called irrational riots, repeatedly called disorders or disturbances at the time. Therefore the most banned literature in the Punjab was related to religion, while a considerable amount of Congress writing circulated freely in the region. All in all, voluntary movements that participated in the public sphere and kept to law and order could expect to be protected under the government's policy of religious neutrality declared in Queen Victoria's proclamation. Those who questioned British authority, however, were suspect and subject to official control.

As said earlier, compared to the Hindu and Muslim communities, the British did not have much trouble with the Sikhs. They even harnessed the Tat Khalsa identity to service in the British Indian army by insisting that all Sikh soldiers should have long hair and a beard. Also every army division had its own scripture reader and gurdwara attendance was made obligatory.[54] Nonetheless, this mutual loyalty was threatened with the Akali movement. Since annexation, the British always had supported the traditional custodians of the Golden Temple. Hence, when in 1905 Sikh reformers succeeded in removing Hindu statues from its precincts, the government became increasingly involved in contemporary Sikh politics. In 1911, for instance, David Petrie of the British government's Criminal Investigation Department (CID) compiled a secret memorandum on contemporary Sikh politics and in particular was negative about Tat Khalsa reformers (including Bhai Vir Singh), whom he labelled as 'neo-Sikhs' who had much in common with Arya Samaj politicians.[55] The First World War cooled things down but in 1920 a proclamation was made from the Golden Temple that a committee was to be set up to manage all Sikh shrines, the Shiromani Gurdwara Parbandhak Committee (SGPC). Almost simultaneously some Sikhs voluntarily organized themselves to wrest gurdwaras away from their custodians. The Akali Dal (band of immortals) clashed with the Army and was declared illegal. Mahatma Gandhi praised the self-sacrifice of the Akalis as exemplary for the struggle against British rule and hence the SGPC temporarily associated itself with the national movement. Finally, the battle was won in the Punjab Legislative Council with the support of non-Sikh (Hindu and Muslim) nationalist leaders. In 1925 the Sikh Gurdwara Act was passed and placed gurdwaras in the custody of the SGPC. Statutory restraints were placed on the participation of the SGPC in politics but in practice the Akali Dal (as a political party) and the SGPC (as custodian of the shrines) generally worked together. In fact, the first established complete control over the latter and so put the Gandhian hierarchy of values upside down.

Unlike their stand on the Sikhs, the British were suspicious about the Arya Samaj almost from the beginning. Officially the movement was in no way political, but the domination of the Punjab Congress (from 1898 until 1907) by the Samaj and its militancy in general made that it was closely watched by the government. This particularly during the so-called disturbances of 1907 which led to the six-month deportation of Lala Lajpat Rai to Burma. The trouble centred on proposals for higher charges and stricter regulations for settlers in the canal colonies. The measures were an additional burden for already hard pressed farmers and provoked an unforeseen wave of agitation which united Punjabi landowners and peasants. Newspapers protested and there were meetings attended by thousands and addressed by Lajpat Rai and other political leaders. For the first time since 1857, the government was confronted by a widespread popular movement that, and this was deeply alarming, was gaining ground among the peasantry. Lieutenant-Governor Ibbetson thought that the protests were signs of a massive conspiracy. He deported the leading agitators and imposed press censorship. Afterwards, however, the potential danger to the loyalty and discipline of Punjabi soldiers in particular made Viceroy Minto veto the Punjabi legislation. The lesson to be learned was that the Raj could no longer take for granted the passive acquiescence of those thought to be its most faithful supporters. After his return from Burma and following the disintegration of the Punjabi Congress after the national split between moderates and extremists, Lajpat Rai laid the foundation for Hindu politics as an alternative to Congress politics. He opposed separate electorates and felt that the Congress had let down the Hindu community, especially in the Punjab where the Hindus were in a minority. On the whole, the Arya Samaj shaped the political attitudes of Punjabi Hindus by giving them an interpretation of India's past, providing a vision of and pride in the Hindu nation (*Arya Varta*) and suggesting remedies for India's miserable economic conditions. Lajpat Rai said he was first a Hindu and then an Indian. Also he argued that in order to create *Arya Varta*, Indians had to stop mimicking the West and instead should rely upon their own traditions and go for *swadeshi* and *swaraj*.[56] Japan's victory over Russia in 1904, being the first time an Asian country defeated a Western one, undoubtedly served as a source of inspiration to extend the call for *swadeshi* towards that of *swaraj*. Interestingly, it is this call combined with the British promise of self-government that, indeed in opposition to the earlier mentioned idea that 'nations do not make states and nationalisms but the other way around',[57] subsequently made Lajpat Rai (and probably most Indian nationalists) question state hegemony:

The German theory of the supremacy of the State over the nation must be repudiated, and the future citizen should be trained to think that the nation is superior to and in every way the master of the State. She determines the form of the State and is free to change it as, in her corporate capacity, and by her corporate will, she wishes to.[58]

In his writings Lajpat Rai reinterpreted the Hindu tradition to make it suitable to the times. In *The Message of the Bhagavad Gita* (1908), he argued that a nation's prosperity and success depended 'upon wisdom like that of Krishna and on bravery like that of Arjuna' and accordingly that Indians would find salvation in the disinterested performance of their duty, without attachments to its fruits, at any cost and any risk: 'if ever any nation stood in need of a message like that of Krishna, it is the Indians of today' and so 'let them invoke his aid by acting up to his message'.[59] In 1909, prominent Aryas founded the Punjab Provincial Hindu Sabha, which in 1915 became the Sarvadeshik (pan-regional) Hindu Sabha and in 1921 the all India Hindu Mahasabha (great council). The latter actively nurtured the Hindu extremists of the Rashtriya Swayamsevak Sangh (better known as RSS), founded in 1925. Hence, it is through the Hindu Mahasabha, that the Arya Samaj and the RSS find a line of historical continuity as Hindu political movements. Thus, despite the fact that, like Mahatma Gandhi, Arya Samajis made available patriotic Hindu terminology to a wider public, the relationship between the Punjab Congress and the Arya Samaj became increasingly tense. Instead of following the politics of Hindu-Muslim cooperation and national unity of the Khilafat movement, Arya Samajis increasingly favoured Hindu politics. This particularly under the leadership of Swami Shraddhanand, who in his *Hindu Sangathan: Saviour of a Dying Race* (1926) exposed the idea of Hindus being a 'dying race' because of conversions, Christian and particularly Muslim, and to which Hindu self-strengthening and solidarity (*sangathan*) was the answer.[60]

As for Mirza Ghulam Ahmad, throughout his life he pointed out to the government that he and his community were loyal subjects, and urged his followers to avoid political agitation and anti-British activity. Out of fear that the government would be misled by his enemies, he stressed that he belonged to a family that had always proved loyal to the British, professed a faith that taught loyalty to the government and condemned *jihad* in his writings because God forbade him to fight one.[61] Obviously, the Ahmadiyahs had more problems with the Muslim *ulema* than with the British. A closely knit organization, they did not belong to the mainstream of Islam, and other Muslims often blamed them for undermining Islamic solidarity and providing assistance to British rule. Ghulam Ahmad, for example, believed that Muslims owed no commitment to the Ottoman Caliph because he was only the symbol of an illegitimate institution.[62]

Accordingly, he showed much disapproval when the Turkish Vice-Consul visited Lahore and Qadian in 1897 (according to his enemies, because the vice-consul found him an imposter).[63] The Ahmadiyahs remained aloof from the Khilafat movement. Most crucial to the attitude of the British government towards the Ahmadiyahs, however, was Ghulam Ahmad's interpretation of the Islamic doctrine of *jihad*. Its centrality was related to the Mirza's involvement in polemic against the Christian missionaries and members of the Arya Samaj, who used the idea of *jihad* to describe Islam in an unfavourable, aggressive light. Ghulam Ahmad countered this idea by tracing the concept linguistically and in the early history of Islam, not just to restore *jihad* to its original meaning but also to make clear that, now that the Promised Messiah had arrived, it was the duty of every true Muslim to hold back from *jihad*.[64] After Ghulam Ahmad's death and especially the 1914 split, however, the Ahmadiyahs became increasingly entangled with the political issues of the day: the growing concern in India with self-government and the problem of Hindu-Muslim relations. In 1931, the earlier mentioned Ahmadiyah achiever *par excellence*, Zafrullah Khan, for example, stepped forward for one year as president of the Muslim League and was later appointed a member of the Viceroy's Executive Council. Increasingly self-conscious criticism of the British government became an element in Ahmadiyah policy. Yet the movement's attitude towards the struggle for independence by the Indian National Congress remained ambivalent. Though Mahmud Ahmad expressed his sympathy, he remained loyal to the British. The most volatile political issue in Ahmadiyah history is probably the declaration of all non-Ahmadiyah as infidels. Following Caliph Mahmud Ahmad's early statement mentioned in Chapter Three, it not only proved to be crucial to the split between the Qadianis and Lahoris but negatively affected the community's relationship with the wider world of Islam.

In sum, all three movements were trying to win British patronage, despite their increasing divisive overtones and transcendent yearnings. Often if actions of individuals threatened the image of loyalty, meetings were held and resolutions passed denouncing co members and pledging support for the Raj. I do not see the importance of an analysis in terms of collaboration, my point being solely to stress the continuity in the acceptance of the terminology of the civilizing mission propagated by the British in the public sphere. By being loyal, Punjabis accepted the supposedly progressive idiom in terms of political representation, elections, constitutional reform or otherwise. Pragmatically, patronage, social status and political participation were taken as crucial by all, particularly after the British gradually had to give in on the terms through which they themselves had defined Indian society. Such, for example, was what Lala Lajpat Rai wrote in his *The Political Future of India* (1919) in response to the Montagu-Chelmsford reforms (announced since 1917). While the reforms suspended *swaraj*, they declared that the introduction of 'responsible government' would be the direction of future imminent reforms. Though Lajpat Rai critically examined the contents of the proposed reforms, he found the often paternalistic political terminology proposed by the British acceptable. For, he argued, 'if the spirit of the announcement is translated into deeds it will be our duty to cooperate actively in constructive thought'.[65] Otherwise, while declaring themselves loyal to the Crown, Indian reformers often stressed that their movements were religious and not involved in politics, that their institutions and practices were pure. In this way, importantly, they adopted the Western notion of religion as separate from the temporal. Significant also remains the fact that British policy advanced divisions and militancy among communities, if only because the structures of the Raj generally encouraged a competitive style of politics. The participation of Arya Samajis in the Congress and subsequently in Hindu politics, encouraged the British to see them as disloyal and to draw economic sanctions against them. When Muslim politicians then also began to picture the Samajis as enemies of the government, Arya Samajis struck out: they described their Muslim accusers not only as greedy job seekers who called Hindus seditious in order to secure posts which under normal conditions they could never have, but accused them also of being disloyal to the British by definition, as the Koran demanded that Muslims would fight their *jihad*.[66] While communities thus increasingly opposed each other, support for the Punjab Congress declined and, instead, Hindu Sabhas, mostly led by Arya Samajis, moved into the public sphere. This was partly to counter similar organizations such as the Punjab Muslim League among Muslims. Otherwise, it remains necessary to emphasize that disputations between members of different communities, willingly or not, generally led to a growth of knowledge about each other. As part of the dominant contemporary Indian social consciousness, the elite absorbed modern scientific ideas and soon also gained knowledge about the wider political changes in the world. The central position of India within the British Empire was most crucial. It allowed the upper-class Indians to study, work or travel to other places in the Empire and, on their return, compare Indian society, with what they had seen elsewhere. In particular those who had studied in Britain after their return adopted British social conventions and moral standards. Yet, even though Indian elites transcended traditional cultural boundaries by incorporating Western thought, because of power differences and the racism of the colonizer and colonized they equally had to accept a respondent role in the making of their modern liberal society.

CONVERSION AND SOCIAL MOBILIZATION

As far as dogmatic high moral thinking is concerned, one's identity is determined by the group(s) one identifies with or, perhaps better, one cannot be disloyal to and still like oneself. Moreover, what makes you loyal to a smaller group may give you reason to cooperate in constructing a larger one, a group to which you may in time become equally or perhaps even more loyal. In reality, of course, the functioning of the individual remains a continuous struggle with ever shifting loyalties and leaving the majority in poor and violent South Asia without much individual choice. Even so, high moral thinking among Indian elites undoubtedly was crucial to the broader social mobilization in the public sphere since the late nineteenth century. To interest people you must provide a fight so that they get excited, take sides, become emotional, feel suspense and charge their moral convictions. Though British policy and the new modes of communication obviously worked as a catalyst in the process, reformers increasingly began to use sacred symbols to mobilize people to defend their own interest and to compete with other communities. Creating a powerful moral imperative, these sacred symbols gave a sense of self-respect and pride to a community as if it were an individual. In this way, as part of the dominant social consciousness among Indian elites, social mobilization more or less followed a growing pre-occupation with the times and often transcended regional interests. On the whole, what happened then in terms of identity formation does not much differ from the identity politics the modern world (obsessed with emancipation since the Enlightenment) has been familiar with.

Most significant to community politics and social mobilization, at least during the period of social reform, was the instance of conversion. Because communities increasingly defined boundaries among themselves and against Christian missionaries through their moral languages, conversion became pivotal to the stirring of Punjabi minds. Within the wider configuration of change in a public sphere under state supervision, community boundaries became directly related to (numerical) competition. This partly because the wider economic and social changes created niches for certain classes and castes to move up in the social hierarchy. Moral languages were important because these provided the material for the rhetoric by which possible converts could be persuaded to join the fold. Conversion thus became a core activity of identity politics, bringing together, for example, competitive adherence to numbers, social work (schools, orphanages, famine relief movements, etc.), education of missionaries and rhetorical polemics. By and large, conversion can be seen both in a spiritual sense (a change of consciousness and experience) as well as social practice ('moving out of one community to another' or 'shifting camp').[67] For a historical discussion, however, it is best to assume that conversion rarely involved an immediate spiritual experience and transformation but instead meant more 'a change of fellowship than of conduct or inner life—although the latter may in time occur'.[68]

The criticisms of Christian missionaries of Indian society created anxiety among indigenous leaders: it led to conflict over converts. Conversion to Christianity followed an earlier pattern taken in the Punjab. First, isolated high caste converts wanted modern education in English, to increase their status, to qualify for government services or legal, medical, engineering or teaching professions. Although they were few in number, they were responsible for far more public attention and reaction to Christian conversion than the numerically superior successes among the oppressed lower and outcastes.[69] The latter, in fact, were the only groups which actively sought out the missionaries. The close linkage between conversion and caste was highly significant. The egalitarian and individualistic notions of the Protestant evangelicals imbued them with a strong hostility to the institution of caste, which they regarded as integral to Hinduism (and to a much lesser extent Islam and Sikhism) and a hindrance to the spread of civilization. Converts therefore were expected to have a total break with their old social milieus, whereas alternatively missionaries hoped in downward filtration of the civilizing mission. The vast majority of Christian converts came from the outcast groups of Camars (leather workers) and Cuhras (sweepers), particularly the latter, in the central districts of the province.[70] Earlier, they had converted to Islam and Sikhism and now they responded to Christian proselytism. Adopting the Christian faith deed was not problematic for them. As one contemporary missionary, for example, put it in relation to the Camars:

They looked on Christianity merely as what they called a *panth*, and *panth* of religion, and not as a brotherhood. They have many of these non-Christian *panths* as followers of Kabir or Ram Dass or Nanak, the founder of the Sikhs; these they can follow without bringing women and children, they can believe in them without being outcast, and their faith in no way interferes with domestic and social customs connected with idolatry.[71]

In a society where the individual counts very little outside his group, conversion usually was a (male) group decision along caste lines, which not only provided much needed support and protection but was also extremely important for social intercourse and marriage among them. Converts continued to live in the same homes, in the same section of the village with the same neighbours and continued to do the same work in almost total dependence upon the landowners of the village. According to G.C. Walker, Cuhras 'generally adopted the religious tenets of the owners of the village in which they are settled'.[72] Traditionally, collective action among the depressed was undermined by their lack of horizontal group solidarity and unusually fragmented character. In fact, often they practised vertical solidarity by espousing the quarrels and factions of their masters. Also, upwardly mobile lower and outcast groups became fiercely competitive among each other. Nonetheless, Christian missionaries discovered that caste links could help rather than hinder evangelicalism. Accordingly, when conversions were in progress in a certain area, they deliberately left it to local initiative and 'confined their own activities to providing further instruction to those who had already made a profession of faith'.[73] The majority of Camars and Cuhras most likely became Christians in order to improve their social status and to remove the stigma of untouchability. As a Superintendent of the 1911 Punjab census, Pandit Harikishan Kaul, put it:

> The number of cases in which conversions are based on an intelligent recognition of the psychological superiority of an religion is never large, and converts to Christianity are not always free from the weaknesses of human nature. The depressed classes are in a condition of peculiar social and religious disadvantage and gain most by the equality of treatment preached and secured by the missions. Their status is raised. An untouchable becomes touchable by adopting Christianity, and has the satisfaction and advantage of receiving spiritual instructions from highly educated and sympathetic clergymen exactly in the same familiar way as his fellow-beings of the highest position. He can receive education and follow better pursuits than his degraded hereditary calling.[74]

Often 'converts also tended to view baptism as entering into a client-patron relationship with the missionaries whom they expected to be their protectors and problem-solvers'.[75] More important in the long term nonetheless was the link with the wider world provided by Christian conversion. First, because

Christian missionaries and subsequently Punjabi reformers preached in the villages, one came to know more about what was happening in their society. Second, because mission schools had low fees and no caste preferences they were particularly attractive for lower and outcastes as a way out to a better life. Third, following the 1901 Alienation of Land Act, conversion to Christianity or the Arya Samaj was about the only possibility for overwhelmingly agricultural Punjabi outcastes to obtain land (mainly in the canal colonies).[76]

As part of the civilizing mission, the freedom of conversion and the protection of the rights of converts was a logical corollary to the official British policy of religious neutrality. In South Asia, the breaking of caste rules and the giving up of one's faith traditionally were serious crimes to be punished, for example, by excommunication and the loss of property or the right to inheritance. It was the duty of the British to protect the victims and, hence, despite many protests and petitions, since the mid-nineteenth century, reforming measures officially guaranteed converts the possession of property and the right to inherit.[77] All the same, as Gauri Viswanathan argues, Anglo-Indian law in many cases insisted on difference: 'even when Hindus or Muslims were converting to Christianity, the decisions made by the civil courts denied that such conscious change occurred, and the Christian convert was treated as essentially someone who had not converted'.[78] Similarly, the official term to describe Christian converts became Native Christian which at least in terms of identity by law left converted Indians 'floating in a nebulous space', neither Hindu, Muslim, Sikh nor Christian.[79] On the whole, however, British rule opened up new socio-economic perspectives for the lower castes. Submission, loyalty and endurance were among the qualities that made them attractive to the British families, though they cannot have had much competition from the other castes, for no one was eager to become a servant. Many also found work as guards and policemen and in the army which offered the possibility of a relatively well-paid job, sometimes complete with housing, and usually the obligation to learn to read and write. So after the 1857 Revolt Cuhras turned Sikhs called Mazhabis were recruited in massive number. Finally, many depressed groups emigrated to other countries. In the Punjab, Camars formed the principal emigrant community, after Jats. None of their new jobs created true wealth but made it possible to sever ties with the village or to save money to send children to school.

The Singh Sabhas, Arya Samaj and Ahmadiyah movements did much to establish an agenda to educate those within their respective traditions and in course created conversion rituals with concise statements of belief. Members of the three movements travelled through the Punjab and eventually beyond to instruct people in the truth of their creed.[80] With the results of the decennial census after 1871 it became clear that because of conversions to Christianity the number of Hindus was falling in proportion to those of other communities. Accordingly, the Arya Samaj, as the self-proclaimed champion of Hinduism, led the counterattack against the Christianization of India. After the death of Guru Datta Vidyarthi, Gurukul Aryas under the leadership of Munshi Ram and Lekh Ram created a plan for educating professional missionaries. In 1896, Arya Samajis of the Ferozepur orphanage made it clear that they accepted any Hindu orphan sent to them from any part of India in order to save the children from being brought up in Christian orphanages. With the same purpose in mind, then, the following year under the leadership of Lala Lajpat Rai, diverse and formerly conflicting Hindu groups were united under the banner of the Hindu orphan relief movement.[81] Hence, when Christian success in converting the marginalized castes furthered Hindu fears, they developed their own ritual of conversion (*shuddhi*). Arya Samajis used this to purify and re-admit Hindus who had been converted to Islam and Christianity, on the basis of a remembered identity. Census operations and the writing of history again were crucial. Through them a large majority of Muslims were recognized as converts who in terms of their practices continued to belong to the larger 'original' Indian (Hindu) tradition. Through *shuddhi*, Arya Samajis more or less transformed Hinduism into a tradition of conversion. Importantly, this transformation 'meant far more than merely the adoption of the necessary ceremonies': 'it meant a shift from a social world based on birth to one founded on voluntary association'.[82] Arya Samajis were particularly successful among the Meghs, an outcaste group and rival of the Cuhras. By 1910 they had purified more than 36,000 of them from the districts of Sialkot, Gujrat and Gurdaspur.[83] Generally, the Arya Samaj opened many schools for outcastes and thus enabled an elite to emerge within these groups. When the rise of the hide trade helped a great number of Camars to improve their lives, Arya Samaj schools became very popular with them.

The main goal of the Singh Sabha movement was to convince Sikhs of the truth of the Tat Khalsa 'rather than bolster diminishing numbers with new converts from non-Sikh faiths'.[84] Therefore it remains particularly interesting that some leading Sikhs initially offered assistance to Samaj attempts to contain the tide of Christian and Islamic conversion and together with it founded the Shuddhi Sabha (purification society). By the early 1890s three groups, the Arya Samaj, the Singh Sabhas and the Shuddhi Sabhas, sometimes in alliance, otherwise independently, performed purifications with increasing frequency. The official division of the Arya Samaj in 1893 led to rift among the supporters of *shuddhi*. The Shuddhi Sabhas under the leadership of radical Sikhs instituted a pork test for converts from Islam: 'if the eating of beef could transform a Hindu into a Muslim', alternately 'the eating of pork would signify the return of a Muslim to Hinduism or Sikhism'.[85] As a result, Gurukul Aryas with their rigid insistence on vegetarianism withdrew all support from the Shuddhi Sabhas and condemned them instead for such degenerate actions. Afterwards, purifications continued (mostly on an individual basis) but now were sponsored independently by two competing groups. On the one hand, the Shuddhi Sabhas with their Arya supporters and on the other the Gurukul Arya Samajis. An important transformation however took place with the extension of the *shuddhi* concept to mass conversion. Partly in response to Christian missionary successes among the oppressed, this was not strictly about re-conversion but, unacceptable in the Indian tradition, the admittance of untouchables to caste privileges. Otherwise, being used to numbers by now, some Sikhs came to see Arya Samaj re-conversion as a direct threat, potentially as dangerous as Christian or Islamic con-

version. As a result, Sikhs started their own *shuddhi* movement
and overall the gap between Hindus and Sikhs widened.

Critical in this context remains the conversion of a group of
Rahtia Sikhs to the Arya Samaj. The community of Rahtia Sikhs
were considered outcastes by other Sikhs and, as a feature of
the newly emerged public sphere, they had unsuccessfully tried
to elevate their status since 1896. Hence they approached Lala
Munshi Ram and in 1900, after a purification ceremony, the
first Rahtias became Arya Samajis. Sikhs were outraged,
especially because of the shaving in public. Bhagat Lakshman
Singh was closely involved in these events and, moreover, as the
editor of the *Khalsa* newspaper, responsible for a confrontation
with Lala Munshi Ram, the then editor of the *Sat Dharm
Pracharak* Urdu newspaper.[86] One of the demands made by the
Rahtias was to be admitted to the Golden Temple in Amritsar,
the stronghold of the orthodox non-Singh Sabha Sikhs. Lakshman
Singh spoke with the leaders of the Rahtias and offered them all
privileges promised them by the Arya Samajis. Yet he also stressed
that, just as Munshi Ram and his party did not represent the
orthodox Hindus and their temples, he only represented the lay
leaders of the Singh Sabha, not the Sikh orthodoxy at the Golden
Temple.[87] In fact, in his *Khalsa* article 'Danger Ahead', Lakshman
Singh appealed to the government for intervention against the
shuddhi activities of the Arya Samaj in order to maintain law
and order in the province. The government did not do anything;
instead the Deputy Commissioner personally told Lakshman
Singh that as a Christian his sympathies were both with him
and the Arya Samajis 'for what was being attempted or done
was for the amelioration of the lot of the depressed people in
the villages'.[88]

In 1889, Ghulam Ahmad made clear the ten conditions on
which he would grant *baiat* to his disciples and afterwards started
a missionary association. Though a timely response to the
widespread Christian missionary activities and *shuddhi* efforts
of Arya Samajis and Sikhs, Ahmadiyah missionaries moved
around in a altogether different world. Their converts mostly
came from orthodox Islam. Initially, Ahmadiyah members
voluntarily went on preaching tours when requested but soon

missionaries were specifically educated and ever since make up the core of the movement. Especially during the six years of Caliph Nur al-Din's leadership the Ahmadiyahs greatly expanded their missionary activities, first in the subcontinent, where converts were most numerous outside the Punjab, in parts of Bengal, the Deccan and Malabar, and later overseas. More interesting, however, remain the Ahmadiyah converts from other traditions. Obviously there were not many of them, but at least they would lead to polemics. Mirza Ghulam Ahmad, for example, ridiculed (as usual in his money-oriented terminology) Arya Samajis for their idea that the change of faith of Hindus who converted to Ahmadiyah Islam was not sincere as they ought to have studied the four Vedas in Sanskrit as well as the sacred literature of Islam: 'I am willing to pay a thousand Rupees to the Arya Samajis if they can prove that even five per cent of their total number are well-versed in the four Vedas in Sanskrit'.[89] In the same article, Ghulam Ahmad sets out to answer the question 'to what extent is research necessary for a change of religion?'[90] In reply, he comes up with three criteria to distinguish a true religion from a false one and afterwards makes clear that:

the merits of every religion can be easily tested by every person who has an ordinary share of common sense without spending years of his life in the study of the gigantic masses of different religious literatures. The principles of every religion are published by its supporters and any one who takes the trouble may test them by the above-mentioned criteria.[91]

The point is that discussions like these go to the core of this study because they feature the idea of individuals making their own rational judgements.

Interestingly, in 1870, before the CMS established a Native Church Council, its leadership declared that they were much in need of indigenous evangelists:

In the Punjab we want men to serve not only as native pastors but as native evangelists. There is a energy and fire about the men of the Punjab which, if sanctified, particularly qualifies them to fall into the front rank with European missionaries. There is no reason why there should not be raised out of such materials an aggressive as well as a pastoral agency.[92]

Imad ud-Din (*c.* 1830-1900) and Abd Allah Atham (1828-96) were two most influential Muslim converts to Christianity at the time.[93] They participated in the Native Church Council (the former in fact gave its inaugural sermon in 1877) and both debated with Mirza Ghulam Ahmad. Abd Allah Atham, who worked as an Assistant Commissioner for the Punjab government, was the adversary of Mirza Ghulam Ahmad in a debate held at the initiation of Henry Martyn Clark in Amritsar in 1893.[94] At the end of a discussion (that lasted for fifteen days!), almost by routine, Ghulam Ahmad made a prophecy that his opponent would die in the near future. The fact that it remained unfulfilled was celebrated by Henry Martyn Clark in several articles in the *Church Missionary Intelligencer*.[95] Even so, when Abd Allah Atham died some years later, Ghulam Ahmad came up with numerous writings in which he explained that his prophecy had been fulfilled.[96] Both Allah Atham and Imad ud-Din particularly deserve to be mentioned because their criticisms and missionary activities were focused on the Muslim community in which they had been born. So Imad ud-Din, who symbolically retained his Muslim name 'Pillar of Faith' after he was baptized by Robert Clark on 29 April 1866 in Amritsar, became a pillar of the nascent Punjabi Christian community.[97] He had been closely connected with William Muir during his school days in Agra when Muir was an examiner in the Agra Government College where Imad ud-Din was a student. His conversion was extremely surprising to Muir and others who had known him earlier because as a young man, he had supported Muslim leaders who criticized the Bible in public debates and had preached against missionaries. During the 1860s and 1870s, generally in collaboration with Robert Clark, he published numerous often controversial tracts in Urdu: criticisms of Islam, works on Christian doctrine, Biblical commentaries for Indian converts and a biography of the Prophet Muhammad. The latter being indeed the task that William Muir had intended to do himself but had failed to accomplish even though he produced two more editions of his *Life of Mohamet* in English. Like Alla Atham, Imad ud-Din played a leading role in public debates against Ahmadiyah 'heretics'. Strangely, however, he criticized them (as well as Sayyid Ahmad Khan) only for their 'alleged "rationalistic" apologetic'.[98] No words by him for example against Mirza Ghulam Ahmad's claim to be Jesus in his second coming. Imad ud-Din certainly belonged to a colonial culture which knew many contradictions. For example also he 'maintained that it was possible and appropriate to follow indigenous customs without jeopardizing the Christian message, and he was criticized by some missionaries for keeping his own wife, also a convert, in purdah'.[99] In the end, however, the activities of Abd Allah Atham and Imad ud-din proved not so profitable. Not only did their activities result in few converts; under the influence of Indian nationalism (that some missionaries supported) their way of assertive preaching and writing against Islam soon lost ground. Furthermore, the subsequent phase of mass conversion among Muslims occurred not in Punjabi urban areas but in the villages where Urdu tracts 'must have remained unread by the mainly illiterate low castes and outcastes who sought baptism'.[100]

All things considered, conversions were critical to the Singh Sabha, Arya Samaj and Ahmadiyah movements. This particularly because the focus on competitive numerical expansion, social identity and mobilization directly featured their public side. Recently defined moral languages proved crucial in terms of the rhetoric by which other communities were to be confronted and converts persuaded to stay in line or join the flock. Ideally, they had to undergo initiation rituals, moral educational programmes and, in the successful cases, contribute their part to the development of their community. The latter could be voluntary work of all sorts but, importantly, it overall took place in an institutional context: schools, hospitals, orphanages, or a local temple, gurdwara or mosque. In reality, however, conversion generally proved superficial and the continuity of local traditions and community behaviour remained strong. Thus, for example, in terms of genuine conversion, the Christian missionaries made few inroads. They remain important therefore because of their pioneering of educational and medical work in the face of widespread apathy and even hostility. Critical to the rhetoric were ideas about what it meant to be a true Hindu, Sikh or Muslim. In this reformers addressed their own community. This could be traditional leaders against whom they firmly positioned themselves or common folk who they perhaps could lure into the fold. More salient of course remain the polemics between different community leaders whereby the contents of speeches and pamphlets changed in accordance with the audience to be tackled. Undeniably, *shuddhi* was a causal factor in the increase of Hindu-Muslim antagonism: most converts came from Islam and the notorious pork test was a slap in the face of Muslims. Still, during the period of social reform, the cow protection movement and the anti-Muslim crusade of the Arya Samaj under the leadership of Lekh Ram proved to be of greater significance than the conversion movement. It was only during the 1920s that under the leadership of Swami Shraddhanand, *shuddhi* created an alliance between Aryas and orthodox Hindus. It became a central feature of Hindu solidarity (*sangathan*) and helped to lay a firm foundation of the influence of the all India Hindu Mahasabha and later the RSS.[101] Before that time, however, conversion was particularly significant because through it a growing number of men and women of the lower sections of Indian society, individually or in a group, 'found it necessary to break with their past and brave the scorn and danger which followed'.[102] In the long term, the mass conversion movement proved critical because it brought a larger part of Indian society into the public sphere that nonetheless remained dominated by a confluence of British and traditional Indian notions of race and class.

CONCLUSION

The focus of this book is the period of social reform and hence I end with describing the emergence of a rational social consciousness that linked moral languages and modern identity politics. To connect moral languages further to religious nationalism seems to be another option.[103] Yet in the light of the complex history of the category religion, such a line of thinking remains difficult: what specifically would make nationalism religious? What is religion more than a moral language motivated and spread by individuals through institutions and practices in the modern public sphere? For what purpose and in whose interest? Indian moral languages not only channelled the aspirations of the elite but almost simultaneously nourished feelings of old patriotisms. Consecutively, then, modern identity politics began to question state power in foreign hands. Be that as it may, it should be stressed that though people sometimes were politically mobilized on the basis of a combination of traditional moral languages and old patriotisms, these were not a necessarily condition and always part of a wider configuration of societal change. On the whole, the newly created moral communities had their images of how the world ought to be. These not only brought them into conflict with other visions of the good society but, importantly, despite points of convergence between colonizer and colonized, the supposedly objective morality of the British civilizing mission which underlined the making of both the colonial state and the public sphere. Thus, because secularization more or less took place within all traditions from the nineteenth century, the boundaries between moral communities were more than ever rationally defined and often led to violence in the challenge of the existing political order.[104] Or to put it in world historical terms, Protestantism and secularism more or less led to the destruction of the transcendent elements in all traditions and dogmatic reasoned moralities in quest of utopian visions have a been a dominant feature of modern politics ever since.[105]

Much of what happened in modern South Asia I believe can be explained through concepts like moral language, civilizing mission, secularization, Anglo-Indian colonial state and liberal public sphere as long as their relative importance is defined in the wider configuration of societal change. What for example became the most important feature of the liberal public sphere in South Asia in the context of a dominant colonial and post-colonial state? As elsewhere, the South Asian public sphere was hierarchical and dominated by modern institutions and practices. Though there certainly was much continuity in terms of caste and traditional leadership, there is the importance of urban lay leadership and, to a much lesser extent, an upward mobility among the oppressed. From the perspective of the upper classes Indian traditions changed during the colonial interaction through an increasing adherence to rationality and a social consciousness that highlighted ideas about improvement. Equally critical was the fact that following the civilizing mission, the definition of moral language went hand in hand with defining oneself as loyal to the colonial state, often in terms of the principle: that 'one should not be content with one's welfare alone, but should look for one's welfare in the welfare of all'.[106] While the relationship between individual and society always is one of moral responsibility within any tradition, in South Asia this relationship particularly was strengthened by the definition of reasoned moralities amongst communities. Hence, importantly, since the nineteenth century different moral communities were continuously respondent towards each other and in striving for state power. In comparison to the West, I wish to emphasize therefore that in South Asia the main feature of the liberal public sphere was not citizenship, rule by law or a distinction between a private and a public domain. Partly because of poverty, overpopulation and a dominant centralized state, the presence of these public features remains uncomfortable in the subcontinent. In their place, I would argue that at least in (British) India electoral politics became the unchallenged legitimate source of a public sphere which, because of the immense importance of Congress' electoral success in securing Independence, persists to this day.[107]

NOTES

1. *Regenerator of Arya Varta*, vol. 1, 20 August 1883, pp. 3-4.
2. Sudhir Chandra, *The Oppressive Present: Literature and Social Consciousness in Colonial India*, New Delhi: Oxford University Press, 1992, p. 138.
3. Barbara D. Metcalf, *Islamic Revival in British India: Deoband 1860-1900*, Princeton: Princeton University Press, 1982, p. 357.
4. The pages on Christianity in the *Satyarth Prakash* remain the definitive source for the criticism of Christianity for Arya Samajis. Interestingly, while Dayanand approached the Bible with a mind more familiar with Islam, he attacked Christians for practices which at the same time were characteristic of Muslim differences with Hindus: eating meat, animal sacrifice, circumcision and the burial of the dead.
5. Kenneth W. Jones, 'Swami Dayananda Saraswati's Critique of Christianity', in *Religious Controversy in British India: Dialogues in*

South Asian Languages, ed. Kenneth W. Jones, Albany: State University of New York Press, 1992, pp. 52-74.

6. Dayanand Saraswati, *Light of Truth*, repr., New Delhi: Sarvadeshik Arya Pratinidhi Sabha, 1991, pp. vi-vii.

7. Bawa Arjan Singh, *Mela Chandapur*, Lahore: Aryan Printing, Publishing & General Trading Co., 1903, p. 31.

8. Ibid., p. 33.

9. Ibid.

10. N. Gerald Barrier, 'Sikh Politics in British Punjab prior to the Gurdwara Reform Movement', in *Sikh History and Religion in the Twentieth Century*, ed. Joseph T. O'Conell et al., Toronto: University of Toronto Center for South Asian Studies, 1988, pp. 176-7.

11. Mirza Ghulam Ahmad, *Jesus in India*, repr., Qadian: Nazarat Nasur-o-Ishaat, 1991. One can still visit this place. In fact, one could do it while going to the famous Hazratbal mosque outside Srinagar on the same day. Supposedly it possesses a hair of the Prophet Muhammad, which has been stolen a few times but was always returned afterwards. In 1913 H.A. Walter visited Srinagar and did not believe it was Jesus who had been buried there but probably some Muslim saint instead. In Spencer Lavan, *The Ahmadiyah Movement: A History and Perspective*, New Delhi: Manohar, 1974, pp. 93-4.

12. Mirza Ghulam Ahmad, *How to get Rid of the Bondage of Sin*, repr., Qadian: Nazir Dawat-o-Tabligh, 1971, pp. 38-41.

13. Ibid., p. 50.

14. Mirza Ghulam Ahmad, *A Review of Christianity from a New Point of View*, repr., Qadian: Nazir Dawat-o-Tabligh, n.d., pp. 1-2.

15. Muhammad Latif, *History of the Punjab from the Remotest Antiquity to the Present Time*, Calcutta: Central Press, 1891, p. 575.

16. Concern for the well-being of cows already was taken up by Sikh Namdharis during the 1860s.

17. Dayanand Saraswati, *Gokarunanidhi*, repr., Ajmer: Paropkarini Sabha, 1993.

18. For the next two paragraphs: Kenneth W. Jones, *Arya Dharm: Hindu Consciousness in Nineteenth Century India*, 1976; repr., New Delhi: Manohar, 2006, pp. 145-53, 193-200; Lavan, *The Ahmadiyah Movement*, pp. 76-87; and the numerous articles in the *Selections from the Punjab Vernacular Press*, 1896-1911.

19. He published *Christian Mat Darpan* in the same year as 'The Epistle of *Jihad*'. In it, Lekh Ram argued that Christ was not sinless but, on the contrary, a cruel illiterate drunkard, liar and thief, who insulted his mother. In *Selections*, 1897, Nur Afshan, 14 May, p. 387.

20. *Selections*, 1897; *Bharat Sudhar*, 13 March, p. 180.

21. Bhagat Lakshman Singh, *Autobiography*, Calcutta: The Sikh Cultural Centre, 1965, pp. 89-93, 160-3.

22. See for example on the reaction in pamphlets by Bhai Ditt Singh: Barrier, 'Vernacular Publishing', in *Religious Controversy in British India*, ed. Kenneth W. Jones, Albany: State University of New York Press, 1992, pp. 212-13.

23. Harald Fischer-Tiné, '"Kindly Elders of the Hindu Biradri": The Arya Samaj's Struggle for Influence and its effect on Hindu-Muslim Relations, 1880-1925', in *Gurus and Their Followers: New Religious Reform Movements in Colonial India*, ed. Antony Copley, New Delhi: Oxford University Press, 2000, p. 111.

24. Jeffrey Cox, *Imperial Fault Lines: Christianity and Colonial Power in India, 1818-1940*, Stanford: Stanford University Press, 2002, p. 60.

25. See especially the articles in Kenneth W. Jones, ed., *Religious Controversy in British India*, Albany: State University of New York Press, 1992.

26. Eric Hobsbawm, *Nations and Nationalism since 1780: Programme, Myth, Reality*, Cambridge: Cambridge University Press, 1992, p. 10.

27. Judith M. Brown, *Modern India: Origins of an Asian Democracy*, New Delhi: Oxford University Press, 1984, p. 67.

28. Richard Temple saw the people of India through the following scheme of four categories that probably was common at the time: those 'actively loyal' (princes and chiefs of native states, banking, trading and industrial classes, landlords); 'loyal but passive' (peasant proprietors, cultivators and labourers); 'many loyal, but some the reverse' (educated classes, native aristocracy in British territories, Hindu and Muslim religious leaders); 'excitable or ready for mischief' (fanatics, hangers-on of courts and camps and, last but not least, the mob!). In *Men and Events of My Time in India*, London: John Murray, 1982, p. 504.

29. As described by Bernard S. Cohn for the 1877 Delhi *darbar* in 'Representing Authority in Victorian India', in *An Anthropologist Among the Historians and Other Essays*, New York: Oxford University Press, 1987 and by Douglas Haynes for public rituals in Surat in *Rhetoric and Ritual in Colonial India: The Shaping of the Public Sphere in Surat City, 1852-1928*, New Delhi: Oxford University Press, 1992, pp. 126-37.

30. Brown, *Modern India*, 67.

31. In *Origins of Nationality in South Asia: Patriotism and Ethical Government in the Making of Modern India*, New Delhi: Oxford University Press, 1998, in Chapter Four: 'Patriotism and Nationalism', C.A. Bayly argues that he finds the term old patriotism preferable to Hobsbawm's idea of proto-nationalism in *Nations and Nationalism since 1780*, because it does not bear the weight of teleology inherent in the suffix 'proto-'.

32. Christopher Shackle and Javed Majeed, eds., *Hali's Musaddas: The Flow and Ebb of Islam*, New Delhi: Oxford University Press, 1998, p. 18. Subtitled 'The Flow and Ebb of Islam', the *Musaddas* exemplified the Aligarh movement in its consciousness of the glories of the Islamic past, its awareness of the decay of the present, and its certainty that Western reason must be embraced for the improvement of society. So great was its impact that it became a kind of Muslim anthem, parts of it usually being recited to inaugurate sessions of Muslim voluntary organizations.

33. Ibid., p. 23.

34. Ibid., p. 76.

35. Ibid., p. 25.

36. Lajpat Rai, *A History of the Arya Samaj: An Account of its Origin, Doctrines and Activities with a Biographical Sketch of the Founder*, repr., New Delhi: Munshiram Manoharlal, 1992, pp. 197-8 and Brown, *Modern India*, pp. 202-23 (M.K. Gandhi and the Enterprise of Swaraj).

37. As cited in Harald Fischer-Tiné, 'National Education, Pulp Fiction and the Contradictions of Colonialism: Perception of an Educational Experiment in Early-Twentieth-Century India', in *Colonialism as Civilizing Mission: Cultural Ideology in British India*, ed. Harald Fischer-Tiné and Michael Mann, London: Anthem Press, 2005, p. 244. See further on the tension between Swami Shraddhanand and Gandhi: J.T.F. Jordens, *Swami Shraddhananda: His Life and Causes*, New Delhi: Oxford University Press, 1981, Chapter Five 'The Call of Gandhi and Politics, 1917-1922'.

38. Metcalf, *Islamic Revival in British India*, p. 5.

39. M.K. Gandhi, 'Hind Swaraj', in *The Collected Works of Mahatma Gandhi*, vol. 10, New Delhi: Publications Division, Government of India, 1958, pp. 22-3 (translation mine).

40. Ashis Nandy, *The Intimate Enemy: Loss and Recovery of the Self under Colonialism*, New Delhi: Oxford University Press, 1983, p. 3. Cf. Chandra, *The Oppressive Present*.

41. D.H.A. Kolff, *Indië en de Wereldgeschiedenis*, Leiden: Universiteit Leiden, 2003, p. 5.

42. Cohn, 'The Census, Social Structure and Objectification in South Asia', in *An Anthropologist* and Kenneth W. Jones, 'Religious Identity and the Indian Census', in *The Census in British India: New Perspectives*, New Delhi: Manohar, 1981, pp. 73-102.

43. In 1867 the Legislative Council passed an Act for the regulation of printing presses and newspapers, which required publishers to submit editorial information and copies of their papers to the government. These materials plus information gathered by the police department served as raw materials for the *Selections*, published between 1867

and 1924, which contain numerous interesting comments from Punjabi newspapers before and after each decennial census.

44. Kenneth W. Jones, 'Religious Identity', p. 87.

45. During census operations, the Lahore Singh Sabha worked together with the British and, importantly, in its claim to Sikh leadership, afterwards brought out the correspondence between them into the open. As stated in N. Gerald Barrier, *The Sikhs and their Literature: A Guide to Books, Tracts and Periodicals (1849-1919)*, New Delhi: Manohar, 1970, p. xl.

46. N. Gerald Barrier, 'The Punjab Government and Communal Policies, 1870-1908', *Journal of Asian Studies*, 27, 1968, p. 532.

47. Ian Talbot, 'State, Society and Identity: The British Punjab 1875-1937', in *Punjabi Identity: Continuity and Change*, ed. Gurharpal Singh and Ian Talbot, New Delhi: Manohar, 1996, p. 14.

48. Ibid., p. 18.

49. *Report on the Administration of the Punjab and its Dependencies*, Lahore: Punjab Government Press, 1904-1905, p. 18.

50. John Strachey, *India: Its Administration & Progress*, London: Macmillan, 1911, p. 5.

51. Separate electorates were also provided for Sikhs and Christians, whereby as Jeffrey Cox put it, 'Indian Christians had rights of representation, and missionaries and Indian Christians were in a state of permanent negotiations over the allocation of those resources, and over the definition of a new phenomenon: a multiracial Indian Christian Church.' In *Imperial Fault Lines*, p. 103.

52. David Gilmartin, 'A Magnificent Gift: Muslim Nationalism and the Election Process in Colonial Punjab', *Comparative Studies in Society and History*, 40, 1998, pp. 415-17.

53. In relation to this Eric Hobsbawm concluded: 'It is by no means evident that Pakistan was the product of a national movement among the Muslims of the then Indian Empire, though it may well be regarded as a reaction against an all-Indian national movement which failed to give adequate recognition to the special feelings or requirements of Muslims, and though, in an era of the modern nation-state, territorial partition seemed to be the only available formula, it is far from clear that a separate territorial state is what even the Muslim League had in mind until very late, or would have insisted on but for the intransigence of Jinnah (who was indeed something like a Muslim nationalist, for he was certainly not a religious believer). And it is quite certain that the bulk of ordinary Muslims thought in communal and not in national terms, and would not have understood the concept of national self-determination as something which could apply to belief in Allah and His Prophet', in *Nations and Nationalism*, 70.

54. Fascinating in this context remains R.W. Falcon, *Handbook on the Sikhs for Regimental Officers*, Allahabad: Pioneer Press, 1896, in which is discussed, for example, how to recognize the true martial Sikh and in which Punjab regions he could be found.

55. Petrie, C.I.D. Memorandum. Cf. Bhagat Lakshman Singh, *Autobiography*, pp. 199-205.

56. During his student days in Lahore, Lajpat Rai still was not so patriotic. On the contrary, as he put it in 'The Story of My Life', in *The Collected Works of Lala Lajpat Rai*, vol. 5, ed. B.R. Nanda, New Delhi: Manohar, 2004, p. 334, 'in Arya Samaj lectures I used to applaud the Government. That was in vogue those days. Besides I believed that the English had rescued us from the tyranny of Mussalmans'.

57. Hobsbawm, *Nations and Nationalism*, p. 10.

58. Lajpat Rai, *The Problem of National Education in India*, London: George Allen & Unwin Ltd., 1920, p. 147.

59. Lajpat Rai, 'The Message of the Bhagavad Gita', in *The Collected Works of Lala Lajpat Rai*, vol. 3, ed. B.R. Nanda, New Delhi: Manohar, 2004, p. 353. The *Bhagavad Gita* (Song of the Lord) contains Krishna's teaching and revelation to the warrior Arjuna. It is the sixth book of the *Mahabharata*, which might be the longest epic in the world. Dating back to the first millennium BC, it always was orally transmitted but extensively popularized during the nineteenth century (for an important part through Orientalist translations for example by Max Müller and Edwin Arnold). Afterwards, it became one of the key texts of Hindu patriotism because, in line with contemporary colonial masculine culture, Krishna taught the importance of selfless devotion to duty in opposition to traditional Hindu quietism, devotionalism and renunciation. Actually, both the *Mahabharata* and the *Ramayana* are epics of unending conflict and military intrigue and most likely therefore, more than the Vedas, they became crucial to modern Hinduism.

60. Swami Shraddhanand, *Hindu Sangathan: Saviour of the Dying Race*, New Delhi: Swami Shraddhananda Sanyasi, 1926.

61. *Selections from the Punjab Vernacular Press*, 1898, *al-Hakam*, 31 March, p. 238.

62. This issue was one of the few about which Mirza Ghulam Ahmad and Sayyid Ahmad Khan agreed.

63. *Selections from the Punjab Vernacular Press*, 1897, Chaudhwin Sadi, June 15 and *Seraj-ul-Akhbar*, 21 June.

64. Mirza Ghulam Ahmad, *Jihad and the British Government*, Lahore: Caxton Printing Works, 1900.

65. Lajpat Rai, *The Political Future of India*, repr., New Delhi: Renaissance, 1988, p. 11.

66. N. Gerald Barrier, 'The Arya Samaj and Congress Politics in the Punjab, 1894-1908', *Journal of Asian Studies*, 26, 1967, p. 378.
67. G.A. Oddie, ed., *Religion in South Asia: Religious Conversion and Revival Movements in South Asia in Medieval and Modern Times*, New Delhi: Manohar, 1977, p. 4.
68. Peter Hardy, *The Muslims of British India*, 1972; repr., New Delhi: Foundation Books, 1998, p. 8.
69. Unlike lower castes, out-caste groups were considered to be outside the caste system. As such they literally were 'untouchables' and denied access to temples and gurudwaras and had to use separate wells.
70. Still today caste names are generally considered humiliating and outcastes avoid using them. Commonly known in north India for instance are the expressions as 'black as a Camar' or 'dirty as a Camar'.
71. As cited in Cox, *Imperial Fault Lines*, 138.
72. *District Gazetteer, Punjab*, Lahore, 1893-4, p. 88.
73. John C.B. Webster, 'Christian Conversion in the Punjab: What has Changed?', in *Religious Conversion in India: Modes, Motivations, and Meanings*, ed. Rowena Robinson and Sathianathan Clarke, New Delhi: Oxford University Press, 2003, p. 357.
74. *Census of India, Punjab*, 1911, p. 192
75. Webster, 'Christian Conversion in the Punjab', p. 358.
76. Ibid., p. 378.
77. Stanley E. Brush, 'Protestant in the Punjab: Religion and Social Change in an Indian Province in the Nineteenth Century', unpublished Ph.D. dissertation, Berkeley: University of California, 1971, p. 142.
78. Gauri Viswanathan, *Outside the Fold: Conversion, Modernity, and Belief*, Princeton: Princeton University Press, 1998, p. 14.
79. Ibid., p. 81.
80. The concept of conversion as spiritual rebirth was and remains unofficial within the Sikh and Hindu traditions.
81. Rai, *A History of the Arya Samaj*, p. 130.
82. Jones, *Arya Dharm*, pp. 129-30.
83. Ibid., p. 212.
84. Louis F. Fenech, 'Conversion and Sikh Tradition', in *Religious Conversion in India: Modes, Motivations, and Meanings*, ed. Rowena Robinson and Sathianathan Clarke, New Delhi: Oxford University Press, 2003, p. 152.
85. As cited in Kenneth W. Jones, 'Ham Hindu Nahin: Arya-Sikh Relations, 1877-1905', *Journal of Asian Studies*, 32, 1973, p. 465.
86. Bhagat Lakshman Singh, *Autobiography*, pp. 160-8 and *Selections from the Punjab Vernacular Press*, 1900, Sat Dharm Pracharak, 29 June; 6 July; 13 July.

87. Bhagat Lakshman Singh, *Autobiography*, pp. 162-3.
88. Ibid., p. 168.
89. Ahmad, 'Religious Conversion and the Respective Merits of Islam, Christianity and Arya Samaj', in *Review of Religions*, March 1903, pp. 89-91.
90. Ibid.
91. Ibid., p. 96.
92. Robert Clark, *The Missions of the Church Missionary Society and the Church of England Zenana Missionary Society in the Punjab and Sindh*, London: Church Missionary Society, 1904, p. 247.
93. Ibid., pp. 39-44.
94. Henry Martyn Clark was the adopted son of Robert and Elizabeth Clark and the biographer of the former. In 1881 he was accepted as a missionary by the CMS and from 1892 onwards he established several medical missions in and around Amritsar. Moreover, together with Bhai Maya Singh he compiled the influential *Punjabi Dictionary* (1895). Cox, *Imperial Fault Lines*, pp. 103, 173.
95. Henry Martyn Clark, 'A Controversy with the Mohammedans', in *Church Missionary Intelligencer*, 19, 1984, pp. 96-105. 'Some Results of the Late Mohammedan Controversy', in *Church Missionary Intelligencer*, 19, 1984, pp. 812-18 and 'Conversions from Mohammedanism in the Punjab', in *Church Missionary Intelligencer*, 25, 1900, pp. 180-2.
96. Yohanan Friedmann, *Prophecy Continues: Aspects of Ahmadi Religious Thought and its Medieval Background*, New Delhi: Oxford University Press, 1988, pp. 6-7, 187-9.
97. Imad ud-Din, who belonged to a well-known Sunni Muslim family from Panipat with strong Sufi associations and a reputation for learning, chose to keep his *maulvi* (Muslim scholar) title even when he adopted that of reverend. Subsequently, he became an ordained deacon in 1868, priest in 1872 and in 1884 the Archbishop of Canterbury conferred on him the title of Doctor of Divinity. He never left Amritsar and died in the same room in which Clark had baptized him. See further: Antony Copley, *Religions in Conflict: Cultural Contact and Conversion in Late Colonial India*, New Delhi: Oxford University Press, 1997, pp. 241-2
98. Avril A. Powell, '"Pillar of a New Faith": Christianity in Late-Nineteenth-Century Punjab from the Perspective of a Convert from Islam', in *Christians and Missionaries in India: Cross-Cultural Communication Since 1500*, ed. R.E. Frykenberg, London: Routledge Curzon, 2003, p. 250.
99. Ibid., p. 253.
100. Ibid.

101. See further: Jordens, *Swami Shraddhananda*, Chapter Six.
102. John C.B. Webster, *The Christian Community and Change in North India*, New Delhi: Macmillan, 1976, p. 272.
103. Mark Juergensmeyer, *Religious Nationalism Confronts the Secular State*, New Delhi: Oxford University Press, 1994 and Peter van der Veer, *Religious Nationalism: Hindus and Muslims in India*, Berkeley: University of California Press, 1994.
104. Ainslee T. Embree, *Utopias in Conflict: Religion and Nationalism in Modern India*, Berkeley: University of California Press, 1990, pp. 131-2.
105. Ibid., p. 123.
106. Explicitly this is one of the ten principles of the Arya Samaj.
107. D.H.A. Kolff, 'Zuid-Azië na 1945', in *De Wereld na 1945*, ed. D.F.J. Bosscher, H. Renner, R.B. Soetendorp and R. Wagenaar, Utrecht: Spectrum, 1992, pp. 496-7. Cf. Gilmartin, 'A Magnificent Gift'.

CHAPTER SIX

Conclusion: Moral Languages Over Time and Seas

SECULARIZATION AND CULTURAL DIALOGUE

Because of broad analogies in socio-political context, I have sometimes compared nineteenth century social reform in the Punjab (if not South Asia at large) with what happened in Europe during the so-called Protestant Reformation. Both phenomena were marked by great political, social and economic change, to which processes of state formation and print culture, including translations of the reformist message into the vernaculars, were decisive. In both cases reformers critiqued the established traditional leadership and accepted one or the other scripture as the authoritative compendium of eternal wisdom to be interpreted on an individual basis. Simultaneously, reformers more or less came to represent an 'arm of the state, enforcing moral and social order', when they began to undermine and control popular culture by printing and preaching uniform ideas about how to improve one's life and to stick to the one and only true tradition.[1] Most likely because of the colonial interaction, the complex of purposes, sometimes contradictory, among the reformers within the greater Sikh, Hindu and Islamic traditions and the Singh Sabha, Arya Samaj, and Ahmadiyah movements in particular, was more varied than that of the sixteenth century reformers of Christendom. The comparison with the European Reformation therefore solely remains illuminating in contrast. In the end, what happened in nineteenth century South Asia had its own internal dynamics and hence a process such as secularization (i.e. the passing of authority from a traditional to a secular source) was different from what happened in Europe. Otherwise, besides above-mentioned parallels, it makes sense to bring up the comparison because it often was made also by the British during the nineteenth century. For them, the 'Indian Reformation', like the European one, was an ongoing process and not some distant historical fact. The difference of course was that in this case the fight was not against Catholicism, but against the excesses of local (especially Hindu) traditions. Indeed, in the eyes of the stalwart Protestant British, both Catholicism and Hinduism encouraged effeminacy in men.

It is in this context that one should situate the British Orientalist myth of Sikhism in decay. Since the annexation of the Punjab and especially after they showed their loyalty during the uprising of 1857, the British showed much respect for the martial Sikhs. Most British found Hinduism abhorrent and, hence, for example, Macauliffe and Monier-Williams spoke of similarities between the Sikh tradition and the European Reformation.[2] In general, the British 'responded warmly to the Sikh scriptural vision of "the One"—true, ineffable, and everlasting—and contrasted this with the baffling array of the Hindu pantheon'.[3] Also the lack of a hierarchy of priests among the Sikhs 'corresponded well with Protestant notions of a priesthood of believers, especially given the highly disparaged clerical order of Catholicism that was deemed as most responsible for the feminization of Christianity'.[4] After the British found that the boundaries of the Sikh community were fluid and often overlapped with that of Punjabi popular culture, however, they came up with their myth of Sikhism in decay. They stressed that the Sikhs would be absorbed by the greater Hindu tradition, if they would not keep to the basics of their tradition. As Macauliffe wrote:

Truly wonderful are the strength and vitality of Hinduism. It is like the boa constrictor of the Indian forest. . . . Hinduism has embraced Sikhism in its folds; the still comparatively young religion is making a vigorous struggle for life, but its ultimate destruction is, it is apprehended, inevitable without State support.[5]

Even though the British compared the Sikh tradition favourably with the European reformation, their ideas apparently were no reason behind the establishment of the Amritsar Singh Sabha, though over time perhaps they might have had some influence on the further developments of the Panth. The Lahori Singh Sabha's reformist goal of educating the community with the vision of the Tat Khalsa, for example, was certainly much in line with the British view of a community in decay. Likewise, the British efforts to foster the Tat Khalsa identity in the British Indian army and the growing importance given by Singh Sabhaites to the Sikh identity in the census reports and Punjabi society remain critical.

On the whole, it remains to be asked as to what extent Indians were influenced by the nineteenth century Protestant versions of Christian history and of the Reformation in particular. Even if the Sikhs perhaps were influenced by the British Orientalist idea of Sikhism in decline, they certainly did not compare themselves to the sixteenth century European reformers. At least until the beginning of the twentieth century, one does not find such references in Indian writings. The more fascinating therefore remains the case of contemporary vernacular Arya Samaj lite-rature wherein Brahmans sometimes are denounced with the English word 'Pope' as supposed mediator between God and men.[6] Undeniably, dissenting Protestantism was central to the processes of secularization, liberalization and because of its images of how the world ought to be, this category of religion emerged simultaneously in Britain and South Asia.

Yet, keeping in mind both the books in English available in South Asia and the state of knowledge of the English language among Indian reformers, the idea that Protestant church history inspired Arya Samajis during the period of social reform seems unrealistic. To begin with, in his chapter on Christianity in the *Satyarth Prakash*, Dayanand Saraswati did not pay any attention to European church history. Instead, as discussed, he interpreted the Bible literally to make it appear a ridiculous book. Be that as it may, Lala Lajpat Rai concluded that Dayanand must have been informed about the Popes of Rome by some of his English-educated followers and, accordingly, applied that name to the Brahmans of India.[7] By the beginning of the twentieth century, therefore, perhaps some general notions about the Reformation became part of South Asian dialogue: Martin Luther's protest against the infallibility of the Pope, translations of the Bible into the vernaculars, individual reading of the scripture and faith in one's own judgement.[8] Certainly more influential than these, however, was the contemporary European discussion about the historical Jesus. This encouraged Indian Muslims to take a different look at their Prophet and most likely also made Sikhs query whether Guru Nanak was a founder of a new tradition rather than a reformer, as the British would argue in line with the European Reformation. All in all, partly because they generally saw all Christian dominations in the subcontinent as one and the same, it seems Indians did know much about European church history and only incorporated some superficial notions that seem helpful to historicize their own identities.

European ideas of the Reformation and the Enlightenment did reach Indian social consciousness but because of time and place Indians wrestled with them on their own terms and so their incorporation differed from what happened in the European mind. Thus, for instance, it would take some more time before the secularization of history reached South Asia. Indians were still far from the liberation of 'historical understanding from theological bias or axiom' whereby, for example, 'the best life of John Calvin was written by a Roman Catholic whereas the best life of the founder of the Jesuits was written by a Protestant'.[9] Or, equally, one came to be aware of the fact that the 'Reformation would have happened without a Luther to make it happen even if not in the way in which it happened; that society depended on deeper movements of economic structure or articulate axioms than could be defined in terms of one man's influence.'[10] As stressed in the Introduction, Indian social consciousness during the period of social reform was informed more by Christian reasoned morality than by the ideas of the Enlightenment. In fact, in hindsight, it seems both Britain and India were not ready for the non-dogmatic insights of the latter. Instead, a growing need was felt for rational and moral explanations about the functioning of nature and society in order to gain progress. Thus Indian elites defined moral languages because they could not just do away with the traditional world they were living in and start anew from scratch, as if it did not mean anything at all. Moreover, under the banner of the civilizing mission, the European Reformation more or less became an ongoing process simultaneously in colony and metropolis.

During the late nineteenth century, the insights of the Enlightenment had been knocking around Christian Europe for almost two centuries. As a result, north-western European Protestant countries in particular gradually acquired secular features that turned the Enlightenment of a few into the secularization of many.[11] Indeed, the fact that Protestantism found ways to incorporate secular forces perhaps partly should be attributed to its growing involvement in missionary activities overseas. Thus from the late eighteenth century onwards, Protestants obtained an outlet for their burning evangelical desire to preach the Gospel. More than in Britain and as a crucial feature of colonial culture, the British in India often could experiment with more extreme versions of contemporary ideas. In Chapter Two, examples have been given of the British reordering of Indian society in accordance with an idealized image of their own class hierarchies as well as Anglo-Indian law. To this may be added that following the training of officials in languages and political economy at the East India Company's Haileybury College, government in India was far in advance of anything in Britain.[12] Throughout the Empire was of course also the acuteness of British racism. Likewise, the Christianity that reached nineteenth century South Asia was of a specific kind because, unlike in Britain, it was not much hampered by secular forces. The British in India and especially in the Punjab were Christians with a civilizing mission. Consequently, Christian morality decisively influenced Indian traditions not only because the British civilizing mission was permeated with it but because Indians furthered its influence by taking to Anglo-vernacular education and with a rising participation in the liberal public sphere. Because of the fast changing conditions, the Indian elite became increasingly preoccupied with the times and willing to take things as they are. Among them there emerged a social consciousness that coped with Western science and Christianity as well as indigenous traditions at the same time. Undeniably the emergence of various state institutions also heavily influenced Indian traditions and the making of a public sphere. Increasingly,

the colonial state demanded rationality (census/scientific definitions) for different reasons (land revenue, political representation, and the establishment of a system of law). Actually, the
definition of moral languages and the making of rational public
identities show an intense preoccupation of Indian elites with
the present, if not with change for the better, and, on the whole,
therefore the period of social reform has an almost millenarian
tinge. Critical was the influence of the urgent call for improvement by the British and Protestant evangelists in particular.
Nineteenth-century Protestant eschatology obviously had mil-
lennial features that were implicit and often overt in evangelical preaching in the Punjab. These in part fell in line with the
British aim to civilize the Punjab and its inhabitants for their
own betterment and to save their souls. It was in this context
that, as Sudhir Chandra has argued, Indian elites increasingly
developed an awareness of the 'oppressive present' of Anglo-
Indian colonial culture:

No generation lives and dreams for itself alone. It engages also in
ventures that it knows will benefit and be carried on by its descendants.
But history also shows generations that seem doomed to work
consciously and almost exclusively for hopes and objectives which can
only be realized by successors still unborn. Those who came of age in
later-nineteenth-century India and felt concerned about the state of
their country and society were all too conscious that this sort of tragic
destiny was theirs. Whichever way they looked, the present seemed
oppressive to them. The problems facing their society seemed so
insuperable that the present could acquire a meaning only with reference
to the past and the future.[13]

Following the activities of those within Indian voluntary movements working through modern disciplinary institutions and
practices, the reconstruction and cultivation of norms to chasten
the individual and the collective life of the community laid the
rational basis for modern identity politics. Hence how inapt it is
that, because of different, colourful and often fluid traditions,
even today South Asia is depicted as a society dominated by
religion, taken indeed as the same unchanging phenomenon over
the centuries. How is this possible after indigenous voluntary
movements have been spreading the word of the civilizing mission

through their moral languages in the public sphere for over a century? Undeniably this has much to do with the dominance and common acceptance of the secular-religious binary opposition between West and non-West. My discussion of the Singh Sabha, Arya Samaj and Ahmadiyah moral languages aimed to make clear that what happened in reality was much more complicated, albeit modern and open to comparison. One of the main propositions of this study has been to replace the use of the category religion with traditions embedded in the flux and continuity of history. During modern times these particularly have much to do with rational knowledge and practice in the context of state formation with the process of secularization as cliffhanger. Thus moral languages put forward the modern features and moral ambiguities of traditions at the same time and, on the whole, remain crucial to the dominant social consciousness in a liberal public sphere for at least three reasons. First, because on the basis of rationality, voluntarism, science and modern institutions and practices, moral languages make possible world historical comparison in terms of secularization. Second, because they show the profound influence of Christian morality, the British civilizing mission as well as Western Orient-alism on modern South Asian identities, despite all continuity in traditional idiom and practice. Third, because they formed the heart of the greater Indian cultural tradition, as defined by Partha Chatterjee and recently again stressed by Dirk Kolff, where the nation already was sovereign, even though the state officially was in foreign hands.[14] Thus the domain of culture became the source of Indian legitimacy from where Indian patriotisms gained their basic moral strength both to stir the public mind and to infiltrate state institutions.

MORAL LANGUAGES IN DIASPORA
AND WORLD HISTORY

Can one also delineate a role for moral languages overseas and in world history at large? Has the influence of tradition abroad, as Sudhir Kakar asks in relation to the idea of culture, ever since been 'so pervasive that even when an individual seems to break away from it, as in states of insanity, the "madness" is still influenced by its norms and rituals'?[15] After the abolition of slavery within the British Empire, one and a half million Indians went overseas during the indentured labour system (1834-1917), mostly to East Africa, the Caribbean and the Fiji islands, and many stayed on after completing the job. As expected, however, migration from the Punjab (mostly from the rural areas of the central districts around Lahore and Amritsar) was not so much the result of the indentured labour system but of military service.[16] Since the beginning of the twentieth century, Singh Sabha, Arya Samaj and Ahmadiyah missionaries followed in the footsteps of those who had emigrated earlier. The first Arya Samaj missionaries arrived in Fiji in 1902 but they were more successful afterwards in the Caribbean and at present particularly in South Africa.[17] The Ahmadiyahs opened the first mosque ever in Great Britain in Woking (Surrey).[18] Afterwards, Ahmadiyahs scattered practically all over the globe and overall displayed a remarkable spirit of enterprise. In the 1980s the movement supported around twenty-five hospitals and thirty-five secondary schools in West Africa alone, ten missionary colleges worldwide and a publishing unit near London with facilities for computer typesetting in thirty languages.[19] Indeed, already from the beginning of the twentieth century the Ahmadiyahs made a critical contribution to the spread of the modern Islamic message through their translations of the Koran in numerous languages.[20] Today, the community may watch the Caliph either on the Ahmadiyah television channel broadcast from London by satellite or on the internet.[21] Better known than the Ahmadiyahs, however, remains the Sikh diaspora. Sikhs are now to be found throughout the world, particularly in the English-speaking countries of the former British Empire and also in the Gulf States.

Obviously Indians abroad had to decide what to keep and what to discard of their home traditions. At first there would not be much change inside the house but over time the children of some emigrants started to question the value of keeping the parental tongue in a strange land, or the traditional custom or meal, preferring to be like their new peer group. Even today the identity markers discussed in this study remain critical. Despite fast changing circumstances, overseas communities do much to stay morally together in terms of tradition, indeed often on the basis of caste. The focus on language and script, for example, becomes increasingly impractical with children growing up speaking and reading English or any other language. Translations of the scriptures bring out not only problems of definition but of the whole relationship between scripture, language and script. Equally, the wearing of traditional clothes and attributes proved problematic (as in the case of Sikh turbans and daggers) and emancipation often questions traditional patriarchal authority (as in the case of educated Indian women opting for marriage outside the community). Also the use of the discipline of history still is much in the frontline. To give two well-known examples of the Singh Sabha legacy: first the controversy between Hew McLeod and the Sikh community about the interpretation of Sikh history and, second, the one concerning the establishment of a Chair for the study of Sikhism in 1987 at the University of British Columbia in Canada, against which many Canadian Sikhs protested. Since the late 1960s, McLeod has written excellent historical accounts on the Sikh tradition. Many Sikhs, however, question the quality of his work because they think the discipline of history alone is unsuited in the study of Sikhism.[22] Similarly, Harjot Oberoi was attacked by Sikhs 'who felt that he was not using his position to promote the cause of Sikhism' after his appointment as the first Chair of Sikh studies by the Canadian government (following a policy of multiculturalism) at the University of British Columbia, Canada.[23] As a result, the author of the best historical work about the making of the modern Sikh tradition withdrew himself completely from Sikh studies. According to McLeod, the contemporary discussion about the Sikh tradition therefore in the end is between sceptical historians, like himself and Harjot Oberoi, and traditional historians, who also could be termed Singh Sabha historians.[24] A recent controversy, with reactions from the Punjab and throughout the Sikh diaspora, concerns McLeod's claim in *Sikhs of the Khalsa* that the five Ks were not part of the Sikh *Rahit* until the Singh Sabha reformation.[25]

On the whole, Indians in diaspora (by now more than 20 million) were confronted with a distinction between religion and culture unfamiliar and incomprehensible to most non-Westerners. Obviously there now are second and third generation settlers who have compartmentalized traditional and cultural life, at least to the extent of separating, for example, their understanding of the Sikh tradition from a Punjabi lifestyle in respect of diet, dress, arranged marriages and language. Continuity of tradition nonetheless partly was secured after the Second World War, when Indian reform movements got hold on the new wave of emigrants from the subcontinent and the second generation overseas Indians to Europe and North America.[26] Many of the Surinamese in the Netherlands, for example, are Arya Samajis or Lahori Ahmadiyahs. Undoubtedly, moral languages had prepared Indians much earlier for what was to come and hence the Singh Sabha, Arya Samaj and Ahmadiyah movements adapted smoothly to changing territorial, political and technological circumstances. When migrants (including those from the West) form closed communities to defend themselves against the wider hostile society and assimilation, moral languages gain in authority. The latter were welcomed as an alternative to full participation in the host societies which follow straightforwardly racist policies. Colonial attitudes increasingly came to the fore with the expanding flow of migrants. In terms of politics of difference, therefore, moral languages remain crucial, while they were clearly defined, respectable and so suitable for pedagogy and identity politics. Hence, members of the Singh Sabha, Arya Samaj and Ahmadiyah movements also can be seen as followers of a canon of reinterpreted nineteenth century traditions. This I experienced for example in Southall, a Punjabi dominated suburb of London, where I talked to Christian, Ahmadiyah and Arya Samaj preachers spreading their word on a busy Saturday afternoon on one of the main streets and during the same week when Sikhs celebrate the Punjabi spring harvest festival and start of the New Year at the local Singh Sabha gurdwara. Many of the arguments brought forward, I knew from nineteenth century sources on religious controversy in the Punjab and indeed also had heard when over the years I talked to Sikhs, Arya Samajis and Ahmadiyahs in India, Pakistan and the Netherlands.

The term diaspora is important because it led to the idea of the Indian/Punjabi homeland. Modern travel facilities and the internet surely boosted this process; equally important are the policies of the Indian government to strengthen ties with migrant Indians overseas. My point is that the continuing search for identity confirms the need for moral languages among Indian migrants after all these years. On the whole, Indians in diaspora increasingly became entangled with politics of difference within the host states (though now generally put under the heading of multiculturalism) and hence continued to define themselves as different from each other and the local populations. As in the nineteenth century, Sikh emigrants mostly remained preoccupied with defining their tradition, though now in terms of a World Religion (we are not Hindus!). Both Arya Samajis and Ahmadiyahs continued their polemics against each other and especially Christian missionaries, though they became much more entangled in internal discussions: Arya Samajis with the followers of the Sanatan Dharm (orthodox religion) about the definition of Hinduism, and Ahmadiyahs with their position *vis-à-vis* Sunni Islam.[27] More significant perhaps remains the fact that overseas Sikhs, Arya Samajis and Ahmadiyahs continued to have ties with the subcontinent (if not physically then at least spiritually and/or, more importantly, financially and politically) and form transnational communities. Particularly since Indira Gandhi's violent suppression of militant Sikhs in the Golden Temple in 1984 (Operation Blue Star), overseas Sikhs for example supported (morally and financially) the agitation for a separate Sikh nation, Khalistan. Thus while nineteenth century and early twentieth century Sikh migrants only had a vague sense of the Indian/Punjabi homeland, since 1984 the idea of the Punjab homeland increasingly came to the fore. A ferocious debate on the collective fate of the Sikh community in diaspora emerged. Sikh activists began lobbying for political rights and representation with local state officials and particularly the United

Nations, leading to 'the World Sikh Organization and the Khalistan Council to proclaim the Sikhs' right for self-determination through many resolutions'.[28] Since the so-called liberalization under Prime Minister Rajiv Gandhi, the ties between the Indian government and Non-Resident Indians (NRIs) and, more recently, Persons of Indian Origin (PIOs) have been strengthened. Hence, in terms of sponsoring, especially since the Bharatiya Janta Party (BJP) came into power, Hindu politics has growing transnational ties. Crucial remains the establishment in 1984 of the Vishva Hindu Parishad (World Hindu Council), which attempts to unite Hindus worldwide to recapture the Indian state from the secularists and to prevent Hindu conversions to Islam. As is well known, the VHP was vital to the financing of the 1992 Ramjanmabhoomi/Babri Masjid campaign, which culminated in the destruction of the latter mosque in the north Indian city of Ayodhya.[29] Indeed, as the mission became an outlet for Protestants in nineteenth century, today overseas connections in a sense function in a similar manner for South Asian traditions, with the blasphemous Ahmadiyahs perhaps as the extreme example.

The case of the Sikhs also makes clear one specific form of identity politics to be found in countries with large minorities (other examples are Israel, Palestine, Nigeria, Malaysia and Sri Lanka, all on the territory of the former British Empire). Modern South Asia saw the combination of the politics of belonging with constructed versions of Hinduism and, partly in reaction to that, Islam, Sikhism and Buddhism. These identifications to a degree developed as alternatives to the secularism of the Indian National Congress and the later Congress party. Since Hindu politics, however, gained power through the VHP and especially the BJP, militant Sikhs and similar movements among other minorities in the subcontinent are also directed against rule by the Hindu majority. All the same, for Ahmadiyahs loyalty in the end has nothing to do with any state, be it Pakistan or Great Britain, but with the true interpretation of Islam. While the Hindu case might seem different, particularly since the BJP became the ruling party of India, at the same time, the tension for most Hindus remains to feel morally comfortable in the modern world. Likewise, if ever there will be a Khalistan, its Sikh inhabitants will have the same problems as their Hindu and Muslim counterparts in India and Pakistan, in accommodating tradition with secular notions about progress, history and individualism.[30]

All over the world, identity politics assertively came to fore out of 'the need to reassert oneself against the real and perceived continued domination by the West'.[31] Whether in the South Asian context this feeling was implanted or nourished by the Anglo-Indian colonial state or not, 'it was based on real inequality which persists even today' and 'the morality-power connection may have been thought of as a partial remedy for that'.[32] Yet, though contemporary identity politics in the subcontinent confirm that the reorientation of community concepts to the needs of (national) economic progress in a way was a passing one, the re-emergence of moral rigour in South Asia today is neither new nor surprising. While it is frequently attributed to disappointment with capitalism, liberalism and secular nationalism, it can be equally explained through its formative roots in the nineteenth century.[33] Whatever the final word, moral languages today are often found useful worldwide as part of criticisms against Western hegemony with its supposedly objective morality and spiritless progress. Despite two World Wars and the rise and fall of communism, the West (now led by the United States) no doubt continues to dominate world politics.[34] Nowadays, the civilizing mission for example can be best detected in the attempts to foist on the world the green agenda under the slogan of sustainable development. Similarly, Non-Government Organizations (NGOs) can be taken as the follow up of nineteenth century Christian missions, as the close relationships between the two often confirm. Moreover, while backed up by multinational commerce, the funding conditions of the World Bank and the disciplinary force of the United Nations (where the Commonwealth, as a pressure group, resembles a club within a club) as a form of extra-territoriality, the West promotes its supposedly objective morality around the world in terms of human rights, democracy, egalitarianism, labour and environmental standards, perhaps more than ever before.

NOTES

1. R.W. Scribner, *The German Reformation*, Basingstoke: Macmillan, pp. 57-8.
2. M.A. Macauliffe, 'The Sikh Religion', 1903, in *The Sikh Religion: A Symposium*, ed. M.A. Macauliffe, H.H. Wilson, Frederic Pincott, John Malcolm and Sardar Kahn Singh, Calcutta: Sushil Gupta, 1958, p. 4 and *The Sikh Religion: Its Gurus, Sacred Writings and Authors*, 1909; repr. Bombay: Oxford University Press, 1963, vol. I, p. xxxiv; Monier Monier-Williams, *Brahminism and Hinduism or Religious Thought and Life in India based on the Veda and Other Sacred Books of the Hindus*, London: John Murray, 1887, p. 161.
3. Doris R. Jakobsh, *Relocating Gender in Sikh History: Transformation, Meaning and Identity*, New Delhi: Oxford University Press, 2003, p. 59.
4. Ibid., p. 60.
5. Macauliffe, 'The Sikh Religion', vol. I, p. lvii.
6. Kenneth W. Jones, *Arya Dharm: Hindu Consciousness in Nineteenth Century India*, New Delhi: Manohar, 1976, p. 110.
7. Lajpat Rai, *A History of the Arya Samaj: An Account of its Origin, Doctrines and Activities with a Biographical Sketch of the Founder*, New Delhi: Munshiram Manoharlal, 1992, p. 54.
8. See for example: Gokal Chand, *Luther of India*, Lahore: Ishwar Chandra Arya Tract Society, 1913.
9. Owen Chadwick, *The Secularization of the European Mind in the Nineteenth Century*, Cambridge: Cambridge University Press, 1975, p. 193.
10. Ibid., p. 203.
11. Ibid., pp. 7, 9.
12. C.A. Bayly, *The Birth of the Modern World 1780-1914*, London: Blackwell, 2004, p. 277.
13. Sudhir Chandra, *The Oppressive Present: Literature and Social Consciousness in Colonial India*, New Delhi: Oxford University Press, 1992, p. 17.
14. Partha Chatterjee, *The Nation and its Fragments: Colonial and Post-Colonial Histories*, New Delhi: Oxford University Press, 1993 and D.H.A. Kolff, *Indië en de Wereldgeschiedenis*, Leiden: Universiteit Leiden, 2003, p. 9
15. Sudhir Kakar, *The Inner World: A Psycho-Analytic Study of Childhood and Society in India*, New Delhi: Oxford University Press, 1981, p. 9.
16. See further: Darshan Singh Tatla, 'Rural Roots of the Sikh Diaspora', in *People on the Move: Punjabi Colonial, and Post-Colonial*

Migration, ed. Ian Talbot and Shinder Thandi, Karachi: Oxford University Press, 2004, pp. 45-59.

17. Like the Ahmadiyahs, Arya Samajis suffered heavily because of the 1947 Partition. They lost their main centre at Lahore and several others permanently and thousands of affluent Punjabi Samajis became refugees.

18. Interestingly, it was originally a Punjab Institute built under the supervision of Dr. G.W. Leitner with money donated mainly by the princess of Bhopal. When the mosque remained closed and deserted after the death of Leitner, Ahmadiyahs got it restored and, with permission of the trustees, transferred their mission from London to Woking in 1913. Muhammad Ali, *The Ahmadiyyah Movement*, Lahore: Ahmadiyyah Anjuman Isha'at Islam, 1973, p. 319.

19. Francis Robinson, 'Prophets without Honour? Ahmad and the Ahmadiyya', *History Today*, June 1990, p. 44.

20. In 1914 Lahori Ahmadiyah leader Muhammad Ali completed his influential translation of the Koran, including English notes, introduction and parallel English and Arabic texts. Interestingly, in 2005, a new translation into Dutch based on Ali's interpretation was published and contested by the larger Muslim community in the Netherlands but welcomed by the Dutch authorities, who do not care to know anything about the heterodox position of the Ahmadiyahs within Islam.

21. Singh Sabhaites, Arya Samajis, Ahmadiyahs and their respective opponents are very active today in creating websites.

22. W.H. McLeod, 'Crisis of Outrage: History versus Tradition in the Study of the Sikh Community', *South Asia Research*, 14, 1994, p. 132.

23. Ibid., p. 122.

24. Ibid., p. 131.

25. See further on these controversies: W.H. McLeod, *Discovering the Sikhs: Autobiography of a Historian*, New Delhi: Permanent Black, 2004.

26. Although there never was a strong missionary emphasis within the Sikh community and an agenda to convert non-Sikhs into the *Panth* never was formalized (see Louis E. Fenech, 'Conversion and Sikh Tradition', in *Religious Conversion in India: Modes, Motivations, and Meanings*, ed. Rowena Robinson and Sathianathan Clarke, New Delhi: Oxford University Press, 2003, pp. 149-80), a trickle of Western converts have become Sikhs through the work of the Sikh Dharm of the Western Hemisphere, founded by Yogi Bhajan in 1971, and its better known educational offshoot 3HO (Happy, Healthy, Holy Organization).

27. Sanatanists in Fiji and Trinidad for example continued to criticize the outdated practice of *niyog* (as discussed in Saraswati's *Satyarth Prakash*) in their debates with Arya Samajis. See: J.E. Llewellyn, *The Arya Samaj as a Fundamentalist Movement: A Study in Comparative Fundamentalism*, New Delhi: Manohar, 1993, p. 146.
28. Darshan Singh Tatla, 'Imagining Punjab: Narratives of Nationhood and Homeland among the Sikh Diaspora', in *Sikh Religion, Culture and Ethnicity*, ed. Christopher Shackle, Gurharpal Singh and Arvind-Pal Mandair, Richmond: Curzon Press, 2001, pp. 163, 181.
29. Like the Hindu extremists of the RSS, the VHP has a broad definition of Hinduism that includes all but the foreign and hostile Muslims and Christians. According to the VHP, a just Hindu society of the ancient Golden Age was conquered and suppressed first by Muslims and then by the British. Hence, following some Western scholars, Hindu religious inclusiveness is called tolerance, while Muslims are seen as fanatical and bigoted, and secularists are anti-national agents of the West.
30. This of course also remains a problem within Christendom.
31. Dietrich Reetz, 'In Search of the Collective Self: How Ethnic Group Concepts were Cast through Conflict in Colonial India', *Modern Asian Studies*, 31, 1997, p. 314.
32. Ibid.
33. Ibid., p. 315.
34. Protestant evangelicals in the United States definitely also can be called religious nationalists or religious fundamentalists, if one wants to use these labels. Demonizing the secular government, these evangelicals have followed a policy of gradual change during the last decades. Stressing electoral victories in local races and chipping away at laws and regulations governing school prayer, creationism and abortion, while the effort to control the Republican Party further shows their continued aim of seeking national power.

Key Dates

1893   Division Arya Samaj; Sikh Shuddhi Sabha Lahore; Hali's *Muqaddima*
1897   Lekh Ram assassinated; Kahn Singh Nabha, *Ham Hindu Nahin*
1898   Death of Dyal Singh Majithia; Bhai Vir Singh, *Sundri*
1899   Khalsa College Amritsar; Ghulam Ahmad, *Masih Hindustan Mein*
1901   Ahmadiyahs mentioned separately in the census; Rudyard Kipling, *Kim*; Punjab Alienation of Land Act;
1902   Chief Khalsa Diwan; *Review of Religions*; Gurukul Kangri Haridwar; Arya Samaj starts mission in Fiji
1904   Japan defeats Russia
1905   Ghulam Ahmad, *Islami Usul ki Falasafi*; Ashraf 'Ali Thanawi, *Bihisti Zewar*
1906   Ghulam Ahmad, *al-Wasiyah*; Muslim League
1907   Punjab Disturbances
1908   Death of Ghulam Ahmad; Nur al-Din first *Khalifah*; Sikh Educational Conference
1909   Morley-Minto Reforms; Max Arthur Macauliffe, *The Sikh Religion*; Anand Marriage Bill; Gandhi, *Hind Swaraj*; Baba Buddh Singh, *Chandar Hari*
1914   Death of Nur al-Din; Mahmud Ahmad second *Khalifah*; Split Ahmadiyah movement; Lajpat Rai, *A History of the Arya Samaj*; Muhammad Ali's translation of the Koran
1919   Jallianwala Bagh massacre, Amritsar
1920   Shiromani Gurdwara Parbandhak Committee (SGPC); Montagu-Chelmsford Reforms
1925   Darling, *The Punjab Peasant*; Gurdwaras Act; Rashtriya Swayam-sevak Sangh (RSS) founded
1930   Kahn Singh Nabha, *Gurushabad Ratanakar*
1931   Ahmadiyah Muhammad Zafrullah Khan, president of the Muslim League conference
1945   Rahit Maryada approved by the SGPC.
1947   Partition of British India into India and Pakistan
1966   Sikh majority Punjabi language state carved from the northern half of pre-existing Indian Punjab (the south becomes Hindu majority Haryana)
1975   Mecca declares Ahmadiyahs as non-Islamic; Pakistan's Constitution amended to exclude Ahmadiyahs from the definition of Muslims

Glossary

Ar. = Arabic
H. = Hindi (Hindustani)
P. = Persian
Pu. = Punjabi
S. = Sanskrit

adab (Ar.)	Literature; respect
Arya (S.)	Of descent from the ancient Aryans; associated with the *rishis* and the Vedas
baiat (Ar.)	Initiation as a disciple through vow of spiritual allegiance
bhakti (S.)	Religious devotion
dharm (S.)	Right moral way of life; duty; righteous rule
doab (P.)	Tract of land lying between two rivers, especially that between the Ganges and Jamuna
fatwa (Ar.)	Legal religious statement
fiqh (Ar.)	Jurisprudence, Islamic law as interpreted by generations of scholars
gurdwara (Pu.)	Sikh temple
Gurmukhi (Pu.)	Punjabi script based on Devanagari
hadith (Ar.)	Body of traditions of the sayings of the Prophet Muhammad
izzat (P.)	Honour; status
jihad (Ar.)	Holy war against non-Muslims
kafir (Ar.)	Infidel; those who do not believe in Islam
karma (S.)	Moral duty; fate as the consequence of previous acts
Khalsa (Ar.)	Sikh order instituted by Guru Gobind Singh
mahdi (Ar.)	Rightly guided one who will come on the last day to save Muslims
masih mawud (Ar.)	Promised messiah
moksha (S.)	Salvation
muhaddath (Ar.)	Person spoken to by Allah or his angels
mujaddid (Ar.)	Renewer of the faith
Nastaliq (Ar.)	Perso-Arabic script used for Urdu

niyog (S.)	Ancient Hindu custom that permitted a widow to bear children; in reinterpreted Arya Samaj practice equivalent to levirate
panth (S.)	Lit. path; system of religious belief and practice; the Sikh community, when spelt with a capital 'P'
purdah (Ar.)	Seclusion of women from public view
pir (P.)	Religious leader of a Sufi order
qissa (Ar.)	Poetic tradition in Punjabi
quam (Ar.)	'People who stand together'; community
Rahit (H.)	*Khalsa* code of belief and conduct
Rahit-nama (H.)	Manual of *Rahit* principles
raj (S.)	Sovereignty with capital 'R' specifically used for period of British rule in India
sannyasi (S.)	Hindu who has renounced all worldly ties and possessions in order to devote himself to the spiritual life, living on alms
sant (H.)	Group of teachers (usually of low caste) who flourished in the fifteenth, sixteenth and seventeenth centuries in north India and were critical about Brahmanical authority
shahid (Ar.)	One who dies for his faith
shaivite (S.)	Follower of the cult of the Hindu God Shiva
shariat (Ar.)	Law based on Islamic scriptures and religious knowledge
Shia (Ar.)	Muslims who believe that religious authority was passed to Muhammad's son in law, Ali, and then through his descendants
shruti (S.)	Sacred book believed to have been revealed by God to wise men and therefore heard by them
shuddhi (S.)	Purification rite which became a vehicle for conversion to the Arya Samaj, alternatively during the late nineteenth and early twentieth centuries used by the Sikhs
Smriti (S.)	Sacred book composed by wise men from remembered tradition
Sufi (Ar.)	Member of brotherhood of people initiated by a *baiat* to a saint, who claims to belong to a spiritual lineage going back to the founder of the brotherhood and ultimately the Prophet himself
sunnah (Ar.)	Customs and traditions associated with the Prophet Muhammad
Sunni (Ar.)	The majority of Muslims who follow the *sunnah*
taqlid (Ar.)	Delegation of authority in Islamic theological context
zail (P.)	Administrative subdivision in the Punjab

Bibliography

PRIMARY SOURCES

Private Papers

British Library, Oriental and India Office Collections, London:
John Beames
Robert Montgomery
Richard Temple

Official and Semi-official Treatises

Arnold, Edwin, *The Marquis of Dalhousie's Administration of British India*, vol. I, London: Saunders, Otley & Co., 1862.

Baden-Powell, B.H., *The Land-Systems of British India*, 3 vols., Oxford: Clarendon Press, 1892.

Beames, John, *Memoirs of a Bengal Civilian*, 1896; London: Eland, 1961.

Census of India, volumes for the Punjab, various dates.

Darling, Malcolm, *The Punjab Peasant in Prosperity and Debt*, 1925; Bombay: Oxford University Press, 1947.

District Gazetteers Punjab, various districts, various dates.

Douie, James M., *Panjab Settlement Manual*, Lahore: Civil and Military Gazette Press, 1899.

———, *The Panjab, North-West Frontier Province and Kashmir*, 1916; repr. New Delhi: Seema, 1974.

Elsmie, G.R., *Thirty-Five Years in the Punjab, 1858-1893*, Edinburgh: David Douglas, 1908.

Falcon, R.W., *Handbook on the Sikhs for Regimental Officers*, Allahabad: Pioneer Press, 1896.

Griffin, Lepel H., *The Punjab Chiefs*, 2 vols., 1865; repr., Lahore: Civil and Military Gazette Press, 1890.

Imperial Gazetteer of India, Provincial Series: Punjab, 2 vols., 1908; repr. New Delhi: Atlantic, 1991.

Indus Valley State Railway: Administration Report, Roorkee, 1879.

Leitner, G.W., *History of Indigenous Education in the Punjab since Annexation and in 1882*, 1883; repr. Gurgaon: Deepak, 1989.

MacMunn, G.F., *The Armies of India*, 1911; repr. New Delhi: Heritage, 1991.

Muir, William, *Records of the Intelligence Department of the North-West Provinces of India during the Mutiny of 1857*, 2 vols., Edinburgh: Clark, 1902.

Petrie, D., 'C.I.D. Memorandum on Recent Developments in Sikh Politics, 1911', as reprinted in *Punjab Past and Present*, 4, 2, 1970, pp. 302-79.

'Queen Victoria's Proclamation, 1 November 1858', in *The Evolution of India and Pakistan, 1858-1947: Select Documents*, ed. C.H. Philips, H.L. Singh and B.N. Pandey, London: Oxford University Press, 1962.

Report by the Panjab Provincial Committee with Evidence Taken Before the Committee and Memorials Addressed to the Education Commission, Calcutta: Government Printing, 1884.

Reports on the Administration of the Punjab and its Dependencies, Lahore: Punjab Government Press, 1898-1906.

Rose, H.A., *A Glossary of the Tribes and Castes of the Punjab and North-West Frontier Province*, 3 vols., 1919; repr. Patiala: Punjab Languages Department, 1990.

Selections from the Punjab Vernacular Press, 1896-1911.

'Sirdar Dyal Singh Will Case in the Chief Court of the Punjab, Probate Case No. 4 of 1899', as reprinted in *Brahmo Samaj and Dyal Singh Majithia*, ed. Madan Gopal, New Delhi: Uppal, 1998.

Strachey, John, *India: Its Administration & Progress*, 1888; London: Macmillan, 1911.

Temple, R.C., *India in 1880*, London: John Murray, 1881.

———, *Men and Events of My Time in India*, London: John Murray, 1882.

———, *The Legends of the Punjab*, 3 vols., 1884-6; repr. Patiala: Punjab Languages Department, 1988.

———, *James Thomason*, Oxford: Clarendon Press, 1893.

Thorburn, S.S., *Musalmans and Moneylenders in the Punjab*, 1886; repr. Lahore: Book Traders, n.d.

———, *The Punjab in Peace and War*, 1883; repr. Patiala: Punjab Languages Department, 1970.

Tupper, C.L., *Punjab Customary Law*, 3 vols., Calcutta: Government Printing, 1881.

Books and Tracts

Ahmad, Mirza Ghulam, *A Clarification*, 1891; repr. Lahore: Ahmadiyya Anjuman Isha'at Islam, 1966.

———, *Jesus in India*, 1899; repr. Qadian: Nazarat Nashr-o-Ishaat, 1991.

———, *Jihad and the British Government*, Lahore: Caxton Printing Works, 1900.

———, *A Misunderstanding Removed*, 1901; repr. Qadian: Nazir Dawat-o-Tabligh, 1974.

———, *A Review of Christianity from a New Point of View*, 1903; repr. Qadian: Nazir Dawat-o-Tabligh, n.d.

———, *The Philosophy of Islam*, 1905; repr. New Delhi: Inter-India, 1978.

———, *The Will*, 1906; repr. Qadian: Nazir Dawat-o-Tabligh, 1970.

———, *How to get Rid of the Bondage of Sin*, n.d.; repr. Qadian: Nazir Dawat-o-Tabligh, 1971.

Ahmad, Nazir, *Taubat an Nussooh* or *Repentance of Nussooh*, tr. M. Kempson, London: W.H. Allen & Co, 1894.

———, *The Bride's Mirror*, tr. G.E. Ward, London: Henry Frowde, 1903.

Ali, Muhammad, *The Ahmadiyyah Movement*, 1931; repr. Lahore: Ahmadiyyah Anjuman Isha'at Islam, 1973.

Amir Ali, Sayyid, *The Spirit of Islam*, 1891; repr. London: Christophers, 1953.

Anon., *Controversy between the Arya Samaj of Wazirabad and Pandit Ganesh Datta Shastri on the Shraddha Ceremony, with the Opinion of F. Max Müller*, Lahore, 1896.

Azad, Muhammad Husain, *Ab-e Hayat: Shaping the Canon of Urdu*, tr./ed. Frances Pritchett and Shamsur Rahman Faruqi, 1880; repr. New Delhi: Oxford University Press, 2001.

Beames, John, *A Comparative Grammar of the Modern Aryan Languages of India*, 3 vols., 1872-9; repr. New Delhi: Munshiram Manoharlal, 1966.

Brown, Percy, *Lahore Museum Punjab: A Descriptive Guide to the Department of Archaelogy & Antiquities*, Lahore: Civil and Military Gazette Press, 1908.

Chand, Gokal, *Luther of India*, Lahore: Ishwar Chandra Arya Tract Society, 1913.

Clark, Henry Martyn, 'A Controversy with the Mohammedans', *Church Missionary Intelligencer*, 19, 1894, pp. 96-105.

———, 'Some Results of the Late Mohammedan Controversy', *Church Missionary Intelligencer*, 19, 1894, pp. 812-18.

———, 'Conversions from Mohammedanism in the Punjab', *Church Missionary Intelligencer*, 25, 1900, pp. 180-2.

———, *Robert Clark of the Punjab: Pioneer and Missionary Statesman*, London: Andrew Melrose, 1907.

Clark, Robert, *The Missions of the Church Missionary Society and the Church of England Zenana Missionary Society in the Punjab and*

Sindh, 1885, ed. Robert Maconachie, London: Church Missionary Society, 1904.

Cunningham, Joseph Davy, *A History of the Sikhs from the Origin of the Nation to the Battles of the Sutlej*, ed. H.L.O. Garrett, 1849; repr. New Delhi: Chand, 1966.

Dass, Lala Dwarka, *Hindi versus Urdu*, Lahore: Arya Press, 1882.

Dilke, Charles W., *Greater Britain: A Record of Travels in English Speaking Countries during 1866 and 1867*, vol. 2, London: Macmillan, 1868.

Elliot, H.M. and J. Dowson, *The History of India as told by its own Historians: The Muhammadan Period*, 8 vols., London: Trübner, 1867-77.

Falcon, S.W., *A New Hindustani-English Dictionary*, London: Trübner, 1879.

Farquhar, J.N., *Modern Religious Reform Movements in India*, 1915; repr. New Delhi: Munshiram Manoharlal, 1977.

Gandhi, M.K., 'Hind Swaraj', 1909, in *The Collected Works of Mahatma Gandhi*, vol. 10; New Delhi: Publications Division, Government of India, 1958, pp. 6-68.

Graham, G.F.I., *The Life and Work of Syed Ahmad Khan*, 1885; repr. Karachi: Oxford University Press, 1974.

Hali, Altaf Husain, 'Assemblies of Women', 1874, in *Voices of Silence*, tr. Gail Minault, New Delhi: Chanakya, 1986.

Iqbal, Muhammad, *The Reconstruction of Religious Thought in Islam*, 1934; repr. Lahore: Muhammad Ashraf, 1954.

———, *Islam and Ahmadism*, Lahore: Anjuman i-Khuddam ud-Din, 1936.

Kipling, Rudyard, *Kim*, 1901; repr. Harmondsworth: Penguin, 1987.

Latif, Muhammad, *History of the Punjab from the Remotest Antiquity to the Present Time*, Calcutta: Central Press, 1891.

———, *Lahore: Its History, Architectural Remains and Antiquities*, Lahore: The New Imperial Press, 1892.

Macauliffe, M.A., 'The Sikh Religion', 1903, in *The Sikh Religion: A Symposium*, M.A. Macauliffe, H.H. Wilson, Frederic Pincott, John Malcolm and Sardar Kahn Singh; repr. Calcutta: Sushil Gupta, 1958, pp. 1-26.

———, *The Sikh Religion: Its Gurus, Sacred Writings and Authors*, 6 vols., 1909; repr. Bombay: Oxford University Press, 1963.

Malcolm, John, 'A Sketch of the Sikhs', 1810, in *The Sikh Religion: A Symposium*, M.A. Macauliffe, H.H. Wilson, Frederic Pincott, John Malcolm and Sardar Kahn Singh; repr. Calcutta: Sushil Gupta, 1958, pp. 84-145.

Mill, James, *History of British India*, ed. Horace Hayman Wilson, 3 vols., 1817; London: James Madden, 1858.

Mill, John Stuart, 'Civilization', 1836, in *The Collected Works of John*

Stuart Mill, vol. 18, ed. J.M. Robson, Toronto: University of Toronto Press, 1977, pp. 119-47.

Monier-Williams, Monier, *Brahminism and Hinduism or Religious Thought and Life in India Based on the Veda and Other Sacred Books of the Hindus*, London: John Murray, 1887.

Muir, William, *Life of Mohamet*, ed. T.H. Weir, 1861; Edinburgh: Grant, 1912.

Mulraj, R.B., *Beginning of Punjabi Nationalism: Autobiography of R.B. Mulraj*, Hoshiarpur: V.V. Vedic Research Institute, 1975.

Platts, John T., *A Dictionary of Urdu, Classical Hindi and English*, 1884; repr. New Delhi: Munshiram Manoharlal, 1997.

Rai, Lajpat, 'Life and Work of Pandit Guru Datta Vidyarthi', 1891, in *The Collected Works of Lala Lajpat Rai*, ed. B.R. Nanda, vol. 1, New Delhi: Manohar, 2003, pp. 143-264.

———, 'The Message of the Bhagavad Gita', 1908, in *The Collected Works of Lala Lajpat Rai*, ed. B.R. Nanda, vol. 3, New Delhi: Manohar, 2004, pp. 329-53.

———, 'The Story of My Life', 1915, in *The Collected Works of Lala Lajpat Rai*, ed. B.R. Nanda, vol. 5, New Delhi: Manohar, 2004, pp. 275-368.

———, 'Young India: An Interpretation and a History of the Nationalist Movement from Within', 1916, in *The Collected Works of Lala Lajpat Rai*, ed. B.R. Nanda, vol. 6, New Delhi: Manohar, 2005, pp. 199-328.

———, *A History of the Arya Samaj: An Account of its Origin, Doctrines and Activities with a Biographical Sketch of the Founder*, 1914; repr. New Delhi: Munshiram Manoharlal, 1992.

———, *The Political Future of India*, 1919; repr. New Delhi: Renaissance, 1988.

———, *The Problem of National Education in India*, London: George Allen & Unwin Ltd., 1920.

Robson, J., *Hinduism and its Relation to Christianity*, London: Oliphant, Anderson & Ferrier, 1893.

The Rules and the Scheme of Studies of the Proposed Gurukula Sanctioned by the Arya Pratinidhi Sabha, Punjab, Lahore: Mufid-i-Am Press, 1899.

Saraswati, Dayanand, *Gokarunanidhi*, tr. Khazan Singh, 1880; repr. Ajmer: Paropkarini Sabha, 1993.

———, *Light of Truth*, tr. Dr. Charanjiva Bharadwaja, 1906; repr. New Delhi: Sarvadeshik Arya Pratinidhi Sabha, 1991.

Scott, T.J., *Missionary Life Among the Villages in India*, Cincinnati: Hitchcock and Walden, 1876.

Shraddhanand, Swami, *Hindu Sangathan. Saviour of the Dying Race*, New Delhi: Swami Shraddhananda Sanyasi, 1926.

Singh, Bawa Arjan, *Mela Chandapur*, 1893; ed. Bawa Chhajju Singh, Lahore: Aryan Printing, Publishing & General Trading Co., 1903.

Singh, Bhagat Lakshman, *Sikh Martyrs*, 1928; repr. Ludhiana: Lahore Book Shop, 1989.

———, *Autobiography*, Ganda Singh, ed., Calcutta: The Sikh Cultural Centre, 1965.

Stocqueler, J.H., *Review of the Life and Labours of Dr. G.W. Leitner*, Brighton: The Tower Press, 1875.

Trumpp, Ernest, *The Adi Granth or the Holy Scriptures of the Sikhs Translated from the Original Gurmukhi with Introductory Essays*, London: Allen & Co., 1877.

Vidyarthi, Guru Datta, *Fragments of Pandit Guru Datta Vidyarthi M.A.'s Criticism on Monier William's Indian Wisdom*, Lahore: Virajanand Press, 1892.

———, *Works of Late Pandit Guru Datta Vidyarthi M.A.*, ed. Lala Jivan Das, Lahore: Punjab Economical Press, 1897.

Vir Singh, Bhai, *Sundri*, 1898; tr. Gobind Singh Mansukhani; repr. New Delhi: Bhai Vir Singh Sahitya Sadan, 1988.

———, *Bijay Singh*, 1900; tr. Devinder Singh Duggal; repr. New Delhi: Bhai Vir Singh Sahitya Sadan, 1988.

———, *Satwant Kaur*, 1900; tr. Ujagar Singh Bawa; repr. New Delhi: Bhai Vir Singh Sahitya Sadan, 1988.

———, *Rana Surat Singh*, 1905; tr. Gurbachan Singh Talib; repr. Chandigarh: Punjab University, 1986.

———, *Baba Naudh Singh*, 1921; tr. Gurbachan Singh Talib, repr. New Delhi: Bhai Vir Singh Sahitya Sadan, 1989.

Walter, H.A., *The Ahmadiya Movement*, 1918; repr. New Delhi: Manohar, 1991.

Yule, H. and A.C. Burnell, *Hobson-Jobson, a Glossary of Colloquial Anglo-Indian Words and Phrases...*, 1886; ed. William Crooke; repr. Calcutta: Rupa Co., 1990.

Periodicals

Punjab Notes and Queries, 1883-7
Regenerator of Arya Varta, 1883-4
Review of Religions, 1902-10
Tribune, 1881-1911

Urdu and Hindi

Ahmad, Nazir, *Ibn-ul-Vaqt*, 1889; repr. Lahore: Ferozsons, n.d.

Das, Lala Jivan, *Do Hindu Beva Auraton ki Baatchit*, Lahore: Arya Pustakalaya, 1891.

Hali, Altaf Husain, *Musaddas*, 1879; repr. Lahore: Ferozsons, n.d.

———, *Hayat-i-Javed*, 1901, repr. Lahore.

Harishchandra, Bharatendu, 'Dilli Darbar Darpan', 1877, in *Hindi and Urdu Since 1800: A Common Reader*, Christopher Shackle and Rupert Snell, London: SOAS, 1990, pp. 101-4.

———, 'Bharatvars ki Unnati Kaise ho Sakti Hai?' 1884, in *Bharatendu Samagra*, ed. Hemant Sharma, Varanasi: Pracarak Granthavali Pariyojan, 1987, pp. 1010-13.

Khan, Sayyid Ahmad, *Asbab-e-Baghavat-e-Hind*, 1859; repr. Lahore: Sang-e-Meel, n.d.

———, *Musafiran-e-Landan*, 1869; repr. Lahore: Majlis-e-Taraqqi-e-Adab, n.d.

Shahid, Dost Muhammad, ed., *Tarikh-i-Ahmadiyah*, 9 vols., Rabwah, n.d.

SECONDARY SOURCES

Adas, Michael, *Machines as the Measure of Men: Science, Technology and Ideologies of Western Dominance*, New Delhi: Oxford University Press, 1990.

Asad, Talal, *Genealogies of Religion: Discipline and Reasons of Power in Christianity and Islam*, Baltimore: John Hopkins University Press, 1993.

Baljon, J.M.S., *Modern Muslim Koran Interpretation, 1880-1960*, Leiden: Brill, 1961.

Ballantyne, Tony, 'Looking Back, Looking Forward: The Historiography of Sikhism', *New Zealand Journal of Asian Studies*, 4, 2002, pp. 5-29.

Barrier, N. Gerald, 'The Arya Samaj and Congress Politics in the Punjab, 1894-1908', *Journal of Asian Studies*, 26, 1967, pp. 363-79.

———, 'The Punjab Government and Communal Policies, 1870-1908', *Journal of Asian Studies*, 27, 1968, pp. 523-39.

———, *The Sikhs and their Literature: A Guide to Books, Tracts and Periodicals (1849-1919)*, New Delhi: Manohar, 1970.

———, 'In Search of Identity: Scholarship and Authority among Sikhs in Nineteenth Century Punjab', in *Language and Society in Modern India*, ed. R.I. Crane and B. Spangenberg, New Delhi: Heritage, 1981, pp. 1-23.

———, 'Sikh Politics in British Punjab prior to the Gurdwara Reform Movement', in *Sikh History and Religion in the Twentieth Century*, ed. Joseph T. O'Conell et al., Toronto: University of Toronto Center for South Asian Studies, 1988, pp. 159-90.

———, 'Vernacular Publishing and Sikh Public Life in the Punjab, 1880-1910', in *Religious Controversy in British India: Dialogues in South*

Asian Languages, ed. Kenneth W. Jones, Albany: State University of New York Press, 1992, pp. 200-26.

———, 'The Formulation and Transmission of Sikh Tradition: Competing Organizations and Ideology, 1902-1925', in *The Transmission of Sikh Heritage in the Diaspora*, ed. Pashaura Singh and N. Gerald Barrier, New Delhi: Manohar, 1996, pp. 193-212.

Bayly, C.A., *Rulers, Townsmen and Bazaars: North Indian Society During the Age of British Expansion, 1770-1870*, 1983; New Delhi: Oxford University Press, 1992.

———, *Empire and Information: Intelligence Gathering and Social Communication in India*, Cambridge: Cambridge University Press, 1996.

———, *Origins of Nationality in South Asia: Patriotism and Ethical Government in the Making of Modern India*, New Delhi: Oxford University Press, 1998.

———, *The Birth of the Modern World 1780-1914*, London: Blackwell, 2004.

Bhattacharya, Neeladri, 'Pastoralists in a Colonial World', in *Nature, Culture, Imperialism: Essays on the Environmental History of South Asia*, ed. David Arnold and Ramachandra Guha, New Delhi: Oxford University Press, 1996, pp. 49-85.

Brass, Paul R., 'Elite Groups, Symbol Manipulations and Ethnic Identity Among the Muslims of South Asia', in *Political Identity in South Asia*, ed. David Taylor and Malcolm Yapp, London: Curzon Press, 1979, pp. 35-77.

Brown, Judith M., *Modern India: Origins of an Asian Democracy*, New Delhi: Oxford University Press, 1984.

Brush, Stanley E., 'Protestant in the Punjab: Religion and Social Change in an Indian Province in the Nineteenth Century', unpublished Ph.D. dissertation, Berkeley: University of California, 1971.

Burke, Peter, *The Art of Conversation*, New York: Cornell University Press, 1993.

Chadwick, Owen, *The Secularization of the European Mind in the Nineteenth Century*, Cambridge: Cambridge University Press, 1975.

Chandra, Sudhir, *The Oppressive Present: Literature and Social Consciousness in Colonial India*, New Delhi: Oxford University Press, 1992.

Chatterjee, Partha, *Nationalist Thought and the Colonial World: A Derivative Discourse?*, London: Zed Press, 1986.

———, *The Nation and its Fragments: Colonial and Post-Colonial Histories*, New Delhi: Oxford University Press, 1993.

Churchill, Edward D., 'Muslim Societies of the Punjab, 1860-1890', *Punjab Past and Present*, 8, 1974, pp. 69-91.

————, 'Printed Literature of the Punjabi Muslims, 1860-1900', in *Sources on Punjab History*, ed. W. Eric Gustafson and Kenneth W. Jones, New Delhi: Manohar, 1975, pp. 253-336.

Cohn, Bernard S., *An Anthropologist Among the Historians and Other Essays*, New Delhi: Oxford University Press, 1987.

————, *Colonialism and its Forms of Knowledge: The British in India*, New Delhi: Oxford University Press, 1996.

Copley, Antony, *Religions in Conflict: Cultural Contact and Conversion in Late Colonial India*, New Delhi: Oxford University Press, 1997.

Cox, Jeffrey, *Imperial Fault Lines: Christianity and Colonial Power in India, 1818-1940*, Stanford: Stanford University Press, 2002.

Dewey, Clive, 'Some Consequences of Military Expenditure in British India: The Case of the Upper Sind Sagar Doab, 1849-1947', in *Arrested Development in India: The Historical Dimension*, ed. Clive Dewey, New Delhi: Manohar, 1988, pp. 93-169.

————, *Anglo-Indian Attitudes: The Mind of the Indian Civil Service*, London: Hambledon Press, 1993.

Dobrée, Bonamy, *Rudyard Kipling: Realist and Fabulist*, London: Oxford University Press, 1967.

Embree, Ainslee T., *Utopias in Conflict: Religion and Nationalism in Modern India*, Berkeley: University of California Press, 1990.

Fenech, Louis E., *Martyrdom in the Sikh Tradition: Playing the 'Game of Love'*, New Delhi: Oxford University Press, 2000.

————, 'Conversion and Sikh Tradition', in *Religious Conversion in India: Modes, Motivations, and Meanings*, ed. Rowena Robinson and Sathianathan Clarke, New Delhi: Oxford University Press 2003, pp. 149-80.

Fischer-Tiné, Harald, '"Kindly Elders of the Hindu Biradri": The Arya Samaj's Struggle for Influence and its Effect on Hindu-Muslim Relations, 1880-1925', in *Gurus and Their Followers: New Religious Reform Movements in Colonial India*, ed. Antony Copley, New Delhi: Oxford University Press, 2000, pp. 107-27.

————, '"The Only Hope for Fallen India": The Gurukul Kangri as an Experiment in National Education (1902-1922)', in *Explorations in the History of South Asia: Essays in Honour of Dietmar Rothermund*, ed. Georg Berkemer et. al., New Delhi: Manohar, 2001, pp. 278-99.

————, 'National Education, Pulp Fiction and the Contradictions of Colonialism: Perceptions of an Educational Experiment in Early-Twentieth-Century India', in *Colonialism as Civilizing Mission: Cultural Ideology in British India*, ed. Harald Fischer-Tiné and Michael Mann, London: Anthem Press, 2005, pp. 229-47.

Freitag, Sandria B., *Collective Action and Community: Public Arenas and the Emergence of Communalism in North India*, New Delhi: Oxford University Press, 1990.

———, 'Introduction', *South Asia*, 14, 1991, pp. 1-13.

Friedmann, Yohanan, *Prophecy Continues: Aspects of Ahmadi Religious Thought and its Medieval Background*, New Delhi: Oxford University Press, 1988.

Gilmartin, David, *Empire and Islam: Punjab and the Making of Pakistan*, New Delhi: Oxford University Press, 1988.

———, 'Democracy, Nationalism and the Public: A Speculation on Colonial Muslim Politics', *South Asia*, 14, 1991, pp. 123-40.

———, 'Models of the Hydraulic Environment: Colonial Irrigation, State Power and Community in the Indus Basin', in *Nature, Culture, Imperialism: Essays on the Environmental History of South Asia*, ed. David Arnold and Ramachandra Guha, New Delhi: Oxford University Press, 1996, pp. 210-36.

———, 'A Magnificent Gift: Muslim Nationalism and the Election Process in Colonial Punjab', *Comparative Studies in Society and History*, 40, 1998, pp. 415-36.

———, 'Partition, Pakistan, and South Asian History: In Search of a Narrative', *Journal of Asian Studies*, 57, 1998, pp. 1068-95.

Grewal, J.S., *The Emergence of Punjabi Drama: A Cultural Response to Colonial Rule*, Amritsar: Guru Nanak Dev University, 1986.

———, *The Sikhs of the Punjab*, Cambridge: Cambridge University Press, 1990.

———, 'Nabha's "Ham Hindu Nahin": A Declaration of Sikh Ethnicity', in *Sikh Identity: Continuity and Change*, ed. Pashaura Singh and N. Gerald Barrier, New Delhi: Manohar, 1999, pp. 231-51.

Guha, Ranajit, 'Dominance without Hegemony and its Historiography', in *Subaltern Studies*, VI, ed. Ranajit Guha, New Delhi: Oxford University Press, 1989, pp. 210-309.

———, *History at the Limit of World-History*, New York: Columbia University Press, 2002.

Hardy, Peter, *The Muslims of British India*, 1972; repr. New Delhi: Foundation Books, 1998.

Haynes, Douglas, *Rhetoric and Ritual in Colonial India: The Shaping of the Public Sphere in Surat City, 1852-1928*, New Delhi: Oxford University Press, 1992.

Hobsbawm, Eric, *Nations and Nationalism since 1780: Programme, Myth, Reality*, Cambridge: Cambridge University Press, 1992.

Jakobsh, Doris R., *Relocating Gender in Sikh History: Transformation, Meaning and Identity*, New Delhi: Oxford University Press, 2003.

Jones, Kenneth W., 'Ham Hindu Nahin: Arya-Sikh Relations, 1877-1905', *Journal of Asian Studies*, 32, 1973, pp. 457-75.

————, *Arya Dharm: Hindu Consciousness in Nineteenth Century India*, 1976; repr. New Delhi: Manohar, 2006.

————, 'Religious Identity and the Indian Census', in *The Census in British India: New Perspectives*, ed. N. Gerald Barrier, New Delhi: Manohar, 1981, pp. 73-102.

————, *Socio-Religious Reform Movements in British India*, Cambridge: Cambridge University Press, 1989.

————, 'Swami Dayananda Saraswati's Critique of Christianity', in *Religious Controversy in British India: Dialogues in South Asian Languages*, ed. Kenneth W. Jones, Albany: State University of New York Press, 1992, pp. 52-74.

Jordens, J.T.F., *Dayananda Sarasvati: His Life and Ideas*, New Delhi: Oxford University Press, 1979.

————, *Swami Shraddhananda: His Life and Causes*, New Delhi: Oxford University Press, 1981.

————, *Dayananda Sarasvati: Essays on his Life and Ideas*, New Delhi: Manohar, 1998.

Juergensmeyer, Mark, *Religious Nationalism Confronts the Secular State*, New Delhi: Oxford University Press, 1994.

Kakar, Sudhir, *The Inner World: A Psycho-Analytic Study of Childhood and Society in India*, 1978; repr. New Delhi: Oxford University Press, 1981.

Kerr, Ian, 'Urbanization and Colonial Rule in 19th-century India: Lahore and Amritsar, 1849-1881', *Punjab Past and Present*, 14, 1980, pp. 210-24.

————, 'British Relationships with the Golden Temple, 1849-1890', *Indian Economic and Social History Review*, 21, 1984, pp. 320-42.

Kishwar, Madhu, 'The Daughters of Aryavarta', in *Women in Colonial India: Essays of Survival, Work and the State*, ed. J. Krishnamurty, New Delhi: Oxford University Press, 1989, pp. 78-113.

Kolff, D.H.A., 'Zuid-Azië na 1945', in *De Wereld na 1945*, ed. D.F.J. Bosscher, H. Renner, R.B. Soetendorp and R. Wagenaar, Utrecht: Spectrum 1992, pp. 475-508.

————, 'A British Indian Circumambulation', *Itinerario*, 16, 2, 1992, pp. 85-100.

————, *Indië en de Wereldgeschiedenis*, Leiden: Universiteit Leiden, 2003.

Lavan, Spencer, 'Communalism in the Punjab: The Ahmadiyahs versus the Arya Samaj During the Lifetime of Mirza Ghulam Ahmad', *Punjab Past and Present*, 5, 1971, pp. 320-42.

————, *The Ahmadiyah Movement: A History and Perspective*, New Delhi: Manohar, 1974.

————, 'Polemics and Conflict in Ahmadiyah History: The Missionaries, the Ulama and the British', in *Essays in Honour of Dr. Ganda*

Singh, ed. Harbans Singh and N. Gerald Barrier, Patiala: Punjabi University Press, 1976, pp. 454-74.

Lee, Harold, *Brothers in the Raj: The Lives of John and Henry Lawrence*, Karachi: Oxford University Press, 2004.

Llewellyn, J.E., *The Arya Samaj as a Fundamentalist Movement: A Study in Comparative Fundamentalism*, New Delhi: Manohar, 1993.

Lutgendorf, Philip, *The Life of a Text: Performing the Ramcaritmanas of Tulsidas*, Berkeley: University of California Press, 1991.

Major, Andrew J., 'State and Criminal Tribes in Colonial Punjab: Surveillance, Control and Reclamation of the "Dangerous Classes"', *Modern Asian Studies*, 33, 1999, pp. 657-88.

Malhotra, Anshu, *Gender, Caste, and Religious Identities: Restructuring Class in Colonial Punjab*, New Delhi: Oxford University Press, 2002.

Matthews, D.J., C. Shackle and Shahrukh Husain, *Urdu Literature*, London: Gora, 1985.

McGregor, R.S., *Urdu Study Materials*, New Delhi: Oxford University Press, 1992.

———, *The Oxford Hindi-English Dictionary*, 1993; repr. New Delhi: Oxford University Press, 1995.

McLeod, W.H., *Who is a Sikh?: The Problem of Sikh Identity*, New Delhi: Oxford University Press, 1989.

———, 'Crisis of Outrage: History versus Tradition in the Study of the Sikh Community', *South Asia Research*, 14, 1994, pp. 121-35.

———, *Sikhs of the Khalsa: A History of the Khalsa Rahit*, New Delhi: Oxford University Press, 2003.

———, *Discovering the Sikhs: Autobiography of a Historian*, New Delhi: Permanent Black, 2004.

Metcalf, Barbara D., *Islamic Revival in British India: Deoband, 1860-1900*, Princeton: Princeton University Press, 1982.

———, 'Introduction', in *Moral Conduct and Authority: The Place of Adab in South Asian Islam*, ed. Barbara D. Metcalf, Berkeley: University of California Press, 1984, pp. 1-20.

———, *Perfecting Women: Maulana Ashraf 'Ali Thanawi's Bihishti Zewar*, Berkeley: University of California Press, 1990.

———, 'Imagining Community: Polemic Debates in Colonial India', in *Religious Controversy in British India: Dialogues in South Asian Languages*, ed. Kenneth W. Jones, Albany: State University of New York Press, 1992, pp. 229-40.

Metcalf, Thomas R., *Ideologies of the Raj*, Cambridge: Cambridge University Press, 1995.

Montgomery, Brian, *Monty's Grandfather: A Life of Service for the Raj*, Poole: Blandford Press, 1984.

Naim, C.M., 'Prize-winning Adab: A Study of Five Urdu Books Written in Response to the Allahabad Gazette Notification', in *Moral*

Conduct and Authority: The Place of Adab in South Asian Islam, ed. Barbara D. Metcalf, Berkeley: University of California Press, 1984, pp. 290-314.

Nandy, Ashis, *The Intimate Enemy: Loss and Recovery of the Self under Colonialism*, New Delhi: Oxford University Press, 1983.

Oberoi, Harjot, 'From Ritual to Counter-Ritual: Rethinking the Hindu-Sikh Question, 1884-1915', in *Sikh History and Religion in the Twentieth Century*, ed. Joseph T. O'Conell et al., Toronto: University of Toronto, Center for Asian Studies, 1988, pp. 136-57.

——, *The Construction of Religious Boundaries: Culture, Identity and Diversity in the Sikh Tradition*, New Delhi: Oxford University Press, 1994.

Oddie, G.A., ed., *Religion in South Asia: Religious Conversion and Revival Movements in South Asia in Medieval and Modern Times*, New Delhi: Manohar, 1977.

Pandey, Gyanendra, *The Construction of Communalism in Colonial North India*, New Delhi: Oxford University Press, 1992.

Panikkar, K.N., *Culture, Ideology, Hegemony: Intellectuals and Social Consciousness in Colonial India*, London: Anthem Press, 1995.

Penner, Peter, *The Patronage Bureaucracy in North India: The Robert M. Bird and James Thomason School, 1820-1870*, New Delhi: Chanakya, 1986.

Perrill, J.P., 'The Anjuman-i-Punjab as a Common Interest Association of Social Change in Nineteenth Century Punjab', *Punjab Past and Present*, 16, 1982, pp. 343-70.

Porter, Roy, *The Enlightenment*, Basingstoke: Macmillan, 1991.

Powell, Avril A., '"Duties of Ahmadi Women": Educative Processes in the Early Stages of the Ahmadiyya Movement', in *Gurus and Their Followers: New Religious Reform Movements in Colonial India*, ed. Antony Copley, New Delhi: Oxford University Press 2000, pp. 128-56.

——, '"Pillar of a New Faith": Christianity in Late-Nineteenth-Century Punjab from the Perspective of a Convert from Islam', in *Christians and Missionaries in India: Cross-Cultural Communication since 1500*, ed. R.E. Frykenberg, London: Routledge Curzon, 2003, pp. 223-55.

Prakash, Gyan, *Another Reason: Science and the Imagination of Modern India*, Princeton: Princeton University Press, 1999.

Pritchett, Frances W., *Nets of Awareness: Urdu Poetry and its Critics*, Berkeley: University of California Press, 1994.

Reetz, Dietrich, 'In Search of the Collective Self: How Ethnic Group Concepts were Cast through Conflict in Colonial India', *Modern Asian Studies*, 31, 1997, pp. 285-316.

Robinson, Francis, 'Islam and Muslim Separatism', in *Political Identity in South Asia*, ed. David Taylor and Malcolm Yapp, London: Curzon Press, 1979, pp. 78-112.

——, 'Prophets without Honour? Ahmad and the Ahmadiyya', *History Today*, June 1990, pp. 42-7.

——, 'Technology and Religious Change: Islam and the Impact of Print', *Modern Asian Studies*, 27, 1993, pp. 229-51.

Rudolph, Lloyd I. and Suzanne Hoeber Rudolph, 'The Coffee House and the Ashram', in *Civil Society and Democracy*, ed. Carolyn M. Elliot, New Delhi: Oxford University Press, 2003, pp. 377-404.

Schimmel, Annemarie, *Islam in the Indian Subcontinent*, Leiden: Brill, 1980.

Scribner, R.W., *The German Reformation*, Basingstoke: Macmillan, 1992.

Shackle, Christopher, 'Making Punjabi Literary History', in *Sikh Religion, Culture and Ethnicity*, ed. Christopher Shackle, Gurharpal Singh and Arvind-Pal Mandair, Richmond: Curzon Press, 2001, pp. 97-117.

Shackle, Christopher and Javed Majeed, eds., *Hali's Musaddas: The Flow and Ebb of Islam*, New Delhi: Oxford University Press, 1997.

Shackle, Christopher and Rupert Snell, *Hindi and Urdu Since 1800: A Common Reader*, London: SOAS, 1990.

Skuy, David, 'Macaulay and the Indian Penal Code of 1862: The Myth of the Inherent Superiority and Modernity of the English Legal System Compared to India's Legal System in the Nineteenth Century', *Modern Asian Studies*, 32, 1998, pp. 513-57.

Smith, Wilfred Cantwell, *Modern Islam in India*, 1946; repr. New Delhi: Usha, 1985.

——, *The Meaning and End of Religion*, New York: Macmillan, 1963.

Stark, Ulrike, 'Educating Women, Educating a Daughter: Babu Navincandra Rai, "Laksmi-Sarasvati Samvad" (1869), and Hemantkumari Chaudhurani', in *Gurus and Their Followers: New Religious Reform Movements in Colonial India*, ed. Antony Copley, New Delhi: Oxford University Press, 2000, pp. 33-56.

Stokes, Eric, *The English Utilitarians and India*, 1959; repr. New Delhi: Oxford University Press, 1992.

Talbot, Ian, *Punjab and the Raj, 1849-1947*, New Delhi: Manohar, 1988.

—— 'State, Society and Identity: The British Punjab, 1875-1937', in *Punjabi Identity: Continuity and Change*, ed. Gurharpal Singh and Ian Talbot, New Delhi: Manohar, 1996, pp. 7-33.

Tandon, Prakash, *Punjabi Century*, London: Chatto & Windus, 1961.

Tatla, Darshan Singh, 'Imagining Punjab: Narratives of Nationhood and Homeland among the Sikh Diaspora', in *Sikh Religion, Culture and Ethnicity*, ed. Christopher Shackle, Gurharpal Singh and Arvind Pal Mandair, Richmond: Curzon Press, 2001, pp. 161-85.

———, 'Rural Roots of the Sikh Diaspora', in *People on the Move: Punjabi Colonial, and Post-Colonial Migration*, ed. Ian Talbot and Shinder Thandi, Karachi: Oxford University Press, 2004, pp. 45-59.

van den Dungen, P.H.M., *The Punjab Tradition: Influence and Authority in Nineteenth Century India*, London: George Allen & Unwin Ltd., 1972.

van der Veer, Peter, *Religious Nationalism: Hindus and Muslims in India*, Berkeley: University of California Press, 1994.

———, 'Writing Violence' in *Contesting the Nation: Religion, Community and the Politics of Democracy in India*, ed. David Ludden, Philadelphia: University of Pennsylvania Press, 1996, pp. 250-69.

———, *Imperial Encounters: Religion and Modernity in India and Britain*, Princeton: Princeton University Press, 2001.

———, 'Religion in South Asia', *Annual Review of Anthropology*, 31, 2002, pp. 173-87.

Viswanathan, Gauri, *Masks of Conquest: Literary Study and British Rule in India*, New York: Columbia University Press, 1989.

———, *Outside the Fold: Conversion, Modernity, and Belief*, Princeton: Princeton University Press, 1998.

Walsh, J.E., *Growing up in British India: Indian Autobiographers on Childhood and Education under the Raj*, New York: Holmes & Meier, 1983.

Washbrook, David, 'South Asia, the World System, and World Capitalism', *Journal of Asian Studies*, 49, 1990, pp. 479-508.

Webster, John C.B., *The Christian Community and Change in North India*, New Delhi: Macmillan, 1976.

———, 'Christian Conversion in the Punjab: What Has Changed?', in *Religious Conversion in India: Modes, Motivations, and Meanings*, ed. Rowena Robinson and Sathianathan Clarke, New Delhi: Oxford University Press, 2003, pp. 351-80.

Yapp, Malcolm, 'Language, Religion and Political Identity: A General Framework', in *Political identity in South Asia*, ed. David Taylor and Malcolm Yapp, London: Curzon Press, 1979, pp. 1-33.

Index